Adobe®
Premiere® Pro
Complete Course

Donna L. Baker

WILEY

Wiley Publishing, Inc.

Adobe® Premiere® Pro Complete Course

Published by:
Wiley Publishing, Inc.
111 River Street
Hoboken, NJ 07030
www.wiley.com/compbooks

Published simultaneously in Canada

For general information on our other products and services or to obtain technical support please contact our Customer Care Department within the U.S. at 800-762-2974, outside the U.S. at 317-572-3993 or fax 317-572-4002.

Library of Congress Control Number: 2003115747

ISBN: 0-7645-4349-0

Manufactured in the United States of America

10 9 8 7 6 5 4 3 2 1

1K/SS/RS/QT/IN

» Credits

Publisher: Barry Pruett

Project Editor: Cricket Krengel

Acquisitions Editor: Michael Roney

Editorial Manager: Robyn Siesky

Technical Editor: Dennis Short

Copy Editor: Gwenette Gaddis Goshert

Production Coordinator: Courtney MacIntyre

Layout and Graphics: Beth Brooks, Sean Decker, Carrie Foster, Joyce Haughey, Jennifer Heleine, Heather Pope

Quality Control: John Tyler Connoley, John Greenough, Susan Moritz, Angel Perez

Indexer: Johnna VanHoose

Proofreader: Vicki Broyles

» Dedication

For Terry.

» Acknowledgments

I would like to thank Michael Roney, Acquisitions Editor at Wiley, for the opportunity to write this book, and my agent, Matt Wagner at Waterside Productions, for managing my affairs. I would also like to thank the editorial and development team at Wiley, with a most special thanks to my one-in-a-million editor, Cricket Krengel.

Thanks to my husband, Terry, for his tolerance and for adding our pizza place to the speed dial, and to my daughter, Erin, for being the inspiring little person she is. Thanks to Deena for the ongoing chats, and to Barb and Bev for support and encouragement.

Thanks to Adobe for its bold move in rebuilding one of my favorite programs, taking it to a whole new level. A very special thanks to Scott Meath at Mediatone Music, Inc. for allowing me to use and introduce you to the Studio Cutz Music Library. Finally, speaking of music, thanks to Tom Waits, for how can you write without a muse?

» About the Author

Donna L. Baker is a seasoned graphics designer, information developer, and instructor. Donna is the author of a number of books, including two other *Complete Course* titles. She writes monthly articles on graphics and web applications for the online magazine WindoWatch. Donna lives in the heart of the Canadian prairies with her husband, Terry; her daughter, Erin; two dogs; and a cat.

» Table of Contents

Introduction	**1**

Confidence Builder　　**7**

Building the Basic Project　8
Adding the Clips to the Timeline　11
Animating the Title Clip　14
Animating the Graphic Image　17
Making Your Movie　20

Part I　Course Setup　　**23**

Premiere Pro Basics　　**25**

Project Overview　　**31**

Part II　Getting Started　　**35**

Session 1　Starting the Project　　**36**
Starting the Project　38
Understanding Project Settings　42
Importing the Project Footage　47
Organizing Clips in the Project Window　49
Setting Durations for Clips in the Project Window　52
Transferring Clips to the Timeline　54
Session Review　58
Other Projects　58

Session 2　Editing Video Clips　　**60**
Adding a Group of Clips to the Timeline　62
Adjusting a Clip's Length in the Project Window　65

Editing a Clip in the Source View Monitor　68
Opening and Editing Clips from the Timeline　70
Reversing Clip Speeds and Previewing the Results　72
Editing a Group of Sports Clips　76
Session Review　81
Other Projects　81

Part III　Editing Footage　　**83**

Session 3　Working with Clips　　**84**
Configuring the Timeline Layout　86
Unlinking and Modifying a Movie Clip　89
Clip Editing Options　91
Using a Rolling Edit on the Timeline　93
Adjusting Clips on the Timeline　96
Editing a Clip Using Multiple Windows　98
Extracting a Clip Segment in the Program View Monitor　101
Completing Some Beach Segment Edits　104
Session Review　107
Other Projects　107

Session 4　Using Transitions　　**110**
Inserting Transitions　112
Using a Transition to Show Two Clips　116
Using Another Push Transition　119
Adding an Iris Transition　121
Organizing Clips and Applying Dissolves　123
Freezing a Video Frame　126
Adding a Pair of Iris Transitions　128
Session Review　131
Other Projects　131

Part IV Working with Audio   133

Session 5 Editing Audio Clips   134

How and Why to Use Audio   136
Organizing the Timeline for Audio   138
Preparing Audio Files   141
Understanding Audio Characteristics   143
Adding Trimmed Audio Clips to the Timeline   145
Editing Audio Clips in the Timeline   149
Adjusting Audio Signal   151
Editing a Group of Clips in the Timeline   152
Applying Sound Transitions   157
Session Review   161
Other Projects   161

Session 6 Mixing Audio and Adding Effects   164

Adjusting Track Volumes Using the Audio Mixer   166
Using Keyframes to Control Settings   169
Fading Volume over Multiple Clips   171
Adding Audio Effects to Tracks in the Audio Mixer   176
Panning Clips   180
Adding Music Clips to the Project   184
Editing the Music Clips   187
Fine-Tuning the Music Tracks   191
Session Review   193
Other Projects   193

Part V Adding Transparency Effects   195

Session 7 Controlling Clips with Fixed and Transparency Effects   196

Resizing Clips Using Fixed Effects   198
Changing Clip Opacity and Stacking Order   202
Adding More Beach Segment Clips   207
Adjusting Transparency Using Luminance
and Screen Keys   211

Using a Garbage Matte Effect   213
Using a Color Keying Effect   218
Session Review   219
Other Projects   219

Part VI Working with Video Effects   221

Session 8 Creating and Animating Titles   222

Creating a Static Title   224
Adding Titles to the Timeline   228
Customizing Title Text   230
Adding the Beach Message   234
Animating a Title Using Fixed Effects   236
Creating More Title Animations   241
Using a Template for a Title   244
Composing a Title Sequence for the Project   246
Session Review   248
Other Projects   248

Session 9 Using Graphics for Special Effects   250

Adding a Title Track Matte   252
Layering Animated Titles   256
Adding More Clips to the Timeline   260
Applying a Matte to Several Clips   262
Adding Graphic Frames to Split Screens   266
Adding Complex Transitions   271
Session Review   274
Other Projects   274

Part VII Using Video Effects and Advanced Techniques   277

Session 10 Using Video Effects   278

Adding Color Tint Effects   280
Focusing the Traffic Lights   284

Adjusting the Drivethrough Traffic Clips — 287
Ending the First Segment with Flair — 289
Correcting and Modifying Color Using Effects — 292
Brightening Palm Tree Backgrounds — 294
Combining Transparency Types — 298
Adding a Color Matte — 300
Session Review — 304
Other Projects — 304

Session 11   More Video Effects   306
Enhancing a Text Title — 308
Finishing the Palm Tree Track Matte Overlay — 310
Transitioning Clips Using Fixed Effects — 312
Improving Color in Two Clips — 314
Cropping the Content of Clips — 318
Using Effects to Create Themes in the Movie — 320
Adding a New Sequence to the Project — 324
Creating Sequences for Animating Bar Titles — 328
Session Review — 333
Other Projects — 333

Part VIII   Final Edits and Exporting   335

Session 12   Nesting Sequences and Exporting Your Movie   336
Nesting Video Sequences in the City Segment — 338
Exporting Single Frames from the Project — 341
Making a Final Splash — 345

Reviewing Your Project — 349
Exporting a Movie Segment — 351
Sharing Your Movie! — 354
Cleaning and Archiving Your Project — 359
Exporting and Archiving Checklist — 361
Session Review — 362
Other Projects — 362

Part IX   Bonus Material: CD-ROM Only

Bonus Session 1   Creating Project Titles and Graphics

Bonus Discussion 1   More Premiere Pro Features

Bonus Discussion 2   More Information on Exporting from Premiere Pro

Bonus Discussion 3   The Finer Points of Premiere Pro Effects

Appendix A   What's on the CD-ROM?   367

Index   373

End-User License Agreement   393

Introduction

Many people, me among them, often have watched television programs or movies and wondered how things were made. How do they make the superhero fly? Why does a dream sequence look dreamy? My particular area of fascination has been music videos, in which you can find every combination of real and imaginary objects and people in a never-ending visual feast.

One of the big changes in recent years has been digital video. Graphic designers and movie folks are making movies, and so are keen hobbyists. Computers have advanced to support complex graphics and animations, and Premiere Pro has changed to take advantage of the hardware power.

You can learn to use a program like Premiere Pro by trial and error. You can certainly learn to use many of the program's functions and create simple video projects. Premiere Pro is a complex piece of software used for creating complex projects. Understanding how to create a project and then how best to approach its design and construction are key elements of your ongoing success.

These key elements are where this book comes in. It uses a project-based approach to teach you how to use Premiere Pro. You learn how to use the tools that make a superhero fly, but you also learn how to use the tools in combination with one another to build a project. You also learn how to plan a project, how to choose specific techniques, and how to choose effects such as transitions.

Each session builds on the previous session. This way, you can see the progressive development of a project and learn to use Premiere Pro in a systematic and practical way. This book is also a structured course that leads you through the project development process, giving you instruction on the intricacies of the program as well as the project design process.

Watching a movie that you created play on the screen in front of you is incredibly satisfying. As you work through the lessons in this book, you will understand this satisfaction even more. By the end of the course, you will have both a finished product suitable for use in a portfolio and a deeper understanding of the intricacies of this very rich program. I also hope that I will have been able to share the fascination I have with the program.

Is This Book for You?

Yes—if you are a creative professional, a digital artist, a motion graphics designer, a passionate hobbyist, a student, or a teacher of Premiere Pro. The sessions offered in this course were designed with you in mind, using projects created by experienced Premiere Pro users who are also designers and teachers. An Instructor's Guide is available to accompany this book. It contains accessory information, answer keys to the session's questions, and other useful information and resources. For more information, contact the author at dbaker@skyweb.ca.

What's in This Book?

This course is divided into eight parts. To introduce you to the program, and to whet your appetite, this book begins with a quick-start tutorial called the Confidence Builder; this is followed by eight sections. Here's an overview of what you'll find in each of these parts.

> » "Confidence Builder" is a hands-on introduction that gives you a hint of what you can create in Premiere Pro. The tutorial introduces you to the program and some of its most impressive features. At the end of it, you will have made your first movie—complete with sound!

» **Part I: Course Setup.** This introductory section of the book contains information about Premiere Pro and this course:

> » "Premiere Pro Basics" includes an overview of what you can create using Premiere Pro and a summary of new features in Premiere Pro.

> » "Project Overview" includes an explanation of the project that you create as you work through this course.

» **Part II: Getting Started.** This is the first of the tutorials that get you started in Premiere Pro. This part has two sessions:

> » Session 1, "Starting the Project," includes tutorials to show you how to start a project in Premiere Pro. You learn how to import clips into the project, how to change the speed or length of the clips, and how to add them to the Timeline, the project assembly window.

> » Session 2, "Editing Video Clips," shows you techniques to edit the length and content of clips used in your movies. You learn to edit clips in different program locations using different techniques.

» **Part III: Editing Footage.** This section includes information that is the heart of any video project. Learn how you do basic editing both visually and in the Timeline:

> » Session 3, "Working with Clips," is where you learn how to work with and manage clips in the Timeline. You learn how to edit clips for length and content, and how to use segments of clips in your movie project.

> » Session 4, "Using Transitions," shows you how to use the first of several categories of effects that you can add to your movie using Premiere Pro. You see how and why to add transitions and also how to use transitions for specific purposes, such as managing the view of other clips.

» **Part IV: Working with Audio.** This part discusses and explains editing and using audio in a Premiere Pro project:

> » Session 5, "Editing Audio Clips," teaches you how to use audio in a movie. You learn how to edit clips and work with them in the Timeline and how to adjust the volume. You also work with multiple copies of your audio clips.

> » Session 6, "Mixing Audio and Adding Effects," shows you how to use the Audio Mixer, which is a real-time audio editor. You also learn to coordinate the audio and video portions of your movie and how to apply audio effects.

» **Part V: Adding Transparency Effects.** This section explores some of the common types of effects that you work with in Premiere Pro. Here you learn how to adjust transparency in your video, using both Timeline settings and video effects:

» Session 7, "Controlling Clips with Fixed and Transparency Effects," introduces you to the fixed effects used with all visual material in Premiere Pro. You learn to use several of the fixed effects in the Effect Controls window, and also how to use special types of video effects called keys to create transparency.

» **Part VI: Working with Video Effects.** In this section, you learn how to use the Title Designer window to create project titles and how to use many of the Title Designer window's settings and features. You also learn how to work with other types of graphic images in Premiere Pro for special effects:

» Session 8, "Creating and Animating Titles," shows you how to work with the Adobe Title Designer. From simple text titles to saving styles and using templates, you see many of the Title Designer features in this session.

» Session 9, "Using Graphics for Special Effects" introduces you to some of the many ways you can use still images and other graphics in a project. You learn how to work with different matte images to create special effects, and add a series of graphic images to segments of the project to frame the picture-in-picture elements.

» **Part VII: Using Video Effects and Advanced Techniques.** This section explores some of the many ways you can work with effects in Premiere Pro. You learn how to use different types of Premiere Pro's many video effects for color correction and repairing clips as well as adding punch to the project:

» Session 10, "Using Video Effects," is a look at using technical effects for correcting color, brightness, contrast, and other image problems. You also work with a range of other effects used to enhance the project.

» Session 11, "More Video Effects," shows you how to work with even more effects. You also learn to work with multiple sequences, or timelines, used for compositing multiple animations in the project.

» **Part VIII: Final Edits and Exporting.** This final section covers some advanced editing techniques and shows you how to do a final review of your project. You also learn how to export a movie.

> » Session 12, "Nesting Sequences and Exporting Your Movie," shows you how to use multiple sequences in the project. You learn to export single frames from the movie to use for creating a final repeating effect in the beach segment of the project. You assemble the final sequences, and learn how to export the finished movie.

Bonus Material on the CD-ROM

There isn't enough room in the book to cover all the information you need to know about Premiere Pro to create a movie and answer some of those "what is?" and "what if?" questions. The CD-ROM that accompanies this book contains several bonus files, including another session, and three collections of discussions on different topics. You can complete the Complete Course project without reading the bonus material or completing the bonus session.

» Bonus Session 1, "Creating Project Titles and Graphics," is an entire session showing you how some of the matte images and other graphics used in the project are constructed. You can create your own versions of some of the graphical elements and other titles using the tutorials in this bonus session.

» Bonus Discussion 1, "More Premiere Pro Features," describes some of the other features you can work with in Premiere Pro such as nesting sequences and workspaces.

» Bonus Discussion 2, "More Information on Exporting from Premiere Pro," covers some of the other methods you can use to export movies and other types of material from a project in formats ranging from audio to filmstrips.

» Bonus Discussion 3, "The Finer Points of Premiere Pro Effects," describes the categories of effects in Premiere Pro. Each category is described and illustrated to give you a reference for choosing effects for your projects.

Confidence Builder

Television programs, movies, interactive presentations—these types of media share many techniques and processes. One of the most common is the use of logos that identify everything from production companies to sneakers. Now it's your turn. In this tutorial, you make an animated logo.

This logo project introduces some of Premiere Pro's tools and techniques so you can get a little taste of what the program can really do. You make a simple animated logo with a background sound effect that runs five seconds. As you work through the book, revisit the logo project occasionally to experiment or add other features. You may also want to experiment with using a different graphic background or creating your own text title.

You can preview the finished movie before you start this project. It is on the CD in the Confidence Builder folder, named `logo.avi`. A finished copy of the project is also on the CD, named `confidence_builder.prproj`.

TOOLS YOU'LL USE
Project window; Timeline; Effect Controls window; Effects window; Opacity, Scale, and Rotation keyframe controls; Lightning effect

MATERIALS NEEDED (From the CD-ROM)
`cymbals.avi`, `diamond_dog.prtl`, `circle.psd`, `logo.avi`, `confidence_builder.prproj`

TIME REQUIRED
60 minutes

Tutorial

» Building the Basic Project

Before you start working with the project, make sure that you view the finished movie so you know what you are building. Copy the `logo.avi` file from the CD to your hard drive. Double-click the file to play the movie in your system's media player. In this tutorial, you create a project folder, start the project, and import your first clips.

1. **Create a new folder on your hard drive where you want to store your project files.**
   Use the folder to store the source files and the finished movie.

2. **Copy the** `cymbals.avi`, `diamond_dog.prtl`, **and** `circle.psd` **files from the Confidence Builder folder on the CD to the new folder.**
   You use the three files—a sound file, a Premiere title, and a Photoshop image—in the project.

3. **Open Adobe Premiere Pro. From the desktop, choose Start→Program→Adobe→Premiere Pro.**
   The program opens with a Welcome screen.

4. **Click New Project.**
   The New Project dialog box opens.

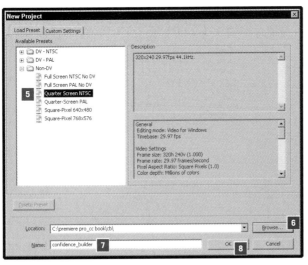

5. **Click the Non-DV heading in the Available Presets column on the Load Presets dialog box to open a list of options. Click Quarter Screen NTSC.**
   A description of the preset options and their settings displays at the right side of the dialog box.

`<TIP>`
Scroll through the list to read the settings included in the preset option.

6. **Click Browse, and locate the folder that you created in Step 1.**
   Store all the project materials in the same folder.

7. **Type a name for the project in the Name field at the bottom of the dialog box.**
   The sample project is named confidence_builder.

`<NOTE>`
Premiere uses the `.prproj` file extension for project files.

8. **Click OK to close the dialog box.**
   The program's interface opens.

Timeline window

History window

Project window   Clip window or Effect Controls window   Monitor window

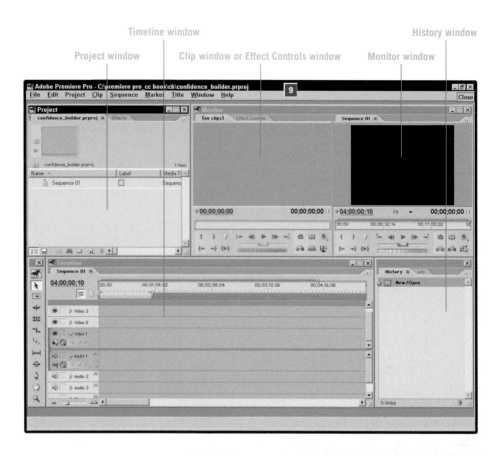

9. **Choose Window→Workspace→Editing.**
   The windows reset their locations and sizes.

<TIP>
Premiere Pro offers several predefined workspaces. You are primarily
editing in this project, and the Editing workspace displays the windows with which you need to work.

10. **Choose File→Import. Browse to the location of the storage folder
    that you created on your hard drive in Step 1. Hold the Ctrl key
    and click the** cymbals.avi, diamond_dog.prtl, **and**
    circle.psd **files, and click Open.**
    The sound and title files are brought into the Project window.
    The Import Layered File dialog box opens for importing the
    Photoshop file.

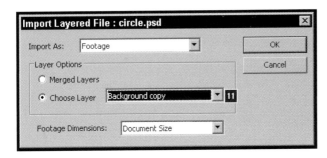

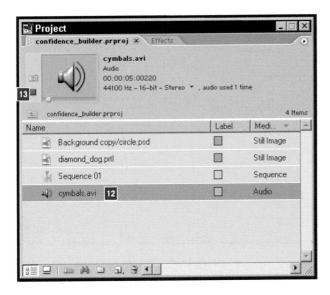

11. **Click the Choose Layer radio button. Click the dropdown arrow, and choose Background copy. Click OK.**

The Photoshop image is brought into the project. You chose a single layer to maintain the transparency of the background.

<NOTE>

In the Project window, you see an element named "Sequence 01." Premiere projects are built on a Timeline, and you can combine several Timelines into one project. Each Timeline is named "Sequence" followed by a number. For this project, you work with only one Timeline.

12. **Click the row containing the** `cymbals.avi` **clip in the Project window to select it.**

A controller and an audio icon (a speaker) display at the top of the Project window.

13. **Click Play to listen to the sound effect.**

The Play arrow changes to a square as the clip plays; click Stop to stop the preview.

14. **Choose File→Save to save your project.**

You started a new project using one of the preset project settings. You added three clips to the project and previewed the audio clip.

Tutorial
» Adding the Clips to the Timeline

You already started and saved a new project and added three clips to the Project window. It's time to add the clips to the Timeline. The Timeline is used to assemble clips for a project and to edit, apply effects, preview, and export your movie.

1. **Click on the** `cymbals.avi` **clip in the Project window to select it.**

   You add the clip to the Timeline.

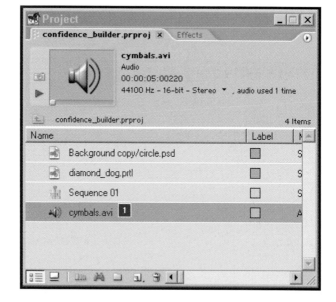

2. **Drag the clip from the Project window to the Timeline. Drop the clip at the start of Audio 1.**

   The sound clips are added to audio tracks.

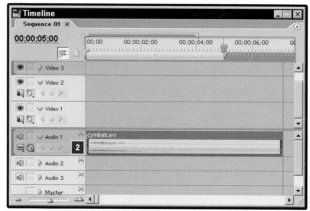

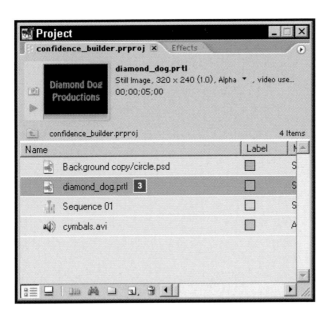

3. **Click the** diamond_dog.prtl **clip in the Project window to select it.**
   You add the clip to the Timeline.

4. **Drag the clip from the Project window to the Timeline. Drop the clip at the start of Video 2.**
   Visual material including video, still images, and titles are added to the video tracks.

5. **Click the name of the** background copy/circle.psd **clip in the Project window.**

   The name of the clip becomes active, and the text is selected.

6. **Delete background copy/ from the name, leaving the clip named as** circle.psd. **Click off the name field to set the name change.**

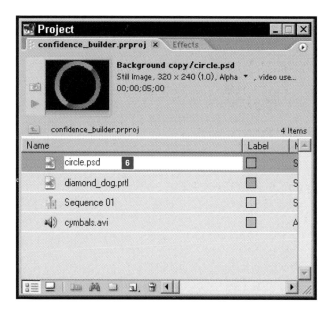

7. **Drag the** circle.psd **clip from the Project window to the Timeline. Locate it at the start of Video 1.**

   The third clip is added to the project. The Photoshop file, although not a video file, is an image file. All visual types of media are used in video tracks.

<NOTE>

The clips are arranged on the Timeline stacked in the order in which the composition should play. The circle background is behind the text title; the circle.psd clip is added to Video 1; the diamond_dog.prtl clip is added to Video 2.

8. **Choose File➔Save.**

   The clips are added to the Timeline; this is a good point to save your project.

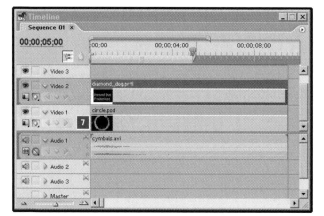

Tutorial
» Animating the Title Clip

You have the three clips for the logo added to the Timeline and have saved the project. In this tutorial, you add some effects to the title clip. The title fades in and out; it increases in size, pauses, and then zooms out toward you. You need to change the layout of the program's interface to work with effects.

1. **Choose Window→Workspace→Effects.**
   The layout of the windows changes.

2. **Make some additional modifications: Close the Tools and the History windows, and then drag the edge of the Monitor window to fill the width of the screen.**
   You aren't working with either tools or the history in this tutorial; close the windows to save screen space. Increase the size of the Monitor window to display its contents more clearly.

3. **Move the CTI (Current Time Indicator) to 00;00;00;00 using one of these methods:**
   » Click the time ruler at the beginning of the Timeline.
   » Drag the CTI left to the edge of the Timeline.
   » Click the time display shown at the top left of the Timeline window, and type in the time location.

<TIP>
You can easily move the CTI using the time display. To move the CTI to the first frame of the Timeline, click the time display to activate it. Then type 00. The CTI jumps to the first frame, and the full-length time notation displays. You don't need to type the entire sequence of 0's.

4. **Click the diamond_dog.prt1 clip on Video 2 to activate it.**
   Effects are added to the selected clip.

5. **In the Effect Controls window, click the arrow to the left of the Motion Effects heading to open a list of effects.**
   You add scale settings to the title clip.

6. **Click the stopwatch to the left of the Scale heading.**
   The stopwatch indicates that keyframes are activated for the scale effect. Keyframes are used to control effects in Premiere.

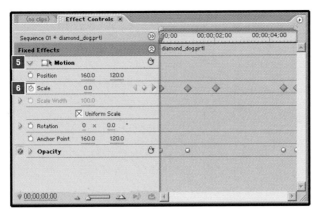

<NOTE>
The Effect Controls window (ECW), Timeline, and Monitor window all show the same information. If you look at each of the three windows, you see the CTI is sitting at the same location on each window.

<NOTE>
The time indicator reads 00;00;00;00, which means the CTI is sitting at 0 hours, 0 minutes, 0 seconds and 0 frames. Your project is only five seconds long, and time references are made to only the seconds and frames locations.

< T I P >

You can view the keyframes in color. If you click the name of the effect, in this case, Scale, the keyframes display in blue rather than gray.

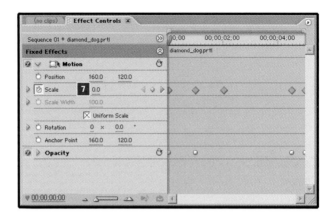

7. Click the Scale value slider, and type 0.

The default size for any object or layer is 100%. Setting the value to 0% means the title starts out invisible.

< T I P >

You can also use the hot text feature. Hold the cursor over the value shown as 100.0 until it changes to a pointing finger, and then click and drag left (to decrease the value) or right (to increase the value).

8. Move the CTI to 01;00 (1 second).

Click the time display shown at the bottom left of the Effect Controls window, and type in the time location.

9. Click the Scale value slider again, and type 40.

At one second, the title text increases in size to 40 percent of its full size.

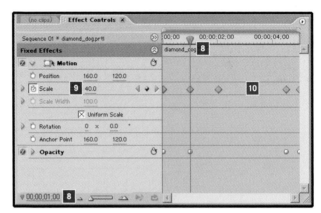

< T I P >

You don't have to add a new keyframe to the ECW Timeline. As soon as you change the value, the keyframe is automatically added.

10. Repeat Steps 8 and 9 to add three more keyframes.

At 02;00 (2 seconds), set the Scale value to 100%.
At 04;15 (4 seconds, 15 frames), set the Scale value to 100%.
At 05;00 (5 seconds), set the Scale value to 200%.

11. Click the arrow to the left of the Motion heading in the ECW to close the list of effects.

12. Click the arrow to the left of the Opacity heading to open the effect settings.

You change the opacity of the diamond_dog.prtl title clip over time.

13. Move the CTI back to 00;00 using one of the methods described in Step 3.

You add the first keyframe at the start of the clip.

14. Click the stopwatch to the left of the Opacity heading.

The stopwatch indicates that keyframes are activated for the Opacity effect.

15. Click the Opacity value slider, and type 0.

A keyframe is added to the ECW. The default opacity for any object or layer is 100%. Setting the value to 0% means the title starts out invisible.

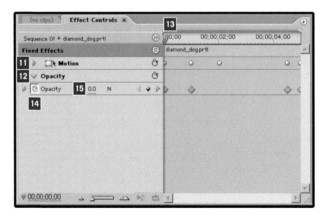

< N O T E >

There are two keyframes with a value of 100%. The scale before the first 100% keyframe increases to that value; the scale of the title after the second 100% scale keyframe increases again. During the period of time between the two keyframes, the title pauses.

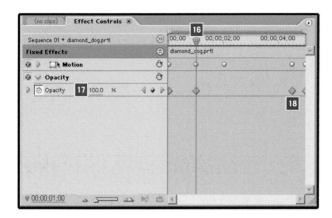

16. **Move the CTI to 01;00 (1 second) using one of the methods described in Step 3.**

You add another keyframe at that location.

17. **Click the Opacity value slider, and type** 100.

A keyframe is added to the ECW Timeline. At one second, the title text visibility increases to 100%.

18. **Repeat Steps 16 and 17 to add two more keyframes.**

At 04;15 (4 seconds, 15 frames), set the Opacity value to 100%. At 05;00 (5 seconds), set the Opacity value to 5%.

<NOTE>

Two keyframes have a value of 100%. The title's opacity increases to the first 100% keyframe at 01;00 (one second) and then stays at the same level until 04;15 (4 seconds, 15 frames), when it starts to become transparent again.

19. **Press Enter on the keyboard to render the clip.**

When the render is complete, the project plays in the Monitor window. Watch the text change its size and opacity in the Monitor window. You can click Cancel to stop the render process. Press the spacebar to start and stop the preview.

<NOTE>

Rendering is a process where the contents of the project, both video and audio, are assembled frame by frame. Rendered files are saved in a storage folder that Premiere Pro adds to your project's folder on your hard drive.

20. **Choose File→Save to save your project.**

You added two effects to the title clip and controlled the effects using keyframes. Leave the windows arranged as is for the next tutorial.

Tutorial
» Animating the Graphic Image

You have animated the title for the project. Now you have to add some effects to the graphic. In this tutorial, you add scale and rotation effects, as well as one video effect. In case you were wondering why the tutorials apply the effects to the title clip first and then to the graphic, it is simpler to add a background graphic after the main subject of the movie (in this example, the title) has been animated and effects applied.

1. **Move the CTI (Current Time Indicator) to 00;00 on the Timeline.**
   You add new keyframes for the `circle.psd` graphic.

2. **Click on the `circle.psd` clip on Video 1 to activate it.**
   Effects are added to the selected clip.

<TIP>
If you are not sure if the correct clip is selected, check the ECW—the name of the clip is written at the top of the window to the left of the time ruler.

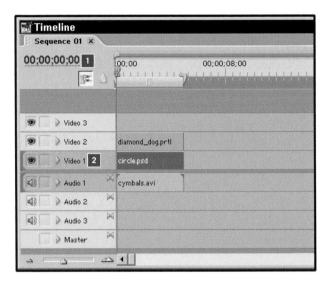

3. **In the ECW, click the arrow to the left of the Motion Effects heading to open the effects list.**
   You add scale settings to the title clip.

4. **Click the stopwatch to the left of the Scale heading.**
   Keyframing for the scale effect is activated.

<TIP>
If you click the name of the effect, in this case, Scale, the keyframes display in blue rather than gray.

5. **Click on the Scale value slider, and type 10.**
   The default size for any object or layer is 100%. Setting the value to 10% means that the graphic starts very small.

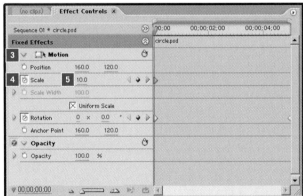

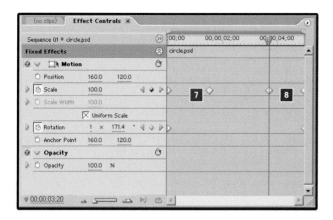

6. **Move the CTI in the Timeline to 01;15 (1 second and 15 frames).**
   You add another keyframe at this location.

7. **Click the Scale value slider, and type** 40**, and then click off the value or press Enter to deactivate the value field.**
   At one second and fifteen frames the title text increases in size to 40 percent of its full size.

8. **Repeat Steps 6 and 7 to add two more keyframes.**
   At 03;20 (3 seconds, 20 frames), set the value to 100%.
   At 05;00 (5 seconds), set the value to 180%.

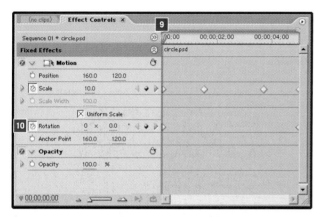

9. **Move the CTI (Current Time Indicator) to 00;00 on the Timeline.**
   You add more keyframes.

10. **Click the stopwatch to the left of the Rotation heading.**
    Keyframing for the rotation effect is activated. The value at 00;00 shows as 0 x 0.0. This means that at the first frame of the movie, the image is not rotated.

<TIP>

The first "0" refers to the number of revolutions, and the second "0" refers to the angle in degrees.

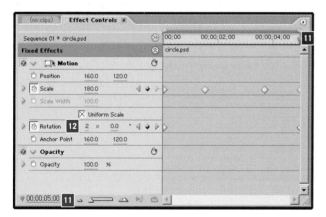

11. **Move the CTI (Current Time Indicator) to 05;00 on the Timeline.**

12. **Click the first value slider to the right of the Rotation heading, and type** 2**.**
    The graphic image rotates two full revolutions from the start to the end of the movie.

13. **Click the Project window to make it active.**

    You see the Effects palette attached to the Project window as a tab.

14. **Click the Effects tab to display it.**

15. **Click the dropdown arrow to display the list of Video Effects.**

16. **Click the dropdown arrow to open the Render folder, and select the Lightning effect.**

17. **Drag the Lightning effect from the Effects palette to the ECW.**

    The effect is applied to the circle image and displays in the ECW under a new heading named Video Effects.

<N O T E>

You don't make any modifications to the basic effect in the tutorial. If you want to see the potential changes that you can make, click the dropdown arrow to the left of the Lightning heading in the ECW to open the list. You can use about 30 different settings with the Lightning effect.

18. **Press Enter on the keyboard to render the clip.**

    When the render is complete, the project plays in the Monitor window. Watch the circle change its size and rotate. You can see the blue lightning bounce back and forth inside the circle.

19. **Choose File→Save to save your project.**

    You added three effects to the graphic clip and controlled the effects using keyframes. You finished the logo's construction.

Tutorial
» Making Your Movie

All your hard work is about to pay off. It's time to finish up and make your clips into a movie.

1. **Choose File→Export →Movie.**
   The Export Movie dialog box opens. The project settings you chose at the beginning of the project are listed at the bottom left of the dialog box. You use these settings for the exported movie. You can scroll through the Summary to read the settings listed.

2. **In the Export Movie dialog box, name your file (the sample is named `logo.avi`) and then click Save.**
   Windows XP uses the `.avi` file format as a default. Your movie is exported, and a copy is added to the Project window so you can check the final movie.

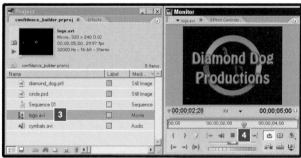

3. **Double-click the `logo.avi` clip in the Project window.**
   Another tab displays a monitor to the left of the original monitor window. The clip's name is shown at the top of the monitor.

4. **Click the Play/Stop toggle in the clip window.**
   The clip plays on a loop, meaning that it plays from start to finish and then repeats. Click the Play/Stop toggle again to stop the playback. The Play toggle is a triangle; the Stop toggle is a square.

5. **Click the** `logo.avi` **clip in the Project window to select it.**

You remove the copy of the finished movie from the project.

<NOTE>

Premiere Pro automatically adds a copy of the finished movie to your project so you can test it. You don't want to keep the copy inside the project as you already have the exported movie. Deleting the copy has no effect on the actual movie, which is saved on your hard drive.

6. **Press Delete or click the garbage can at the bottom of the Project window.**

The movie is removed from the project.

7. **Close Premiere.**

Your logo is finished. Share your video with everyone you know!

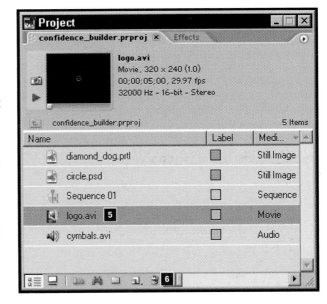

Part I

Course Setup

Premiere Pro Basics   p 25

Project Overview   p 31

Premiere Pro
Basics

An Overview of Premiere Pro

Premiere Pro is a professional program designed for video editing. Its capabilities and potential have expanded with each new version, although the program looked and worked much the same way. Premiere Pro is the first version of the Premiere program to veer dramatically from its original interface. For old-timers, it may take some getting used to, but the new interface is efficient and cohesive.

How do you use Premiere Pro?

Now there's a loaded question, and one that takes the remainder of this book to answer. If you are reading this, you no doubt have an interest in motion graphics. Premiere Pro is an editing program. Therefore, you wouldn't use it to design all parts of a flashy sports program opener. You would use it to assemble, edit, and enhance material from a range of other sources to make the final product.

Some types of source material are best prepared in Premiere Pro, such as video footage. You can work with your audio source materials within Premiere Pro or use an external audio-editing program.

Other types of material commonly used come from illustration or image-editing programs, such as Illustrator or Photoshop. You can format images in an external editor before bringing them into Premiere Pro, or you can use effects in Premiere Pro for image manipulation, such as color balancing or levels.

Graphical animations, such as animated circles, lines, logos, and so on are another element commonly used in visual media. The decision to build these animations in Premiere Pro or to use another program depends on the complexity, time available, and software available. Until Premiere Pro arrived, animations were done in a separate window in Premiere. Although you could essentially animate anything, the process was complex, time consuming, and often better left for a dedicated motion graphics program such as Adobe After Effects. You can create some very sophisticated animation in Premiere Pro, with much less time and effort than previously, as you will learn in the book.

Working with Premiere Pro

As I mentioned, Premiere Pro is an editing program. It uses time lines to organize and control the content of your movies. You add media such as video and audio to the tracks in the Timeline and then edit the material for length, content, and so on. But that's only the beginning. After the basic movie is assembled, you can add titles; transparencies and superimposed tracks; animation; and effects, split screens, and track mattes—the opportunities are almost endless.

After your movie is completed, you have to decide how you want to distribute it. You choose project settings as you start a project, but you can choose different settings for exporting. This feature gives you an enormous amount of freedom.

Suppose that I am hired to design media for a furniture manufacturer. I have to consider what kinds of products the company needs. In all likelihood, the manufacturer wants to use a variety of products that may include consumer or trade show promotions, a training video, material for prospective investors, and online materials. Using Premiere Pro, I can design and export all these different types of material. The projects can be output from Premiere Pro in whatever formats are required, ranging from CD or video formats to DVD and online media such as Windows Media. All these products are created from the same source material. This ability is the power of Premiere Pro.

How far you can go?

Premiere Pro is an advanced piece of software. This course is designed at the introductory to intermediate level. As a result, some features are not explored in the book due either to their level of complexity or to the technical issues involved. For example, one of Premiere Pro's strong features is its ability to capture digital video and audio. However, because incorporating video that you capture into a book-based project is practically impossible, digital video isn't covered.

Another strength of the program in this version is its audio-editing capabilities. Because audio can be used is so many different ways and also can be extended based on your computer's capabilities (using surround sound, for example), the course covers basic audio editing and audio effects.

Premiere Pro can be highly customized based on the way you like to work. You can work predominantly with the mouse or with shortcut keys. You can also define your own set of keyboard shortcuts for many functions. You learn where to do those tasks, but for the most part the project is based on general settings and uses standard mouse and key functions.

Treat what you learn in this course as a starting point. Whether your interests are in HDTV or Web video, there is a great deal to learn beyond what you learn here. The important thing to remember is that this course gives you a good overview of the program, introduces you to editing concepts, and helps you design a workflow that can be used regardless of your area of interest.

New features in Premiere Pro

Premiere has changed considerably over the years. Version 6.0 had some interesting new features, including digital video support, a Storyboard function to lay out a project before adding it to the Timeline, enhanced editing capabilities, and an Audio Mixer for real-time audio editing. Version 6.5 expanded those features and added real-time previews and a snazzy new title editor. Premiere Pro takes the software to an entirely new level. Unlike earlier versions of Premiere, Premiere Pro works only on Windows XP to take advantage of its architecture—no Mac version of Premiere Pro is available.

Motion and animation

Version 6.0 introduced the Effect Controls window, and that window is much expanded in Premiere Pro. The new Effect Controls window allows you to set keyframes for individual parameters of the effects that you apply to your clips. Not only can you control effects more easily, but the same Effect Controls window is used to create motion paths and animations using more precise controls than those available in the Motion window in earlier versions of Premiere. Premiere Pro also has hundreds of video and audio effects.

Multiple time lines

You can create and use multiple time lines, known as sequences. Use multiple sequences to create complex layered and repeating effects or to organize large projects into segments.

Real-time viewing

Premiere Pro uses real-time viewing for all aspects of a project. See your edits, effects, titles, color correction, and animation in real-time as you are working. This means as you work on a project, you can see the effects immediately and you don't have to wait to produce a preview.

Expanded audio tools

The audio tools were enhanced in Versions 6.0 and 6.5, and they take a leap forward in Premiere Pro. You can record audio, such as a voiceover track, directly to the Timeline. You can create audio in surround sound for your projects. The Audio Mixer now includes options to apply effects to an entire track and to submix tracks. Premiere Pro supports the VST plug-in architecture, which is an industry standard for audio filters.

Color management

Premiere Pro uses a wide range of tools and processes for modifying and managing color. The color correction tools can be used to precisely adjust hue, saturation, and lightness, or even replace one color with another throughout a clip. Premiere Pro includes waveforms and vectorscopes to monitor your clips for legal color compliance if you are creating broadcast video.

An expanded range of export options

Premiere Pro has more export options than any previous version. You can export Adobe Premiere Pro projects directly to DVD for distribution. Create output in DV, DVD, CD, VCD, SVCD, Web, and broadcast formats.

These changes are very good ones. I have worked with Premiere since Version 2, and my skill and enthusiasm have evolved along with the program. Premiere Pro is a new and better way to work with video.

Integration into Adobe's digital video suite

Premiere Pro is the cornerstone of Adobe's digital video suite. You can perform a wide range of activities in Premiere Pro, as you will learn, and can expand the scope of your work with the other products in the suite. Design animations in Premiere Pro, or use After Effects to develop complex motion graphics. Work with audio in Premiere Pro or use the new Adobe Audition for complex audio development. You can export DVD-formatted material directly from Premiere Pro, or use the new Adobe Encore program for designing interactive DVDs.

System Requirements

The first step begins before you even install Premiere Pro. Many programs put your computer's capabilities to the test, and Premiere Pro is certainly one of them. Make sure that your computer meets the *required* hardware and software capabilities—and preferably the recommended capabilities. Nothing is as frustrating as waiting and waiting and waiting for your computer to catch up to you. I have long viewed an underpowered computer as an enormous inspiration killer. After all, how do you sustain your enthusiasm and artistic vision when you have to wait to see it? By the time the machine catches up to you, you have forgotten what you wanted to do!

Your system should meet the requirements as listed here to properly run with Premiere Pro.

- » Intel Pentium III 800MHz processor (Pentium 4 3.06GHz recommended)
- » Microsoft® Windows® XP Professional or Home Edition with Service Pack 1
- » 256MB of RAM installed (1GB or more recommended)
- » 800MB of available hard-disk space for installation
- » CD-ROM drive
- » Compatible DVD recorder (DVD-R/RW+R/RW) required for Export to DVD
- » 1024x768 32-bit color video display adapter (1280x1024 or dual monitors recommended)
- » Optional: ASIO audio hardware device; surround speaker system for 5.1 audio playback

You don't need digital video capture capabilities to do the project in this book.

- » OHCI-compatible IEEE 1394 interface
- » Dedicated 7200RPM UDMA 66 IDE or SCSI hard drive or disk array

Project
Overview

The Complete Course Project

This book is a tutorial-based course in Premiere Pro for students, educators, and design professionals. You can use this book in two ways. For those of you who have been using Premiere, this is a handy reference and is very useful for learning the new features and working with the new interface of Premiere Pro. I recommend that you start with the Confidence Builder tutorial, which is an overview of the program. Although you may not need confidence building per se, you can see how different Premiere Pro is from earlier versions of the program and what areas you want to learn more about.

If you are new to Premiere Pro, welcome to a new world! I recommend that you take a different approach to learning Premiere Pro. First, carefully work through the Confidence Builder. This series of tutorials shows you the highlights of the program. It also walks you through producing an animated logo that you can modify and use for visually signing your projects. Keep in mind that this introductory tutorial, though it touches on many of the program's features, is not elaborate.

Understanding the project story

A video project requires a number of stages. First and foremost is the stage in which you define the purpose of the video. Using this book, you create a video that runs for roughly 90 seconds. The video concept is a travel association promoting tropical resort vacations to the harried, overworked office crowd. This project is similar to those you may create in the real world. Videos are very commonly used for tradeshows and for public display. This travel video could be used as a promotion at a consumer trade show, such as a lifestyle or travel show.

Here's the story. The video opens with different aspects of congested city life: traffic, crowds, more traffic, more crowds. The images and video of city life are accompanied by a heavy drum soundtrack, as well as common city noises such as telephones, traffic, and vehicle horns. This runs for about 15 seconds. The first part fades to black.

The movie segues to the second section, which opens with the sound of waves crashing against the shore. A lovely tropical beach appears, and then you see a happy, carefree young woman running down a beach. A slightly exotic and active musical score begins. Over the next minute, various scenes appear and disappear. Clips of water sports, such as surfing and sailing, are interspersed with clips of tropical resorts. The movie ends with an understated message about how vacations can restore your perspective on life.

Essentially, the project is two separate segments connected by the theme and intent of the video. When you run the video, you see that the two segments are very different in their look and visual effects. This range of material allows you to use more of the program's editing and effects features while building your project.

When you picture a tropical vacation, what do you think about? You probably envision sun and fun—a relaxing situation. This is the theme of the second segment of the movie. The first segment of the movie creates a sense of tension by showing the fast pace, noise, and crowds of everyday city life. Think how much more you would wish for a vacation under those circumstances. The message of the video is much stronger when you use two contrasting segments.

Developing the project

Through the process of building this project, you pass through several stages of development. These stages correspond with the sections in this book.

» **Project creation and assembly of materials:** This includes creating the project and custom project settings, and importing and organizing the set of clips used in the project.

» **Basic editing:** This includes organizing and trimming the clips to fit the length of the project, as well as adding transitions between clips.

» **Using audio:** This includes adding sound effects, music, and audio effects. The first section of the video uses sound effects from the CD; the second section uses sound effects and a musical score provided by Studio Cutz Music Library.

» **Adding other visual elements:** Titles, transparency, animation, and video effects are added.

» **Exporting the movie:** This is the final stage of a project when you distribute the finished movie and show it to others.

Working with the tutorial files

The CD-ROM that accompanies this book contains a folder called footage. This folder houses all the material that you need for finishing the Complete Course project and the Confidence Builder tutorials.

Before you work on the tutorials, copy the files to your computer. Make a folder on your hard drive to store the project folders and files. Open the footage folder, which contains eight folders and a number of files, from the CD-ROM. One folder is named confidence builder; this folder contains the source files, project file, and completed movie from the introductory tutorial, the Confidence Builder. The remaining files and folders are used in the Complete Course project. The simplest way to use the files is to copy the entire contents of the footage folder to your hard drive. The footage folder contains several subfolders and a series of project files named session*xx*.prproj (where *xx* is the session number; there are 12 in total).

Each session has its own project file. The beginning of each tutorial picks up where the last one leaves off. For example, if you want to start working on Session 4, open the `session4.prproj` file. If you want to see what the project layout looks like at the end of Session 4, open the `session5.prproj` file. More instructions for copying files and folders to your computer are located in the CD Appendix.

Rename the project file when you save it. This way, if you need to start over or make changes, you can start again with the original project file or with your project file from the previous session.

The footage folder on the CD contains a subfolder named samples. This folder contains a collection of movie files showing the finished work from each session. Some sessions have single completed files, while other sessions have two or three movie files.

Make notes in the margins as you work through the project. The hallmarks of a good tutorial book are generous slatherings of highlighter, scribbles in the margins, and wrinkles in the pages. Above all, experiment as you learn.

Part II

Getting Started

Session 1 **Starting the Project**   p 36

Session 2 **Editing Video Clips**   p 60

Starting the Project

Tutorial: **Starting the Project**

Discussion: **Understanding Project Settings**

Tutorial: **Importing the Project Footage**

Tutorial: **Organizing Clips in the Project Window**

Tutorial: **Setting Durations for Clips in the Project Window**

Tutorial: **Transferring Clips to the Timeline**

Session Introduction

Making a movie starts before you open the program. You cannot make a movie until you decide how it should work technically. When you start a new project, you choose settings according to the project's purpose and the types of media that you are using, such as different video formats.

You learn how to import and organize the clips used to make your movie. The tutorials on importing and organizing your project's clips point out a key ingredient of successful movie-building: You must organize your source material both for smooth program operation and to remember what material you have to work with!

In this session, you learn how to add individual clips to the Timeline, which is Premiere Pro's main work area—this is where it all happens. Clips are edited, manipulated, and enhanced after they are sited on tracks in the Timeline.

A sample movie is included in this session, named `session01.wmv`. It is on the CD in the footage folder in a folder named samples. Play the movie from the CD, or copy it to your hard drive and have a look before you start the session.

TOOLS YOU'LL USE
Clip Speed/Duration dialog box, CTI (Current Time Indicator), General preferences, Import Folder command, Info window, New Bin command, New Project window, Project Settings dialog box, Project window, Project window view buttons, Save Project command, Still Image preferences, time indicator, Timeline, Welcome window, Workspace command

CD-ROM FILES NEEDED
Contents of folders premierecc_video and premierecc_audio

TIME REQUIRED
90 minutes

Tutorial
» Starting the Project

You have many, many ways to start a project using a wide range of settings. Not only can you choose from a range of project presets, but you can also create your own custom settings. In this tutorial, you start your project using a project preset. After you're in the program, you make a project setting change and check and modify some preferences.

1. **Choose Start→Programs→Adobe→Premiere Pro to open the program.**
   The Welcome window opens. You see the options to start a new project, open an existing project, or Exit the program.

2. **Click New Project at the left side of the Welcome window.**
   The New Project window opens.

<TIP>

The option chosen for the project is one of the most generic. When you create other projects in the future, you may need to change the settings depending on your requirements. For example, you should use a DV (digital video) preset if you are capturing and using your own digital material.

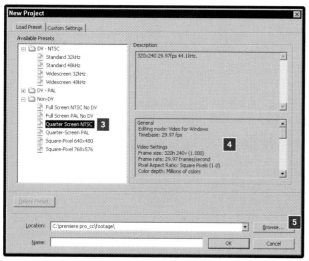

3. **Click Non-DV in the Available Presets to open the folder. Click Quarter Screen NTSC.**
   Premiere includes a collection of presets that you can use to save time when starting a project. The presets are included in one of three editing modes, including DV-NTSC, DV-PAL, and Non-DV. The project uses media from a number of sources, including QuickTime, still images, and VFW (Video for Windows) formats. Because the final project isn't intended to be a full-screen size, starting with a quarter-screen size helps keep the project preview file size manageable.

4. **Review the settings in the Description area for the selected option.**
   The general description includes information on major settings, such as the frame rate and frame size. You can scroll down the list to see the rest of the settings.

5. **Click Browse to open the Browse For Folder dialog box.**
   You have to specify a storage location for your project and its files.

<NOTE>
You can also create custom settings for a project. Click the Custom Settings tab, and select options as required. You can save the options as a custom preset, which is then included with the program's preset listings. A discussion of the project settings follows this tutorial.

6. **In the Browse For Folder dialog box, select the folder you want to use to store the project. Click OK to return to the New Project dialog box.**

<TIP>
If you don't have a storage location, select the folder in which you want to insert a new storage folder for the project files and click Make New Folder.

7. **Type a name for the project file.**
In the figure, the project is named session01. Each session has its own folder and its own project file so you can follow along or check your work. You may want to name the file using a single name. You use this project file throughout the course.

<NOTE>
You can save the project using the default name Untitled. However, that is not a good practice. If you don't name the project and save it in the default path, the next time you start a new project and save it with the default name, you overwrite the original Untitled project. Besides, it is much simpler to keep track of projects if you use descriptive names.

8. **Click OK to apply the settings.**
The New Project dialog box closes, and you are finally in the program itself.

9. **Choose Project→Project Settings→General to open the Settings dialog box.**
You modify one of the project settings.

<NOTE>
The title for your project can be descriptive, catchy, or utilitarian. The important thing is to save it in the same location as your source files. This saves time, both yours and your computer's. If you do lots of Premiere work in the future, collecting everything for one project in one place saves you time searching for files. From the program's perspective, if the project file is in the same location as the source files, it can link to them more quickly and start, process, and save faster.

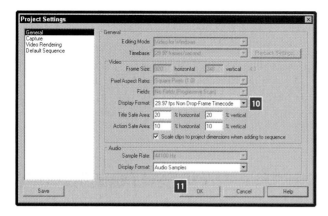

10. **Click the Display Format dropdown arrow to open a list of options. Choose 29.97 fps Non Drop-Frame Timecode.**
    Your project is short and is going to be used for the Web or CD-ROM; select the timecode standard that is simpler to use.

<TIP>
Read more about timecode in the sidebar "Where do Frames Go When You Drop Them? Or, Understanding Timecode."

<TIP>
The Display Format setting can be set as you create a project, or it can be set by changing the option in the Custom Settings panel of the New Project dialog box.

11. **Click OK to close the dialog box.**
    You changed a display setting. Now the Timecode displayed in the program corresponds with the output planned for your project.

12. **Choose Edit→Preferences, and click AutoSave in the Preferences dialog box.**
    Make sure that the Automatically Save option is selected. You can leave the default save time at 20 minutes. The Maximum Project Versions, or number of copies, is set at 5 by default.

<NOTE>
AutoSave saves a numbered copy of your project according to the time you specify. You can also specify the total number of copies to be saved at any time. Project files are quite small, so saving copies is a good way to protect your work in case of computer problems.

Where Do Frames Go When You Drop Them? Or, Understanding Timecode

You alter the Display Format setting in the General project settings in this tutorial, choosing the Non Drop-Frame Timecode option. Your project uses the NTSC standard timebase of 29.97 frames per second, yet you count frames in 30 frames per second. When you use drop-frame timecode, Premiere Pro drops two frames from the counter for each minute, except for every tenth minute. For

example, the frame after 59:29 is labeled 1:00:02. Although it is precise, drop-frame timecode can be confusing. If the precise duration isn't critical, as in the case of your project, choose the non drop-frame timecode, which doesn't renumber any frames. In drop-frame timecode, the frames aren't actually lost, only the frame numbers are changed.

Timebase Notation

Your project uses standard timebase notation at a frame rate of 30. Standard timebase notation uses 00:00:00:00, which indicates hours/minutes/seconds/frames. You can write the entire string, or shorten it to match the length of the clip you are describing. For example, a 2 1/2 second clip can be written as 02:15, and means the clip is 2 seconds and 15 frames long using the project's frame rate of 30. One-half second is 15 frames, and is written as 00:15 (0 seconds, 15 frames). It is natural to think that one-half second should be written as 00:30, but in timebase notation, this is actually the same thing as writing 01:00, or 1 second. Rest assured that over time the translation becomes second nature!

13. **Click Still Images from the list of preferences in the Preferences dialog box.**
    The Still Images settings display.

14. **Click the text in the Default Duration field, and type** 60.
    The default is 150 frames, which is 5 seconds long; you don't use any still images in the project at that length. Changing the preference now saves time as you work with the clips in your project.

15. **Click OK to close the dialog box.**
    You modified preferences before starting your project.

16. **Choose File➔Save to save the project.**
    Even though you haven't added any material to the project yet, you have changed settings that need to be saved. You started a new project file, customized the settings, and changed some program preferences. Time to get the show underway!

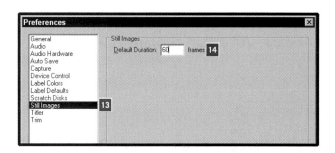

Discussion

Understanding Project Settings

Understanding what the settings include and what they mean is important. You can change the settings in the Custom Presets as you create a new project, as mentioned in the preceding tutorial. You can change some of the settings after a project is opened in Premiere Pro. To change settings, choose Project→Project Settings and select a settings group—choose from General, Capture, Video Rendering, and Default Sequence. You cannot change the basic characteristics of the project, such as changing from the quarter-screen NTSC used in this project to DV (digital video).

Here is a brief rundown of the settings. More information about the settings is included throughout the book as you work through different aspects of the project.

General settings

The General settings include options for video and audio as shown in the figure below.

The editing mode and timebase are selected when you choose a project preset. The editing mode is the type of video method used to playback video from the Timeline. If you choose a DV preset, the Playback Settings option is active.

The project uses Video for Windows editing mode. The timebase corresponds with the editing mode. Timebases are divisions used in the program to identify the position of each edit. There are variations in the timebase depending on the type of output you are planning as well as the part of the world in which your project is used. If you are planning broadcast output in Europe, use a timebase of 25 frames/second; for motion picture film, the timebase is 24 frames/second.

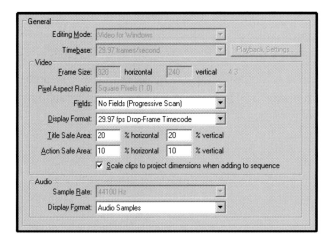

Video options

The video section of the General Settings dialog box includes several options:

» Frame Size is the dimension, in pixels, of the frames when you play them in the program. Your project uses a standard-sized 320x240-pixel frame size. The conventional aspect ratio for television is 4:3. This means that there are 4 units horizontally for every 3 units vertically, as you can see in the following image. The ratio constrains the size of your movie regardless of how you resize it. For example, a size of 400x300 pixels uses the same ratio as a size of 800x600 pixels.

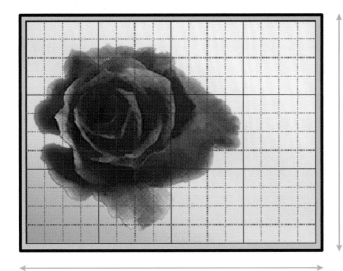

You need 3
vertical units

To use a 4:3 ratio,
for every 4 horizontal units...

» Pixels also have an aspect. In the project, you use square pixels, which means the pixels have the same width and height. Other pixel aspects are available for different formats, such as digital video or widescreen TV. Widescreen TV used in North America, for example, uses a ratio of 1.2.

» Video used for television is broadcast using two fields, or sets of horizontal lines, that lace together to make one complete screen image. The default is progressive scan, or no fields. This means that the video is drawn on your screen as a series of lines from the top to the bottom of the screen.

» The Display Format refers to the way time is displayed throughout the project. The options relate to video and motion-picture film editing standards. You changed this option in the preceding tutorial.

» Safe Areas refer to the area at the edges of the screen that are distorted when viewed on a television. Both an area for titles and screen action are configurable.

» Automatic scaling resizes imported video and stills to fit within the frame if they are larger or smaller than the frame size used for the project.

Audio options

The audio sample rate is chosen when you create the initial project. The default value is 44100 Hz, which is a high-quality setting. Sample rate refers to the speed used to play, or sample, the sound. Audio quality is better at higher sampling rates. The Display Format options include Audio Samples (the default setting) as well as milliseconds. The display format refers to how audio is displayed in the Monitor window.

Capture options

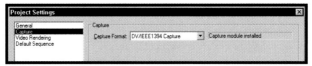

The capture settings list the types of video capture devices connected to your computer that can be used to import digital media into Premiere Pro. You are not working with video capture in the project.

Formats are listed in a drop-down list and display a status in the dialog box, such as "capture module installed."

Video rendering

Premiere Pro uses special program components for building previews and exporting your finished movie. A codec (compressor/decompressor) is a program that compresses the video data in your project using a variety of processes and then decompresses it for playback.

Your choice of codec depends on several things. The editing mode that you choose limits the available codecs. That is, if you choose Video for Windows as the editing mode, you do not have the same number of codecs that are available when using DV Editing. Choose a codec based on video capture, hardware requirements, or the speed of the codec. The default codec chosen with the project preset, Indeo 5.10, produces good quality compression.

Color depth

For the most part, a codec or the editing mode that you choose controls color depth. Some codecs allow you to create custom palettes. If you are building a project for Web display and are having problems with file size or playback, changing the color depth to an 8-bit (256-color) palette may help. You sacrifice color quality when changing color palettes. For example, look at the following images. The image at the left uses a depth of millions of colors. The same image on the right uses a 256-color palette.

The final Video Rendering option deals with still images. Leave this option selected bcause it saves processing time and file size.

One frame for the duration
of the still image

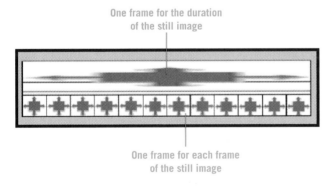

One frame for each frame
of the still image

If you have a still image in your project, rather than creating duplicate images for each frame of the video that uses the still image, one single image is created and reused.

Default sequence

The default sequences describe the number of video and audio tracks used in the project. The defaults, shown in the figure, are three tracks for video and three tracks for stereo audio.

The options also include options to use submix tracks and Surround Sound (shown as 5.1 options).

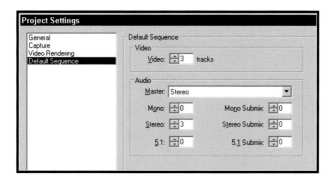

Storing Your Files

Storing all the media required for a project can use a great deal of processing power. The more memory available to Premiere Pro, the easier it can perform. Project editing is processed in RAM. If you don't have enough RAM (Random Access Memory, used for reading and writing processes to perform the work of your programs), Premiere Pro uses some hard drive space as a work area, called a *scratch* disk. The program also requires a storage location for preview files. If you have multiple hard drives, you can set different locations for your storage areas. Choose Edit→Preferences to open the Preferences dialog box. Select Scratch Disks and Device Control to view the settings shown here.

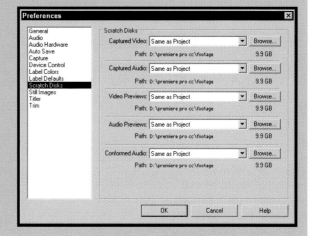

The first two options are for storing captured audio and video. The last three apply to the work you do in the book's project. To move Video Previews, Audio Previews, or Conformed Audio storage to a different location, click the drop-down arrow and choose Custom. Then click Browse to open the Browse For Folder dialog box. Select the new storage location, and click OK.

Tutorial
» Importing the Project Footage

In this tutorial, you organize the program windows and import your project's files. The project files should be copied from the CD to your hard drive as instructed in the Project Overview. If you haven't copied the files, read about the storage process and how to copy the files in the book's appendix and in the Project Overview. The program should be open if you are continuing from the preceding tutorial. If not, choose Start→Programs→Adobe→Premiere Pro. In the Welcome screen, choose your project file, session01.prproj, and the program opens.

1. **Click the window to make it active, and then resize the Project window by dragging the resize handle at the bottom right of the window.**

2. **Choose File→Import to open the Import dialog box. Browse to the location where you stored the files copied from the CD.**
   You should have the files copied to your hard drive. The storage process is described in the book's appendix and discussed in the Project Overview.

3. **Select the premierecc_audio folder and the premierecc_video folder.**
   You can import the content of an entire folder at once, or you can select individual files.

4. **Click Import Folder.**
   The Import dialog box closes, and the files are imported into Premiere Pro. The folder's names are retained, and the folders are called bins in the Project window.

5. **Click the spindown arrow to the left of premierecc_audio.**
   The files are listed. Eight sound files are added to the project in the folder.

<NOTE>
All the files for the project are contained in folders, so importing the entire folder is easiest. You can also import single files. Choose File→Import. When the Browse dialog box opens, locate the file you want to import, select it, and click OK in the dialog box. The file is added to your project into whatever bin is selected. You can also import several files the same way (if they are located in the same folder) by using Shift+click to select them.

6. **Click the folder name to select it.**
   The name becomes highlighted, and a cursor is active.

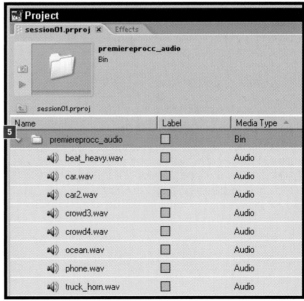

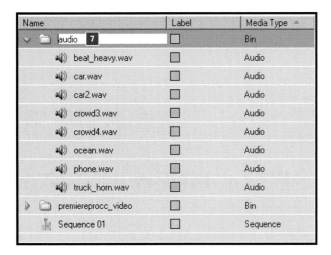

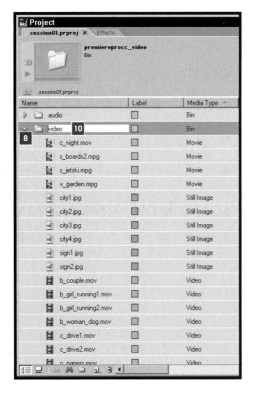

7. **Rename the folder** audio**. Click elsewhere in the window or the program interface to deselect the name.**

8. **Click the spindown arrow to the left of premierecc_video.**
   Scroll through the list, and note the different types of files listed.

<TIP>
The video folder includes still image, movie, and video formats. Each file is labeled both with a colored swatch and a name according to its file type; each file shows a corresponding icon in the Project window before its name. By the way, a movie file is one that contains both video and audio; a file containing video alone is called a video file.

9. **Click the folder name to select it.**
   The name becomes highlighted, and a cursor is active.

10. **Rename the folder** video**. Click elsewhere in the window or the program interface to deselect the name.**

11. **Choose File→Save to save the project.**
    You added the project's audio, video, and still image files.

<NOTE>
As you work through the book, you add other items to the Project window, including titles and music. The collection of files that you have added so far are all you need to work with until Session 6.

Naming Project Files

All the video files are prefaced by a single letter and an underscore. Each letter refers to a segment or type of clip used for the project. In this project, the names mean the following:

» **c_ refers to city footage; the clips are used in the first segment of the movie.**

» **b_ refers to beach footage; all these clips show people on a beach.**

» **s_ refers to sports footage; all the clips show people participating in different water activities.**

» **v_ refers to view; these clips show scenery, palm trees, and so on.**

Naming the clips using a defined structure helps you keep track of your footage. It also helps you to sort the content of your Project window if you use a method similar to the one in this project.

Tutorial

» Organizing Clips in the Project Window

Now your files are inside the program, and the project is saved. In this tutorial, you learn how to customize the layout of the Project window and how to preview the clips. You add another folder, or bin, to the project to hold the still image files. The term "bin" was originally used in film editing to refer to sections of film. Film strip segments would be placed on a table and dangle down into trash bins (not used for trash!) to keep the film clean and orderly. The term is now used to describe folders of material used in NLE (non-linear editing) programs such as Premiere Pro.

1. **Click the Folder icon at the bottom of the Project window.**
   A new bin is added to the Project window.

2. **Type** stills **in the bin name field. Click off the field to deselect the name.**
   The new bin is named and added to the project.

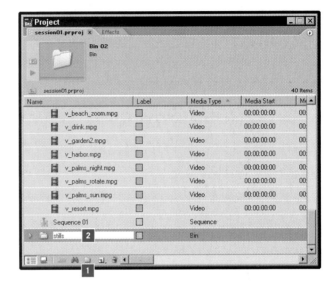

3. **Click Media Type to sort the contents of the bin according to their file format.**
   You select a group of files of the same type.

4. **Scroll down the listing in the Project window until you display the still image files in the Media Type column.**
   The six files are all .jpg files; Still Images are assigned a lavender label.

5. **Click the first** .jpg **image in the list; hold the Shift key and click the last** .jpg **image in the list to select the group of six image files.**
   The files are named city1.jpg, city2.jpg, city3.jpg, city4.jpg, sign1.jpg, and sign2.jpg.

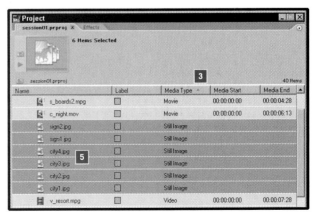

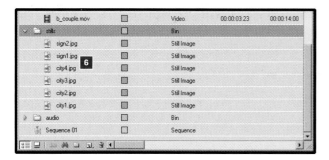

6. **Drag the set of files down the Project window, and drop them into the stills bin.**

   As you drag, the cursor changes to a bent hand. The set of still images display in their new bin location.

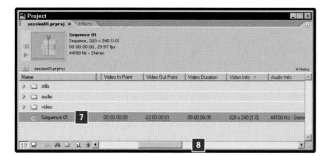

7. **Click Sequence 01 in the Project window.**

   The sequence details display at the top of the Project window. Read the details; you notice that the sequence uses the settings you chose for the project in the first tutorial.

   < N O T E >

   Each project contains one sequence by default. The sequence is the actual content used on the Timeline as well as the effects, edits, and other alterations made to the clips in the Timeline. You can use multiple sequences in the same project; each has its own Timeline. The Project window contains the sequences as well as all the media that you have imported for use in the project.

8. **Drag the horizontal scroll bar right.**

   Read the information about your project's sequence. You see a variety of headings. The headings can be customized.

   < T I P >

   Refer to the sidebar "Managing Project Window Data" for information on configuring the Project window contents.

9. **Open the video bin. Click a clip to select it.**
   You preview the clip.

10. **Preview the clip in the Project window by clicking the play arrow.**
    When you select a clip, an active preview displays at the top of the Project window. The type of preview depends on the type of clip. For example, video and audio clips have a play controller; still images have no controls.

11. **Click the play slider (the gray square) under the image of the clip and drag it further to the right to move the preview to a location partway through the clip.**
    It isn't necessary to preview the entire clip. Move the play slider right to a location partway through the clip. You can view segments this way to find the approximate time of a clip segment that you plan to use. You can click the horizontal slider at any location to jump the play to the clicked location, or you can click the square indicator on the horizontal slider and drag it to a location you want to preview.

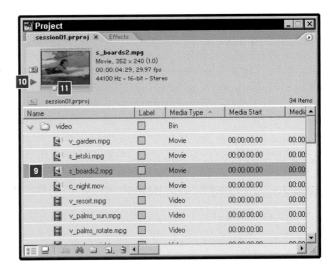

<NOTE>
Look through the other clips in your project to familiarize yourself with their contents using the process described in Steps 10 and 11.

12. **Choose File→Save, or use the Ctrl+S shortcut key combination.**
    You created an additional bin for storage of a separate file type and learned how to preview your clips in the Project window.

Managing Project Window Data

The Project window contains lots of information about the clips in your project. If you look at the clips in the list view, you can scroll through a large number of information headings.

» Click and drag any of the headings to reorder the information display.

» You can identify your clips on the basis of their data rather than how they look visually. For example, you can have a number of audio clips with similar names that are easily identified on the basis of their duration. To make the identification process simpler, drag the duration column to follow the name of the clip.

» Drag the vertical bar on the right of the column headings. Expand and shrink the size of columns to show information as you work with your clips. Expand the columns to read the content, and then shrink them to conserve space on the screen.

Tutorial

» Setting Durations for Clips in the Project Window

In this tutorial, you look more closely at the contents of the clip's descriptions in the Project window. You learn how to change the duration or speed of the clip in preparation for adding your first set of clips to the Timeline. Clips have some basic characteristics. A clip has a duration, that is, a length of time that it runs. It also has a speed, which is how fast the clip moves in relation to its default speed of 100 percent. You adjust the speed of some of the clips in your project for effect.

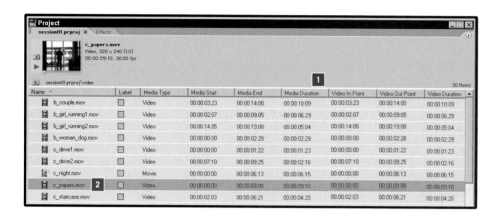

1. **Extend the Project window to nearly the full width of your screen.**
   You need to see a variety of settings. Make sure that the columns from the Name to the Video Duration are displayed.

2. **Click c_papers.mov in the Project window to select it.**
   The clip is highlighted in the Project window. Look for the Media Duration = 09:10 value, which is the length of time the clip runs. You change this time in the next steps.

< N O T E >

Time notation is written as 00:00:00:00 meaning 0 hours, 0 minutes, 0 seconds, and 0 frames. In this book, time is abbreviated; that is, unless there are hour or minute values, the time is written as 00:00. In the clip described in Step 3, the value is written as 09:10, or 9 seconds and 10 frames.

3. **Right-click the c_papers.mov name, and select Speed/Duration.**
   The Clip Speed/Duration dialog box opens. You see that the Speed is set to 100%, and the Duration is listed as 09:10.

< N O T E >

Speed and duration are inversely proportional. A clip with a duration of two seconds at 100% speed extends to four seconds if you slow the clip down to a speed of 50%. On the other hand, if you increase the speed to 200%, the duration drops to one second. Changes in speed or duration have no effect on the content of the clip, only on how long it takes to view it.

4. **Click the 100% speed setting to convert it to an active field, and then type** 180 **as the new percentage.**
   This means that the man in the clip throws the papers into the air at almost twice the speed of the original clip.

<TIP>
When you enter the new percentage value, the Duration decreases to 05:05.

5. **Click OK to close the dialog box.**
   The new speed is set.

<NOTE>
Check the Media Duration in the Project window again; you see that the value is now displayed as 05:05.

6. **Reset the speed for** c_subway.mov. **Repeat Steps 3 and 4, typing** 400 **for the percentage in the Speed setting. Click OK.**
   The Speed/Duration dialog box closes, and the clip's duration decreases from 10:14 to 02:18.

7. **Reset the speed for** c_subway2.mov. **Repeat Steps 3 and 4, typing** 200 **for the percentage in the Speed setting box. Click OK to close the Clip Speed/Duration dialog box.**
   When you check this clip's duration in the Project, you see that it drops from 13:16 to 06:22.

8. **Choose File→Save to save the project.**
   You adjusted the speeds of three clips in the project and saved the new settings.

Tutorial
» Transferring Clips to the Timeline

So far, you have added clips to the project and organized them. You adjusted the speed some of the clips play. In this tutorial, you add several clips to the Timeline. The clips that you use are all part of the city segment of the movie. Before you start, click the Name column heading in the Project window to organize the clips alphabetically.

1. **Choose Window→Workspace→Editing to reorganize the Premiere Pro window.**
   The Project window resizes itself, and several other windows display and arrange themselves to fill the screen. You work with the Project window, Timeline, and Info window.

2. **On the Timeline, drag the zoom slider to approximately the center mark.**
   You zoom in to the Timeline to see the content more clearly for placement.

3. **Move the Current Time Indicator (CTI) to 00:00.**
   The CTI is the blue tab and vertical line over the time ruler on the Timeline. Drag the CTI as far left as you can. You want the clip to start at the beginning of the Timeline.

<TIP>
The Current Time Indicator (CTI) defines the location in time where any editing you do takes place. The CTI is found in several locations including the Timeline, Source view, and Program view monitors.

<NOTE>
The time ruler in the Timeline also shows a beige horizontal bar, known as the Work Area bar. This bar is used to define segments of the Timeline to use for exporting.

4. **Click c_night.mov in the Project window to select it.**
   You add the clip to the Timeline.

5. **Drag the clip from the Project window to Video 1, and place it at the far left of the Timeline.**
   The video portion of the clip displays on Video 1; the audio portion of the track displays on Audio 1.

<TIP>
You don't have to deal with the audio track separately—it moves with the video portion automatically.

<NOTE>
The Timeline contains tracks—horizontal bars where you place clips, and apply edits and effects. Each track is named at the left side of the track by number. The default settings use three video tracks, named Video 1 to Video 3; Video 3 is the uppermost track. Audio uses three tracks and a Master track as defaults; again, the tracks are numbered, with Audio 1 being the uppermost track. In the book, each track is referred to by name, as in Video 1, instead of referring to it as the Video 1 track.

6. **Repeat Steps 4 and 5 to add another copy of the** c_night.mov **to the Timeline.**

   Place it to the right of the first copy on Video 1.

7. **Drag** c_drive1.mov **and** c_drive2.mov **into the Timeline following the second copy of the** c_night.mov **in Video 1.**

   You have four clips on the Video 1 track starting at 00:00 and ending at 17:07.

8. **Click the time indicator at the top left of the Timeline to make the field active. Type** 400.

   The CTI (Current Time Indicator) jumps to 04:00.

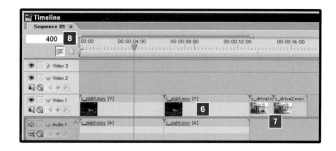

<NOTE>

You don't have to type 04:00 to move the CTI to the 4 second mark; typing 400 tells the program that you want to go to the 4 second, 0 frame location. If you want to go to a particular frame, for example, 04:15, type **415**.

9. **Select** c_subway2.mov **in the Project window. Drag the clip to the CTI location on the Timeline in Video 2.**

   The clip snaps into location starting at the CTI location 04:00.

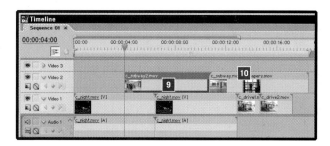

<NOTE>

If the clip doesn't snap to the CTI location, check the snap feature. Below the time indicator at the top left of the Timeline is a button that looks like a magnet. This is the snap feature. It is selected by default.

10. **Add** c_subway.mov **and** c_papers.mov **following the** c_subway.mov **clip on Video 2.**

    You have three clips on the Video 2 track starting at 04:00.

<NOTE>

When you preview the movie for this session, session01.wmv, you see only the content in the uppermost track. If content is in Video 1 only, that's what you see. If content is in Video 2 overlaying Video 1, you see the content in Video 2. The same applies to other video tracks.

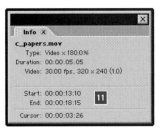

11. **Click the** c_papers.mov **to select it. Check the ending time for the final clip on Video 2 in the Info window.**
Look at the Info window to the right of the Timeline. The times for the selected clip are displayed. You see the clip's duration, as well its starting and ending times. The clip starts at 13:10 and ends at 18:15.

< T I P >
Make sure to check locations frequently in the Info window. It is a simple way to see where your project's content is at all times.

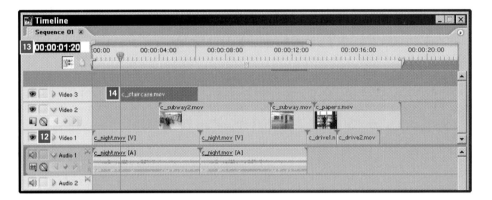

12. **Click the spindown arrow to the left of the Video 1 track title.**
The arrow points right, and the content in the lower portion of the track is hidden, or collapsed. Video 3 is visible in the Timeline window.

< T I P >
You can scroll vertically using the scroll bar at the right side of the Timeline window; collapsing Video 1 lets you see all three tracks. In its collapsed state, you cannot see a thumbnail image of the clip.

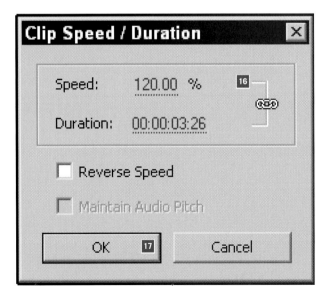

13. **Click the time indicator to make it active. Type** 120**, and click off the indicator.**
The CTI jumps to 01:20.

14. **Click the** c_staircase.mov **clip in the Project window to select it. Drag the clip from the Project window to snap into position at 01:20 on Video 3.**

15. **Right-click the** c_staircase.mov **clip on the Timeline, and choose Speed/Duration from the shortcut menu.**
The Clip Speed/Duration dialog box opens. This is the same dialog box that you used earlier with clips in the Project window.

16. **Click the 100% Speed value to make the field active. Type** 120**.**
You increase the speed of the clip, and the duration of the clip drops to 03:26.

17. **Click OK to close the dialog box.**
The clip resizes itself on the Timeline, now running from the CTI at 01:20 to 05:16.

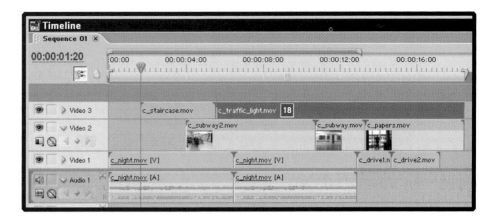

18. **Click the** c_traffic_light.mov **clip in the Project window to select it. Drag the clip from the Project window, and drop it to follow the** c_staircase.mov **clip on Video 3 starting at 05:17 and ending at 18:15.**

19. **Choose File→Save.**

    You added the first set of clips to the Timeline on three tracks. You added content to the video tracks, as well as audio attached to the c_night.mov clips.

»Session Review

This session introduced you to working with Premiere Pro . You learned how to start a new project, how to choose Project Settings, and how to save the project. After you were into the program, you learned how to change some project preferences. You imported project files and learned how to view the files in the Project window. You learned how to organize clips and how to organize the clips using bins.

You have adjusted the duration of some clips both in the Project window and Timeline by changing their speed. You added several clips to the Timeline in three tracks. The clips that you added are in the first segment of the movie, which contains city scenes and activity. The first image in this session shows the night traffic scene in the city. The final image in this session shows the end of the sequence that you added to the Timeline—the traffic lights.

The following questions are to help you review the information from this session. The answers to the questions are in the tutorials noted in parentheses.

1. Can you open Premiere Pro without opening a project or starting a new project? (See Tutorial: Starting the Project.)

2. Can you start a new project without naming it? What is the default name assigned by Premiere Pro? Is it a good idea to use the default? Why or why not? (See Tutorial: Starting the Project.)

3. What is project editing mode? How are editing mode and Timebase related? (See Discussion: Understanding Project Settings.)

4. What is an aspect ratio? How is it defined? What does it apply to? (See Discussion: Understanding Project Settings.)

5. What is a codec? What does it do? (See Discussion: Understanding Project Settings.)

6. How do you rename a bin in the Project window? (See Tutorial: Importing the Project Footage.)

7. What kinds of information can you read about a clip in the Project window? (See Tutorial: Organizing Clips in the Project Window.)

8. How many sequences are in a new project? (See Tutorial: Organizing Clips in the Project Window.)

9. How do you preview a clip in the Project window? Do you have to run the entire clip? (See Tutorial: Organizing Clips in the Project Window.)

10. How are clip speed and duration related? (See Tutorial: Setting Durations for Clips in the Project Window.)

11. How can you easily move the Current Time Indicator to a specific location on the Timeline? (See Tutorial: Transferring Clips to the Timeline.)

12. How is the snap feature used? Where is it located? (See Tutorial: Transferring Clips to the Timeline.)

13. Where is the zoom slider, and how is it used? (See Tutorial: Transferring Clips to the Timeline.)

14. What information is displayed in the Info window? (See Tutorial: Transferring Clips to the Timeline.)

» Other Projects

In the tutorial, you learned how to preview a clip in the Project window. Preview all the audio, video, and movie footage to familiarize yourself with it.

Session 2

Editing Video Clips

Tutorial: **Adding a Group of Clips to the Timeline**

Tutorial: **Adjusting a Clip's Length in the Project Window**

Tutorial: **Editing a Clip in the Source View Monitor**

Tutorial: **Opening and Editing Clips from the Timeline**

Tutorial: **Reversing Clip Speeds and Previewing the Results**

Tutorial: **Editing a Group of Sports Clips**

Session Introduction

In the first session, you started your project, added the first folders of clips, and then added some clips to the Timeline. You also edited the speed/duration of some clips both in the Project window and in the Timeline.

In this session, you add more clips to the Timeline. Instead of adding them one at a time, you reconfigure the Project window, assemble a collection of clips, and then add them to the Timeline all at once. You learn how to adjust clips for length in the Source view monitor and how to use markers to identify specific locations in the project's Timeline.

One core function of Premiere is editing. In this session, you begin the editing process and learn to work with the Source view monitor for previewing and trimming a clip. You also learn how to adjust modified clips in the Timeline.

The sample movie for this session is named `session02.wmv`. It is on the CD in the samples folder.

TOOLS YOU'LL USE
Automate to Sequence command, Source view monitor, CTI (current time indicator), In point tool, Info window, Out point tool, Play In to Out button, Play/Stop button, Program view monitor, Project window, Program view monitor buttons, Save Project command, Speed/Duration commands, time indicator, Timeline, Take Video toggle

CD-ROM FILES NEEDED
Session 1 project file that you created or the `session01.prproj` file from the CD-ROM

TIME REQUIRED
90 minutes

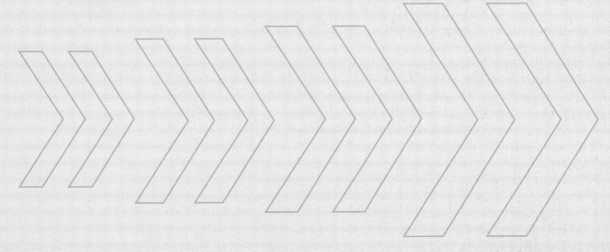

Tutorial
» Adding a Group of Clips to the Timeline

In the preceding session, you learned how to add individual clips to the Timeline from the Project window. In this tutorial, you reconfigure the Project window to work with the clips visually, and you reorganize a group of clips.

1. **Open Premiere Pro. When the Welcome window opens, choose** session01.prproj.
   The Welcome window closes and the project is loaded into the program.

<NOTE>
If you didn't do the tutorials in Session 1, copy the session01.prproj file from the CD to your hard drive. In the Welcome window, choose Open Project. Browse to the location where you stored the copied project file, and select Open. Then resave the project in Premiere Pro as session02.prproj (or use another filenaming convention).

2. **Choose File→Save As. Resave the project file as** session02.prproj.
   Follow the same naming convention that you used in Session 1. The name of the new project version displays at the top of the program window.

<NOTE>
If your file is named session01.prproj, rename it as session02.prproj. The important thing is to distinguish one session project file from another.

3. **On the Timeline, click the time indicator and type** 5600. **Press Enter to move the CTI (current time indicator) to the 56:00 mark.**
   You add a sequence of clips to the project starting at that location.

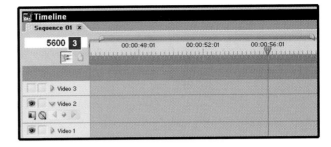

4. **In the Project window, click Icon view at the bottom of the Project window.**
   The three bins and sequence display as icons.

5. **Double-click the Video bin.**
   The contents display as a group of icons instead of a list of files.

6. **Drag the resize handle at the bottom right of the Project window to display a larger number of icons.**

<TIP>
You can choose from three icon sizes. Click the arrow at the top right of the Project window to open the Project menu. Choose Thumbnails, and select a size option from the Small, Medium, and Large icon sizes. The figure shows the icons at Medium size.

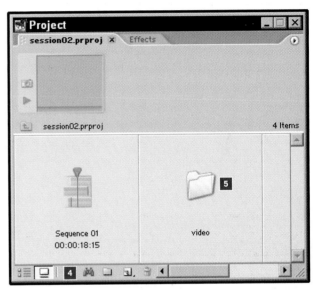

7. **Drag the four clips listed into a sequence.**
   The location of the sequence in the Project window isn't important as long as the four clips follow one another:
   v_palms_sun.mpg
   v_garden.mpg
   v_drink.mpg
   v_palms_night.mpg

8. **Click the Automate to Sequence icon (to the right of the Icon view).**
   The Automate to Sequence dialog box opens; you set options for the set of clips.

<NOTE>
Adjusting clips in the Project window is like playing cards. You move one thumbnail, shuffle others, and then arrange the final results. If you find the shuffling process difficult (or annoying), you can also select the clips individually.

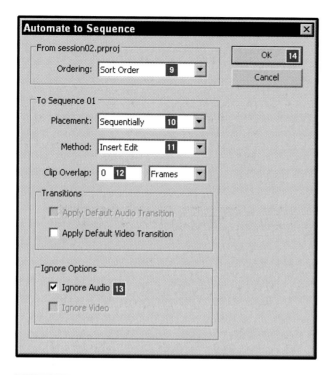

9. **Choose Sort Order from the Ordering options.**
   The second option is Selection Order. You sorted the set of clips in Step 7.

10. **Choose Sequentially from the Placement options (the default option).**
    The second option is to add the clips at unnumbered markers; you haven't added any markers to the Timeline yet.

11. **Choose Insert Edit from the Method options (the default option).**
    The second option is an Overlay edit. An Insert edit moves any clips in the Timeline further in time (to the right) while an Overlay edit replaces the content that may exist in the Timeline.

<N O T E>
Much more on Insert and Overlay editing appears in Session 3.

12. **Click the Clip Overlap field, and type 0.**
    The default process uses a transition, or a type of effect that is used to replace one clip with another visually. In this tutorial, you add clips without transitions because the clips require editing before adding effects.

13. **Click Ignore Audio in the Ignore Options.**
    One of the clips in the selected set, v_garden.mpg, also has an audio track. The audio isn't needed in the project.

14. **Click OK.**
    The Automate to Sequence dialog box closes.

15. **Check the clips on the Timeline.**
    The set of four clips is added to the Timeline in Video 1 starting at the CTI location that you set in Step 3; only the video track from the v_garden.mpg file is added to the Timeline. The first clip, v_palms_sun.mpg, starts at the CTI (56:00) and the last clip, v_palms_night.mpg, ends at 01:29:18. If the locations on your Timeline aren't correct, check the CTI location that you set in Step 3.

<N O T E>
You can either deselect the Apply Default Video Transition option or leave it selected; because the clips are being placed in sequence without overlap on the Timeline, it won't make a difference.

<T I P>
Clips in the Timeline can be nudged right or left one frame at a time. Select the clip, and then press Alt+, (comma) to move it left one frame; press Alt+. (period) to move right one frame. Use the keyboard keys, not the number pad keys.

16. **Choose File→Save, or use the shortcut Ctrl+S.**
    You reconfigured the Project window and selected and added a group of clips to the Timeline using the Automate to Sequence process.

Reorganizing Your Project's Contents

Sometimes, you reorder the content in the Project window and reorganize the program window to show different options, different arrangements, and layouts. The simplest way to keep track of your project contents is to use one system. Click the List icon at the bottom of the Project window to reset the project contents into a list. Then click the Name column heading to reorder the clips alphabetically. That takes care of the Project window.

Tutorial
» Adjusting a Clip's Length in the Project Window

In the preceding tutorial, you reconfigured the layout of the Project window and added a set of clips to the Timeline using the Automate to Sequence process. In this tutorial, you learn a handy way to reorganize the Project window and the program. You also edit a clip for length in the Project window and add it to the Timeline. Each clip has a starting frame and an ending frame. You can use the entire length of a clip in a project or only portions of the clip. If you designate a frame where the clip first appears in your movie to any frame but the first, you have set the In point; if you set the location where the clip disappears from the movie to any frame but the last frame, you have set the Out point. Unless you set different locations, the first frame is also the In point, and the last frame is also the Out point.

1. **Click the List button at the bottom of the Project window.**
   The icon view is replaced by a list of clips.

2. **Click the Name column.**
   The clips are reorganized by name.

<NOTE>
Because the clips are named using an alphabetical system, they can be quickly reorganized so you can see what you are working with at all times.

3. **Choose Window→Workspace→Editing.**
   The program's layout is reorganized, and all windows are returned to their default sizes and locations.

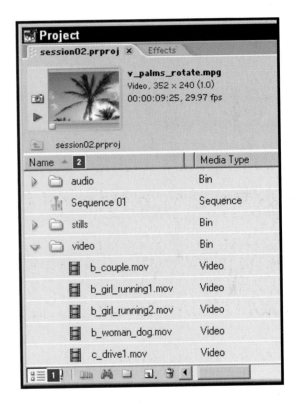

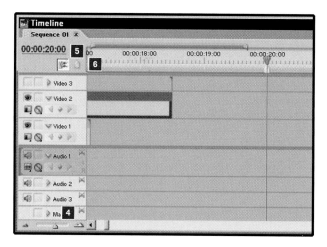

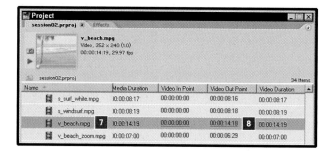

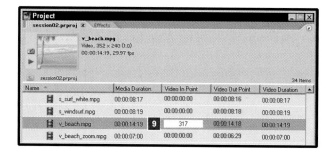

4. **Drag the zoom slider to the right to magnify the Timeline.**
Move the slider approximately 3/4 of the way to the right to see the Timeline more closely.

< N O T E >

Drag the zoom slider left to zoom out of the Timeline and right to zoom into the Timeline. You can also click the icons to the left and right of the slider to decrease or increase the zoom. Zoom in and out as you require to see the Timeline contents and time ruler clearly. Other ways to change the magnification include the Zoom tool (magnifying glass) on the toolbar or the menu commands available by choosing Sequence→Zoom In or Zoom Out. Finally, you can also use keyboard shortcut keys. Press = (equal sign) to zoom in, and press - (minus sign) to zoom out.

5. **On the Timeline, click the time indicator, type** 2000, **and press Enter.**
This moves the CTI (current time indicator) to the 20:00 mark.

6. **Click the Unnumbered Marker icon to add a marker to the Timeline, or click the * (asterisk) on the number pad.**
A marker is added to the Timeline's time ruler at the CTI position. You use this marker to identify the approximate location in your movie where the city scene ends and the beach scene begins.

7. **Click the** v_beach.mpg **clip in the Project window to select it.**
You adjust its length in the Project window.

8. **Scroll to the right to view the Video In and Video Out points as well as the Video Duration.**
You see the Video In is listed at 00:00, the Video Out is listed at 14:18, and the Video Duration is 14:19.

< N O T E >

You may want to increase the width of the Project window to see all the values as shown in the figure.

9. **Click the Video In Point value to activate the field. Type** 317.

Understanding Frames and Durations

Premiere Pro uses a consistent way to refer to time and durations for a clip. The length of a clip is the total number of frames for the entire clip. However, the duration is the number of frames plus one, because the first frame's duration doesn't occur until the first frame has played, and the last frame must play to complete the specified duration. In the example, the upper row shows a set of 10 frames. The In point is at 00:00, and the Out point is 00:10. The duration, as shown in the lower row, ends after 9 frames, or at 00:09.

For many types of editing, one frame difference isn't critical; in other cases, as with some of the editing you do in the next session, the duration is critical and the differences must be considered.

Each frame is numbered and counted

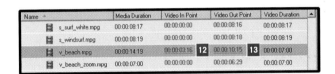

A frame is counted for the duration AFTER it is played.

10. **Click off the field, and read the value.**
The Video In Point is reset to 03:16, meaning that the clip displays in the movie starting at the 3 second and 16 frame point.

11. **Click the Video Out Point value to activate the field. Type** 1016.

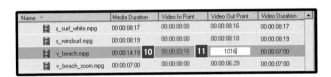

12. **Click off the field and read the value.**
The Video Out Point is reset to 10:15, meaning that the clip stops its display in the movie after the 10:15 frame is shown.

13. **Check the Video Duration value.**
The v_beach.mpg clip has a duration of 7:00 seconds.

14. **Drag the clip from the Project window to the Timeline at the CTI location.**
The clip snaps into place starting at the CTI and marker location at 20:00.

15. **Choose File→Save, or press Ctrl+S to save the project.**
You added a marker to the Timeline. You edited one clip for length in the Project window and added it to the Timeline at the marker location.

Tutorial
» Editing a Clip in the Source View Monitor

Editing a clip for length in the Project window is easy to do. However, unless you know exactly what the clip contains and where the edits are required, you need to edit in other locations. In this tutorial, you edit a clip in the Monitor window's Source view and then add it to the Timeline. The Monitor window contains two views. The left view, the Source view, shows the content of a selected clip; the name of the clip appears at the top of the monitor view. The right view, the Program view, shows the content of the Timeline, and the name of the sequence is shown at the top of the monitor view. The Effect Controls window (ECW) is tabbed with the Source view for the workspace you are using. Before editing, you modify the way the clips are displayed on the Timeline.

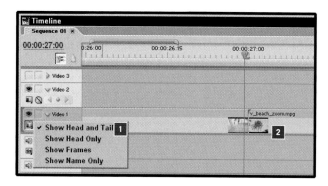

1. **Click the Set Display Style icon for Video 1 to open the options list. Choose Head and Tail.**
   The list closes, and now you see the first and last frames of a clip.

2. **Drag the** v_beach_zoom.mpg **clip from the Project window to the Timeline to follow the** v_beach.mpg **clip on Video 1.**
   The clip starts at 28:00.

3. **Double-click the clip on the Timeline.**
   The clip, named Sequence 01: v_beach_zoom.mpg, opens in the source view monitor.

4. **Click the arrow at the top right of the Source view in the Monitor window.**
   The Monitor window menu opens.

< N O T E >
You see light blue lines above and below the Monitor window, indicating that the monitor is active.

5. **Click Single View.**
   The menu closes, and the Sequence 01 Timeline view monitor closes, leaving only the Source view monitor. Drag from the left side of the window to resize it in the upper-right area of the screen.

6. **Click the Source view monitor's time indicator, and type** 00.
   The CTI moves to the start of the clip. The Clip monitor has its own CTI, shown on the time ruler below the monitor. The position of the CTI is shown above the time ruler at the left; the length of the entire clip is shown above the time ruler at the right.

CTI   Time indicator   Time ruler

7. **Click the time indicator, and type** 404.
   The CTI jumps to the 04:04 frame.

8. **Click the Set Out point icon.**
   The Out point is added to the clip's time ruler, and the ruler beyond the Out point changes from blue to white, indicating the end of the visible clip.

<NOTE>

On the Timeline, the v_beach_zoom.mpg clip resets its length when you modify the In or Out point in the Clip monitor. The clip starts at 27:00 and ends at 31:05.

9. **Choose File➔Save, or press Ctrl+S to save the project.**
   You added one clip to the Timeline after editing in the Source view monitor.

Set in point   Set out point   Out point set on time ruler

Tutorial
» Opening and Editing Clips from the Timeline

You have added a number of clips to the Timeline so far. In this tutorial, you add two more clips. You add the clips to the Timeline and then open them in the Source view monitor for editing. You also edit the Timeline's video track using a Ripple Delete, a method of editing that removes and shuffles content on a Timeline track.

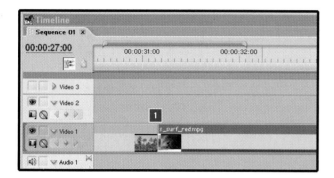

1. **Drag the** s_surf_red.mpg **clip from the Project window to the Timeline. Drop the clip to follow the** v_beach_zoom.mpg **clip on Video 1 starting at 31:05.**

2. **Right-click the** s_surf_red.mpg **clip on the Timeline, and choose Speed/Duration.**
   The Clip Speed/Duration dialog box opens.

3. **Click the 100% Speed indicator to activate the field, and type 125. Click OK to close the dialog box.**
   The s_surf_red.mpg clip length decreases to 02:05.

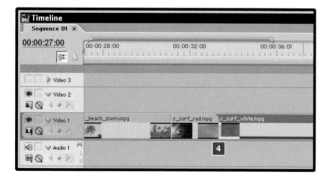

4. **Drag the** s_surf_white.mpg **clip from the Project window to the Timeline. Drop the clip to follow the** s_surf_red.mpg **clip starting at 33:11 on Video 1.**

5. **Repeat Steps 2 and 3 with the** s_surf_white.mpg **clip.**
   The clip's length decreases to 06:26 from 08:17, and the action speeds up.

6. **Double-click the** s_surf_white.mpg **clip on the Timeline to open it in the Source view monitor.**
   You reset the In point for the clip; that is, you specify the frame that first appears when the clip plays in the Timeline. The start of the clip shows the surfer at a distance; resetting the In point means the clip starts playing when the surfer is closer to the camera.

7. **Click the time indicator to make it active, and type** 21.
   The CTI moves to 00:21.

8. **Click the In point marker.**
   The In point is set at the CTI location, and the area prior to
   the CTI on the time ruler changes from blue to gray. The clip's
   length is decreased to 06:05. A blank area appears before the
   s_surf_white.mpg clip on Video 1 in the Timeline indicating that frames are removed at the start of the clip.

9. **Right-click the blank space to display a command named Ripple
   Delete. Click Ripple Delete.**
   The blank space is removed as the s_surf_white.mpg
   clip moves left to butt against the right edge of the
   s_surf_red.mpg clip. The clip starts at 33:11 and ends
   at 39:16.

10. **Choose File→Save, or press Ctrl+S.**
    You adjusted the Monitor window views and added two more
    clips to the project. You made speed, length, and Timeline
    track edits.

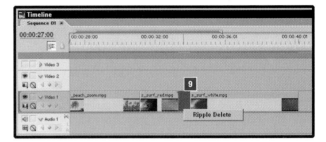

Understanding the Monitor Window

The Monitor window is used to display both the content of a single
clip and the content of the Timeline at a specified location. The
default workspaces show the Source view monitor at the left and the
Program view monitor at the right of the Monitor window. The name
of the clip displayed in the Source view monitor is shown at the top
of the Source view monitor; the name of the sequence is shown at
the top of the Program view monitor. When you double-click a clip

from either the Timeline or the Project window, it is displayed in
the Source view monitor. You can edit the clip in the Source view
monitor. The location of the CTI in the Timeline is shown in the
Program view monitor. The ECW (Effect Controls window) is tabbed
with the Source view monitor in the Editing, Effects, and Audio
workspaces. The ECW is tabbed with the Project window in the
Color Correction workspace.

Tutorial

» Reversing Clip Speeds and Previewing the Results

You have added a number of clips to the Timeline so far. In this tutorial, you add three more clips. You also add a specific form of speed control and view the results of your edits in the Source view monitor as well as the Program view monitor. You can reverse the speed of a clip, which essentially means the clip runs backwards. The Speed/Duration dialog box contains a setting for reversing clips. The Source view monitor shows the clip running in its default direction; the Program monitor view shows the clip as it will appear in your movie; that is, the motion in the clip is reversed.

1. **Choose Window→Workspace→Editing.**
   The project windows realign, and both the clip and program monitors display. Later in the tutorial, you experiment with a clip and have to view it in both windows.

2. **Select** v_palms_rotate.mpg **from the Project window. Drag it to the Timeline to follow the** s_surf_white.mpg **clip on Video 1 starting at 39:16.**
   The clip has a duration of 09:25 and ends at 49:11.

3. **Right-click the** v_palms_rotate.mpg **clip, and choose Speed/Duration from the shortcut menu.**
   The Clip Speed/Duration dialog box opens.

4. **Click the 100% Speed value to activate the field, and type** 80.

5. **Click Reverse Speed. Click OK to close the dialog box and apply the settings.**
   The v_palms_rotate.mpg clip's new duration is 12:09. Reversing the speed means the clip plays backwards, and plays for 12:09.

<NOTE>
A clip uses a speed of 100 percent as default. Increasing the value speeds up the clip; decreasing the value slows down the clip. Changing speed/duration settings works whether the clip runs in its default direction or whether you reverse direction.

6. **Right-click the** v_palms_rotate.mpg **clip in Video 1 again to open the shortcut menu. Click Reveal in Project.**

The Project window scrolls itself to the clip's location, and the v_palms_rotate.mpg clip is selected in the Project window.

< T I P >

Use the Reveal in Project command to quickly find clips in the Project window. It saves time scrolling through the list or opening bins.

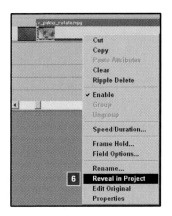

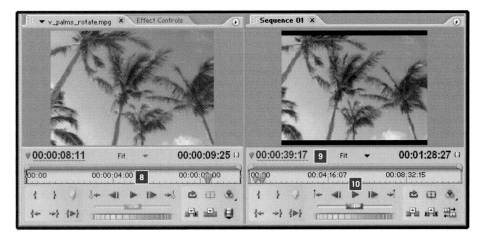

7. **Double-click the selected** v_palms_rotate.mpg **clip in the Project window.**

The clip opens in the Source view monitor.

< N O T E >

The Program view monitor plays the Timeline content; the Clip view monitor plays the clip that you select in the Project window or the Timeline.

8. **Click the Play button in the Source view monitor.**

Note that the palm trees rotate clockwise.

9. **On the Program view monitor, click the time indicator and type** 3917.

You move the CTI to display the first frame of the v_palms_rotate.mpg clip.

10. **Click Play on the Program view monitor.**

You see the palm trees rotate counterclockwise and at a slower rate than that of the original clip.

11. **In the Project window, double-click the** v_harbor.mpg **clip.**

The clip opens in the Source view monitor.

12. **Click the time indicator in the Source view monitor, and type** 102.
    The CTI on the Source view monitor moves to 01:02.

13. **Click the In point icon to set the In point for the**
    v_harbor.mpg **clip.**
    The portion of the time ruler beyond the In point changes
    to blue.

14. **Repeat Step 12, typing** 421.
    The CTI on the Source view monitor moves to 04:21.

15. **Click Out point to set the Out point for the** v_harbor.mpg **clip.**
    The portion of the time ruler beyond the Out point changes to
    gray. The final clip length is shown in black below the image
    in the Source view monitor.

16. **Click the clip image in the Source view monitor, and drag it to the Timeline. Drop the** v_harbor.mpg **clip to start at 51:25 in Video 1 following the** v_palms_rotate.mpg **clip.**
    The clip starts at 51:25 and ends at 55:15, running for a duration of 03:20.

<NOTE>

Dragging from the Source view monitor is an easy way to add an edited clip to the Timeline.

17. **Right-click the** v_harbor.mpg **clip on the Timeline, and choose Speed/Duration.**
    The Clip Speed/Duration dialog box opens, showing a speed of 100% and a duration of 03:20.

18. **Click the Duration text to make the field active, and type** 500.
    You change the duration of the clip to 05:00. The speed drops to 73.41%.

19. **Click OK to close the dialog box.**
    The v_harbor.mpg clip on the Timeline is adjusted to a duration of 05:00 starting at 51:25 and ending at 56:25.

20. **Drag the** s_surf_girl.mpg **clip from the Project window to Video 1.**
    Place the clip to follow the v_harbor.mpg clip, starting at 56:25.

21. **Double-click the** s_surf_girl.mpg **clip to open it in the Source view monitor.**
    You edit its In and Out points.

22. **Click the time indicator in the Source view monitor, and type** 300.
    The CTI on the Source view monitor moves to 03:00.

23. **Click the In point button to set the In point for the** s_surf_girl.mpg **clip.**
    The portion of the time ruler beyond the In point changes to blue.

24. **Click the time indicator again, and type** 825.
    The CTI on the Source view monitor moves to 08:25.

25. **Click the Out point button to set the Out point for the** s_surf_girl.mpg **clip.**
    The portion of the time ruler beyond the Out point changes to gray. The final clip duration is 05:26.

26. **Choose File→Save, or press Ctrl+S to save the project.**
    You added two clips. You reversed the direction of one clip and compared the clip before and after editing in the Source view and Program view monitors. You also edited another clip and modified its duration.

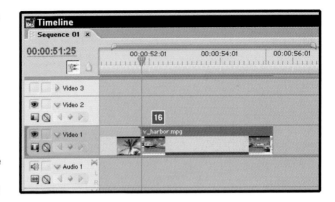

Tutorial
» Editing a Group of Sports Clips

In this tutorial, you edit a group of four clips—more sports clips used in the beach segment of the movie. You learn how to add markers in the Source view monitor, and then edit the clip directly on the Timeline. You learn how to add additional tracks to the Timeline and how to add only the video portion of a movie clip.

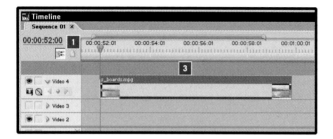

1. **On the Timeline, click the time indicator and type** 5200.
   The CTI moves to 52:00.

2. **Select** s_boards.mpg **in the Project window.**
   You add the clip and another track to the Timeline at the same time.

3. **Drag the clip to the gray area below the work area bar on the Timeline ruler, and release the mouse.**
   A new track, Video 4, is added to the Timeline. The s_boards.mpg clip is added to Video 4 starting at 52:00.

4. **Double-click the** s_boards.mpg **clip on Video 4.**
   The clip opens in the source view monitor.

5. **Click the Play button to play the clip.**
   You add clip markers as the clip plays.

6. **At the frame when the wakeboard first appears, at approximately 00:25, click the Set Unnumbered Marker icon or click * (asterisk) on the number pad.**
   A marker is added to the clip.

<NOTE>
In the figure, the CTI is moved to show you both markers on the time ruler in the Source view monitor.

7. **Repeat Step 6 at the point in the clip when the wakeboard passes across the camera, at approximately 06:25.**
   A second marker is added to the clip.

<NOTE>
When you add markers to the clip in the Source view monitor, they display over the clip on the Timeline as well.

8. **Move the mouse slowly over the left edge of the** s_boards.mpg **clip on the Timeline in Video 4.**
   The cursor changes to a red bracket with a black double-ended arrow.

Unnumbered marker button

9. **Slowly drag the left edge of the** s_boards.mpg **clip right toward the marker set in Step 6.**

   The left edge of the clip snaps to the marker location. The frames from the start of the clip to the marker location you set at 00:25 in the Source view monitor are removed from the Timeline. In the figure, the left margin of the clip has not been reset to the marker location, so you can see the icon clearly. The track has been collapsed in this figure to show you the markers clearly.

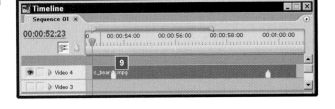

10. **Repeat Step 9 from the right side of the** s_boards.mpg **clip, moving the right margin of the clip left to the marker added at 06:25 in Step 7.**

    The right edge of the clip snaps to the marker location, removing the frames from the Timeline. The clip ends at 58:23.

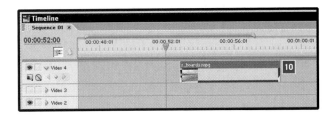

<NOTE>
Check the edited length in the Info window. The length should be 06:00. If not, adjust the In or Out points in the Timeline or the Clip monitor.

11. **Click the Play In to Out button in the Source view monitor.**

    The clip starts at the location of the first marker and ends at the location of the second marker. On the Clip monitor's time ruler, the edited portion of the clip displays in blue; the frames before and after the In and Out point are gray.

12. **Double-click the** s_boards2.mpg **clip in the Project window to open it in the Source view monitor.**

    You edit the clip's length and select only the video track to add to the Timeline.

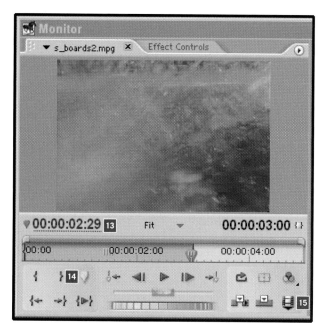

13. **Click the time indicator to activate it and type** 229.
The CTI jumps to 02:29.

14. **Click the Out point button to set the Out point at 02:29.**
The final duration of the clip is 03:00.

<NOTE>
You don't have to change the In point from the first frame of the clip.

15. **Toggle the Take Audio Video icon to Video.**
The switch toggles among Audio (a speaker), Video (a film-strip), and Audio Video (both speaker and filmstrip).

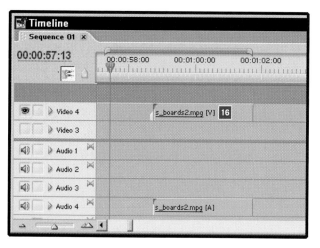

16. **Drag the** s_boards2.mpg **clip to Video 4 to follow the** s_boards.mpg **clip.**
The clip starts at 58:23 and ends at 01:01:23. Note the color of the clip on the Timeline; the color key for a movie clip (one containing both audio and video) is green. Also note the name of the clip is underlined and its component (audio or video) is indicated in brackets following the clip name.

17. **Right-click the** s_boards2.mpg **clip and choose Unlink Audio and Video from the shortcut menu.**
You separate the two components of the clip. The underline is removed from the clip's name on the Timeline, and the audio/video indicator initials are removed.

18. **Click the audio portion of the** s_boards2.mpg **clip in Audio 4 and press Delete.**
    You remove the audio component of the clip.

19. **On the Timeline, click the time indicator and type** 010123**.**
    The CTI moves to the end of the s_boards2.mpg clip at 01:01:23. You add another clip at this location in the next steps.

<TIP>
Whether you type 010123 or 10123, the CTI moves to the same location, that is, 01:01:23. To make the values you type simpler to understand and to correlate more precisely with the time indicator, the first "0" is added in the steps as required.

20. **Double-click the** s_jetski.mpg **clip in the Project window to open it in the Source view monitor.**
    You adjust its In and Out points.

21. **Click the time indicator to activate it and type** 17**.**
    The CTI jumps to 00:17.

22. **Click the In point button to set the In point for the** s_jetski.mpg **clip.**

23. **Click the time indicator to activate it and type** 511**.**
    The CTI jumps to 05:11.

24. **Click the Out point button to set the Out point for the clip.**
    The edited duration of the clip is 04:25.

25. **Toggle the Take Audio Video icon to Video.**
    The Video switch uses a filmstrip icon.

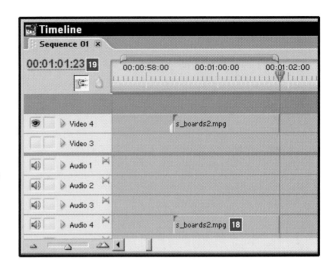

26. **Drag the** s_jetski.mpg **clip from the Source view monitor to Video 4 to follow the** s_boards.mpg **clip at the CTI.**
    Drop the clip to start at 01:01:23 following the s_boards2.mpg clip at the CTI location; the clip ends at 01:06:18.

27. **Drag the** s_sail.mpg **clip from the Project window to the Timeline to follow the** s_jetski.mpg **clip starting at 01:06:18.**
    You edit the clip's In and Out points.

28. **Double-click the** s_sail.mpg **clip to open it in the Source view monitor.**
    You edit its In and Out points.

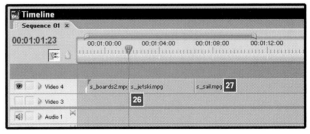

29. **Click the time indicator to activate it and type** 109.
The CTI moves to 01:09.

30. **Click the In point button to set the In point for the clip.**

31. **Click the time indicator to activate it and type** 1213.
The CTI moves to 12:13.

32. **Click the Out point button to set the Out point for the clip.**
The duration of the clip is 11:05.

33. **On the Timeline, drag the clip left to butt against the**
s_jetski.mpg **clip again.**
When you reset the In point, the first 01:09 of the clip is
removed, leaving a gap on the Timeline.

<NOTE>
You can also click the blank space, right-click to display the Ripple
Delete command, and click to delete the space.

34. **Right-click the** s_sail.mpg **clip on Video 4 starting at**
01:06:18, and select Speed/Duration from the shortcut menu.
The Clip Speed/Duration dialog box opens.

35. **Set the duration to** 07:00**, and the speed changes to slightly less**
than 160%. Click OK.

36. **Choose File→Save, or press Ctrl+S to save the project.**
You added three more clips to the project. You also added
another track to the Timeline. You learned how to add only one
portion of a movie track and how to edit on the Timeline.

» Session Review

This session was all about the beach. As you learned to perform different types of editing, you added numerous clips to the Timeline, starting with the beach footage shown in the first image for this session. You learned to edit clips for length, speed, and duration. You also learned to edit clips in the Project window, Timeline, and Source view monitor. You learned how to add tracks to the project and how to view a clip in both the Source and Program view monitors, shown in the final image in this session.

Answer these questions to review the information in the session. The answer to each question is in the tutorial noted in parentheses.

1. Is there a specific location to place the clips when you arrange a group of clips in the Project window? (See Tutorial: Adding a Group of Clips to the Timeline.)

2. How do you adjust the size of the thumbnails when you use the Icon view in the Project window? (See Tutorial: Adding a Group of Clips to the Timeline.)

3. What are the different ways to zoom in and out of the Timeline? (See Tutorial: Adjusting a Clip's Length in the Project Window.)

4. When using an unedited clip, why is the clip's Out point always one frame less than its duration? (See Tutorial: Adjusting a Clip's Length in the Project Window.)

5. How do you change a clip's appearance on the Timeline? (See Tutorial: Editing a Clip in the Source View Monitor.)

6. How can you tell whether a monitor (Source or Program) is active? (See Tutorial: Editing a Clip in the Source View Monitor.)

7. What happens to a clip on the Timeline if you edit its In and Out points in the Clip window? (See Tutorial: Opening and Editing Clips from the Timeline.)

8. What is a Ripple Delete? (See Tutorial: Opening and Editing Clips from the Timeline.)

9. What is a quick way for finding a clip in the Project window when you are working in the Timeline? (See Tutorial: Reversing Clip Speeds and Previewing the Results.)

10. What's the difference between viewing a clip in the Source View monitor and in the Project view monitor? (See Tutorial: Reversing Clip Speeds and Previewing the Results.)

11. How do you add a track and a clip to the Timeline at the same time? (See Tutorial: Editing a Group of Sports Clips.)

12. How do you edit a clip for length on the Timeline? How can you use unnumbered markers to assist in editing? (See Tutorial: Editing a Group of Sports Clips.)

» Other Projects

Experiment with the editing techniques that you learned in this session; try editing in different locations, and try working with unnumbered markers. Save an extra copy of the project for experimenting.

Part III

Editing Footage

Session 3 **Working with Clips**   p 84

Session 4 **Using Transitions**   p 110

Session 3

Working with Clips

Tutorial: **Configuring the Timeline Layout**

Tutorial: **Unlinking and Modifying a Movie Clip**

Discussion: **Clip Editing Options**

Tutorial: **Using a Rolling Edit on the Timeline**

Tutorial: **Adjusting Clips on the Timeline**

Tutorial: **Editing a Clip Using Multiple Windows**

Tutorial: **Extracting a Clip Segment in the Program View Monitor**

Tutorial: **Completing Some Beach Segment Edits**

Session Introduction

When you look at the project you have created so far, you can see clips spaced and grouped in different ways along the Timeline. These clips make up much of the basic movie, on the first few tracks in any case. In this session, you work mainly with the clips in the city portion of the movie, as well as clips at the end of the beach segment.

You continue working with different types of editing in this session. You learn how to do Extraction edits, where you delete sections of one clip to make a shorter clip. You unlink the audio and video tracks of a movie clip to work with only the video portion of the movie. You work with other types of edits such as Overlay and Rolling edits. You also learn some project management skills like configuring the Timeline for specific types of work and using markers in different locations for reference.

You can view the movie for this session before you start. It is named session03.wmv, and is on the CD in the samples folder. The movie contains material from both the beginning and the end of the project.

TOOLS YOU'LL USE
Extract Edit tool, Play tools, positioning handle, Program view monitor, Razor tool, Rolling Edit tool, Selection tool, Set Display Style menu, Source view monitor, time ruler, Timeline window, track lock, track visibility toggle, unnumbered markers, zoom slider

MATERIALS NEEDED
Session 2 project file that you created or the session02.prproj file, session03.avi

TIME REQUIRED
90 minutes

Tutorial
» Configuring the Timeline Layout

In this tutorial, you reorganize the Timeline to work with the set of clips for the city segment of the project. You change the view and resize the tracks and Timeline to hide tracks not being used.

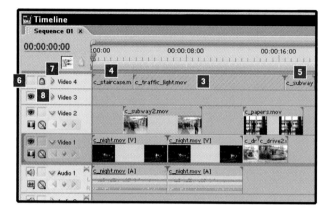

1. **Open Premiere Pro. When the Welcome window opens, choose** `session02.prproj`.
   The Welcome window closes, and the project is loaded into the program.

<NOTE>

If you didn't do the tutorials in Session 2, copy the `session02.prproj` file from the CD to your hard drive. In the Welcome window, choose Open Project. Browse to the location where you stored the copied project file, and select Open. Then resave the project in Premiere Pro as `session03.prproj` (or use another filenaming convention).

2. **Choose File→Save As, and resave the project file as** session03.prproj.
   The name of the new project version displays at the top of the program window.

3. **Select the** `c_traffic_light.mov` **on Video 3 starting at 05:17. Drag the clip up to Video 4.**
   You work with the clip later in the session.

4. **Select the** `c_staircase.mov` **clip on Video 3. Drag it to Video 4.**
   You work with this clip later in the session as well.

5. **Select the** `c_subway.mov` **clip on Video 2. Drag it to Video 4.**
   You work with this clip in a later session.

6. **At the left of the Timeline, click the visibility toggle (the eye icon) for Video 4 to hide it.**
   The Video 4 track is hidden. Now when you work with the clips on lower tracks, you can preview them without seeing the traffic lights.

7. **Click the spindown arrow to the left of the Video 4 label to collapse the track.**
   You collapse the track to use less space on the Timeline.

8. **Click the spindown arrow to the left of the Video 3 label to collapse the track.**
   You need to collapse Video 3 if you opened the track in previous sessions.

9. **Click the box to the left of the Video 4 track name. A lock displays in the box.**

   The track displays gray hatched lines, indicating that Video 4 is locked and that you can't make changes to it.

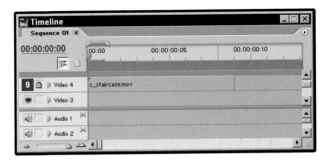

<NOTE>

It isn't necessary to lock a track. However, as you develop work habits while working through the sessions, this is a good one to develop. When you work with 10 or 12 or more tracks in a project, it is very simple to modify content on tracks accidentally, and you often don't notice until making previews or exporting movies. Repairs can be complicated and time-consuming, and they take much longer than clicking the track lock.

10. **Minimize the Project window to open more room on the screen, and resize the Timeline to fill more of the screen.**

    You need space to see the material with which you work in this session, but you don't need any clips from the Project window.

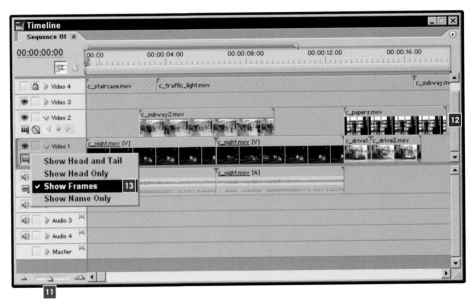

11. **Drag the zoom slider right to fill the Timeline view area with the clips in the first segment of the movie.**

    You need to see the content more clearly.

12. **Scroll down the vertical scroll bar to display Video 1 and Video 2 in the Timeline window.**

    You work with the two tracks in the first part of this session.

<NOTE>

The track's contents must be visible to see frames. Check the Collapse/Expand arrow to the left of the track name. If the arrow points downward, the track content is visible.

13. **Click the Set Display Style icon on Video 1 to open the list of options, and choose Show Frames from the menu.**

    The clip display on the track shows a sequence of frames for easier recognition of the clips' contents.

14. **Repeat Step 13 on Video 2.**

15. **Move the cursor over the dividing line between Video 1 and Video 2.**

    The cursor changes to a height adjustment icon.

16. **Drag upward to increase the height of Video 1.**

17. **Move the cursor over the dividing line between Video 2 and Video 3, and drag upward to increase the height of Video 2.**

    You can clearly see the contents of both tracks with which you are working.

18. **Move the cursor over the dividing bar between the Audio and Video tracks to display the height adjustment icon. Drag downward to increase the space allocated to the Video tracks.**

<TIP>

You can adjust the Timeline's audio/video track space from either the line between Video 1 and Audio 1 or the area between the Audio and Video scroll bars at the right side of the Timeline.

19. **Choose File→Save to save the project.**

    You moved three clips and modified the Timeline's layout in preparation for editing.

Tutorial
» Unlinking and Modifying a Movie Clip

Now that you have reconfigured the Timeline layout, you can see the track content more clearly. In this tutorial, you are going to adjust the In point for the night traffic movie on Video 1, separate the audio and video segments, and edit the video segment further. You can edit entirely from the Timeline in this tutorial. Preview your work as you go. Move the CTI to a point before your edits. In the Program view monitor (the right view in the Monitor window), click Play to view the project in real time.

1. **Click the time indicator in the Timeline, and type** 20.
   The CTI jumps to 00:20.

2. **Drag the left margin of the** c_night.mov **clip on Video 1 starting at 00:00 to snap to the CTI at 00:20.**
   The In point of the clip is trimmed.

<TIP>
You can check the duration of a blank space. Click the space on the Timeline, and check the Info window. The type is called nonmedia, and the duration, start time, and end time are displayed, just as with footage.

3. **Right-click the** c_night.mov **clip now starting at 00:20 on Video 1, and choose Unlink Audio and Video from the menu.**
   You separate the two elements of the movie so you can edit only the video component and leave the audio track intact.

<NOTE>
Look closely at the two copies of the c_night.mov clip. The second copy of the clip displays the label for both Audio and Video tracks underlined. After a clip is unlinked, the name is no longer underlined (as you can see in the first copy, starting at 00:20).

4. **Click the time indicator, and type** 513.
   The CTI jumps to 05:13.

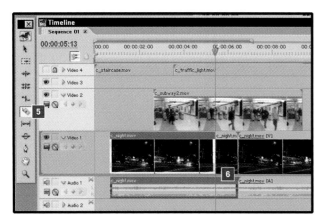

5. **Click the Razor tool on the toolbar to select it.**
   You cut the c_night.mov clip, separating it into two individual clips; the first clip ends at the razor cut line, the second starts at the cut. Rather than resetting the In or Out point, you can also cut the clip.

<NOTE>
Sometimes it doesn't matter whether you cut a clip or reset its In and Out points. For certain effects, such as transitions, you need to keep extra frames before the In point or after the Out point to use in the effect.

6. **Move the tool over the c_night.mov clip at the CTI position, and click to cut the clip. Click the Selection tool on the toolbar to switch from the Razor tool.**
   The clip is now divided into two distinct segments.

7. **Click the segment of the c_night.mov clip following the CTI position at 05:13. Press Delete to remove the cut segment from the Timeline.**
   The audio track is unaffected because you unlinked the tracks in Step 3. Don't close the gap; in the next tutorial you use a special edit to add a clip to the blank space.

<TIP>
The location of the Razor cut is called the cut point. The term also applies to the location between any two clips on a track.

8. **Choose File→Save, or press Ctrl+S to save the project.**
   You trimmed a clip in the Timeline and removed a segment of the video track of the movie clip after unlinking the tracks.

Discussion
Clip Editing Options

For the most part, the methods and locations that you use for editing clips depend on your personal preference as well as the structure of your project. If you are in the finishing stages of the project when most of the clips are assembled and edited precisely, you must edit more cautiously than when you are doing the initial assembly of the clips.

The names of edits correspond to how a clip added to a track interacts with the clips before and after it in the track. Some types of edits have no effect on the overall length of the project, while others change the times. In the discussion below, in all cases the clips are shown before the edit in the top part of the image, and after the edit in the bottom part of the image.

These are the basic types of edits:

Rolling edit—This is used with two clips. Frames added to or subtracted from Clip A are added to or subtracted from Clip B. The program duration doesn't change. The clips are shown before the edit in the top of the image, and after the edit in the bottom part of the image. The blue squares represent frames of the clip being edited; the green rectangles represent the clips preceding and following the edit.

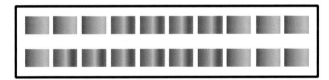

Ripple edit—Adding frames to or subtracting frames from a clip adds frames to or subtracts frames from the entire project. You used this type of editing when you did ripple delete edits in the Timeline. The clips are shown before the edit in the top of the image, and after the edit in the bottom part of the image. The blue squares represent frames of the clip being edited; the green rectangles represent the clips preceding and following the edit.

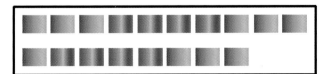

Slip edit—This edit works with single clips and shifts the starting and ending frames of a clip forward or backward. This doesn't affect the length of the project, just the content of the clip that is visible in your project. In the image, the visible frames are shown as dark blue rectangles, and the entire clip's length is shown as pink rectangles. The shifted frames are shown in the bottom part of the image.

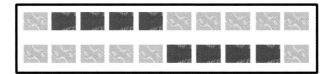

Slide edit—This edit works with clips surrounding a selected clip. Suppose that you have three clips: Clip A, Clip B, and Clip C. In the top part of the image below, the visible frames of each clip are shown as blue or green rectangles. If you use the slide edit tool with Clip B and drag left, the Out point of Clip A moves by the number of frames you move Clip B (in the bottom part of the image, the Out point is moved 2 frames), and the In point of Clip C moves by the same number of frames. A slide edit doesn't affect the length of the project.

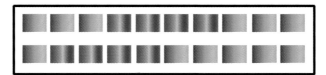

Lift edit—This edit is used with an area defined by In and Out points. The defined segment is removed and a gap remains. The duration of the project doesn't change. In the image below, the yellow rectangles represent the entire clip; the red rectangles indicate the area defined by the In and Out points. In the lower part of the image, you can see the gap that remains when the segment is removed.

Extract edit—This edit is used with an area defined by In and Out points. The defined segment is removed and the content to the right of the removed area ripples left to close the gap. The duration of the project changes. In the image below, the yellow rectangles represent the entire clip; the red rectangles indicate the area defined by the In and Out points. In the lower part of the image, you can see the gap is closed when the segment is removed, shortening the clip by the number of frames defined by In and Out points.

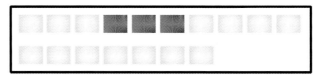

Tutorial
» Using a Rolling Edit on the Timeline

In the preceding tutorial, you deleted a segment of the first copy of the c_night.mov clip on Video 1. The blank space left is 01:01 in length. In this tutorial, you edit the c_subway2.mov clip in the Timeline. You use a special edit to add the clip to the Video 1 track in the blank space, adjusting the end and start frames for the affected clips.

1. **Right-click the** c_subway.mov **clip on Video 2 starting at 02:20, and choose Speed/Duration.**
   The Clip Speed/Duration dialog box opens.

2. **Click the Speed setting (200%), and type** 400.
   Click OK to close the dialog box. The clip speed is changed, and the duration decreases to 01:20.

3. **Click the time indicator to activate the field, and type** 513.
   The CTI jumps to 05:13, the beginning of the blank space in Video 2.

4. **Press * (asterisk) on the number pad to add a marker to the CTI location.**
   Use this location for reference as you work on the edits.

5. **Click the time indicator to activate the field, and type** 620.
   The CTI jumps to 06:20.

6. **Press * (asterisk) on the number pad.**
   You add a second marker on the Timeline at the 06:20 CTI location.

<NOTE>
The CTI location at 06:20 is used as a reference later in the tutorial. The blank space on Video 1 is 01:01 long, and you want the final pair of clips to meet at the 06:20 mark.

7. **Right-click the** c_night.mov **clip starting at 06:14, and click Unlink Audio and Video on the shortcut menu.**
   The audio and video tracks of the clip are separated.

<TIP>
You can see the margins of a clip in the Timeline. A gray triangle at the top-left corner of the first frame means that the first frame of the clip is displayed; a triangle at the upper-right corner of the last frame indicates that the final frame is displayed.

8. **Drag the** c_subway2.mov **clip from Video 2 to the blank space in Video 1 starting at 05:13 and ending at 07:04.**
   The clip drops into place and overlaps the copy of the c_night.mov clip, which started at 06:14.

9. **Click the Rolling Edit tool on the toolbar.**
   You use this tool to adjust the frames where the first clip ends and the second begins.

10. **Move the cursor over the end of the last frame of the** c_subway2.mov **at 07:04 on Video 1.**
    The Rolling Edit tool is activated, indicated by the vertical red bar on the tool.

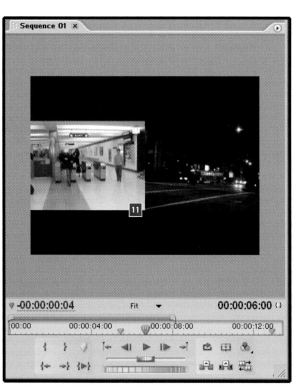

11. **Drag left to adjust the frames for both clips. Watch the changing frames in the Program view monitor as you drag.**
    The last frame of the first clip, c_night.mov, and the first frame of the c_subway2.mov clip, are shown side by side when the edit tool is active.

12. **Continue to drag left until the Rolling Edit tool snaps to the CTI at 06:14.**

    The clips' Out and In points are adjusted.

13. **Click the Selection tool on the toolbar.**

    You are finished with the Rolling Edit tool.

14. **Choose File→Save to save the project.**

    You completed some complex edits. You changed the speed of a clip and added it to another track, adjusting the duration of a pair of clips using the Rolling Edit tool.

Editing Space Options

A workspace is a layout of Premiere windows and palettes for specific purposes. Several different workspaces are available. You have worked with the Editing workspace so far. You work with the other workspaces throughout the book. You can create and save your own workspaces as well.

1. Organize the windows as you want them on the screen.

2. Choose Window→Workspace→Save Workspace.

3. You are prompted for a name. Name the workspace, and click Save.

Aside from saving a named workspace, whenever you modify the layout of the program and then save your project, the next time the project reopens, you see the windows in the same configuration and sizes as they were when saving.

Tutorial
» Adjusting Clips on the Timeline

You are making your way through the clips in the first segment of the movie. The last two clips to modify are the pair of drive-through traffic clips on Video 1. In this tutorial, you adjust the clips from the Timeline again. You change the speed, and then set the In and Out points on the Timeline.

1. **Click the time indicator, and type** 1108.
   The CTI moves to 11:08.

2. **Press * (asterisk) on the number pad.**
   An unnumbered marker is added to the Timeline; you use the marker as a reference location.

3. **Drag** c_drive1.mov **left over the** c_night.mov **clip, and snap it to the CTI.**
   The clip is moved, and the c_night.mov clip is cut. The audio track of the c_night.mov is unaffected because you unlinked the tracks in the preceding tutorial. A small portion of the c_night.mov clip appears to the right of the c_drive1.mov clip on the Timeline. You can select the clip segment and delete it; however, moving the c_drive2.mov clip (which you do in Step 6) deletes the segment automatically.

4. **Right-click the** c_drive1.mov **clip, and choose Speed/Duration from the shortcut menu.**
   The Clip Speed/Duration dialog box opens.

5. **Change the speed to** 200%, **and click OK to close the dialog box.**
   The clip's duration decreases to 00:20.

6. **Drag** c_drive2.mov **left to butt against the** c_drive1.mov **clip on Video 1.**
   The clip starts at 11:29 and ends at 14:15.

7. **Repeat Steps 4 and 5.**
   The c_drive2.mov clip's duration decreases to 01:08.

8. **Click the time indicator to make it active, and type** 1220.
   The CTI jumps to 12:20. You use this CTI location to edit the clip's Out point on the Timeline.

9. **Drag the right margin of the** c_drive2.mov **clip left to snap to the CTI.**
   Dragging the margin resets the clip's Out point; the clip's duration decreases to 00:21.

10. **Select the** c_papers.mov **in Video 2 starting at 12:28. Drag the clip to Video 1, and butt it against the** c_drive2.mov **clip starting at 12:20.**

11. **Choose File→Save to save the project.**
   You edited several clips in the Timeline, adjusting speed and length. Working only in the Timeline, you adjusted the second drivethrough movie clips' Out point.

Tutorial
» Editing a Clip Using Multiple Windows

In the preceding session, you learned how to edit clips in the Source view monitor. In this tutorial, you use both the Source view monitor and the Program view monitors simultaneously to perform a complex edit. In this tutorial, you trim the clip and set markers in the clip.

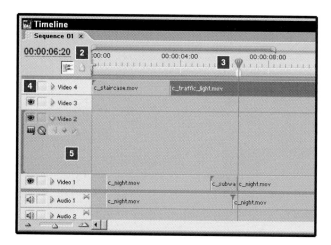

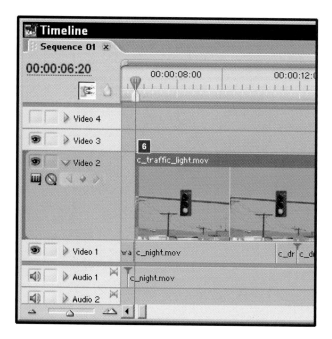

1. **Right-click the time ruler on the Timeline to open a shortcut menu. Choose Clear Sequence Marker→All Markers.**
   The markers that you used in previous tutorials for clip placement are removed from the Timeline.

   <NOTE>
   You can access the same shortcut menu for managing markers from any Timeline.

2. **Click the time indicator to make it active, and type** 620.
   The CTI jumps to 06:20.

3. **Press * (asterisk) on the number pad to add a new marker.**
   You assemble clips according to the marker location.

4. **Click the Lock on Video 4 to deselect it.**
   The Video 4 track is unlocked.

5. **Collapse all tracks except for Video 2.**
   You are working only in Video 2 in this tutorial.

6. **Drag the** c_traffic_light.mov **from Video 4, and drop it at the CTI location on Video 2.**
   The clip starts at 06:20 on Video 2.

7. **Double-click the** c_traffic_light.mov **in Video 2 to open it in the Source view monitor.**
   You perform the edits in the Source view monitor. Although the original clip is nearly 13 seconds long, the finished edits result in a pair of clips of only 01:19.

8. **Click the time indicator in the Source view monitor to make it active, and type** 326.

   The CTI moves to 03:26 on the clip.

9. **Click the Set In Point button to add the In point for the clip.**

   The area to the left of the In point on the time ruler turns light gray, indicating that it is excluded from the edited clip.

10. **Click the Play In to Out button to view the remaining clip segment, now 09:02 in length.**

   You see that the traffic light changes from green to amber quickly after the beginning green light segment is removed.

11. **Click the Go to In Point button to return the CTI to the In point in the Source Monitor view.**

   You preview the first edit.

12. **Click the time indicator in the Source view monitor to make it active, and type** 1128.

   The CTI moves to 12:28.

13. **Click the Set Out Point button to add the Out point for the clip.**

   The area to the right of the In point on the time ruler turns gray, indicating that it is excluded from the edited clip. The clip length is now 5:17.

14. **Click the Play In to Out button to preview the remaining clip.**

   Note how the time during which the amber light is displayed is far longer than either the green or red lights due to the edits that you have made.

15. **Click the time indicator in the Source view monitor, and type** 425.
    The CTI moves to 04:25.

16. **Press * (asterisk) on the numeric keypad, or press Unnumbered Marker on the Source view monitor.**
    A marker is added to the clip at 04:25. You can't see the marker on the clip itself in the Source view monitor; however, a visible marker is displayed on the clip in the Timeline.

17. **Repeat Steps 15 and 16, adding a second marker at 08:22.**
    The two markers display on the Timeline and are used to identify a segment of the clip that you are going to extract in the next tutorial.

18. **Choose File→Save, or press Ctrl+S to save the project.**
    You edited the c_traffic_light.mov clip for length, setting In and Out points. The traffic lights use long sequences between color changes. To use the clip in the project, you have to cut out segments of the green and amber light footage. You added two markers to use as guidelines for removing the extra footage, which you do in the next tutorial.

Tutorial
» Extracting a Clip Segment in the Program View Monitor

In the preceding tutorial, you trimmed the traffic lights clip for length and added markers to define an area to remove. In this tutorial, you transfer the markers to the Timeline and perform the edits in the Program view monitor. Finally, you use the Timeline for positioning.

1. **On the Timeline, drag the** c_traffic_light.mov **left to the location of the marker that you set on the Timeline in the preceding tutorial at 06:20.**
   The clip moves when you edit the In point.

2. **Drag the zoom indicator to the right to zoom in to the Timeline.**
   You add Timeline markers in the following steps, so you need to see the Timeline clearly.

3. **Click the Set Display Style icon, and choose Show Head and Tail from the menu.**
   You don't want to see the image of each frame; you just need to see the markers clearly.

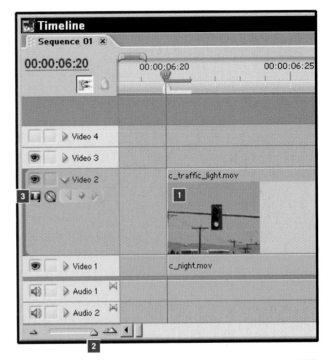

4. **Scroll right through the** c_traffic_light.mov **clip until the first marker is visible.**
   Drag the bottom scroll bar or click the Hand tool on the toolbar, and drag the Timeline content.

5. **Double-click the time ruler at the location of the first marker on the clip, at 07:19.**
   The CTI jumps to the location on which you double-click.

6. **Click the Unnumbered Marker button on the Timeline, or press *** **(asterisk) on the number pad.**
   A marker is added to the Timeline at the same location as that on the c_traffic_light.mov clip.

7. **Repeat Steps 4 through 6 using the second clip marker at 11:16.**
   This transfers both clip markers to the Timeline.

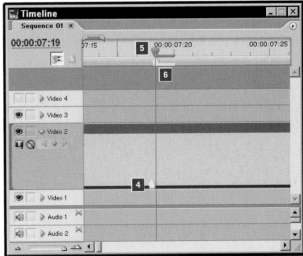

8. **In the Sequence 01 Program view monitor, drag the positioning handle to display the markers that you added earlier in the tutorial.**
   You can see the markers displayed on the Timeline.

<NOTE>

The positioning handle is another way to zoom in or out of the Timeline, and also to scroll along the Timeline. It is used in all monitor windows, on the Timeline, and in other timelines, such as that in the Effect Controls window. In all instances, drag the left or right edge to decrease or increase the zoom; drag the handle left or right to display different segments of the project in the visible area of the Timeline or window.

9. **Click the time indicator to make it active, and type** 719.
   The CTI jumps to the first clip marker that you transferred in Step 6 at 07:19.

10. **Click the Set In Point button to add an In point to the project's Timeline.**
    The area to the left of the marker changes from blue to gray indicating that it is deselected from the editing area.

Click to open Trim window for precision edits

11. **Click the time indicator to make it active, and type** 1116.
    The CTI jumps to the second clip marker that you transferred in Step 7 at 11:16.

12. **Click the Set Out Point button to add an Out point to the project's Timeline.**
    The area to the right of the marker changes from blue to light gray indicating that it is deselected from the editing area.

13. **Click Extract.**
    You have two separate clip segments. The segment of the clip that you identified with Timeline markers in Steps 5 and 7 is removed from the clip. The remainder of the c_traffic_light.mov clip moves left to close the gap created by removing the segment, a process called extraction. If you choose the other editing method available from the Project monitor window (the icon to the left of the Extract icon), the edit is referred to as a Lift edit. This means that the Timeline segment bracketed by the Timeline markers is removed, and the gap remains.

<NOTE>

Click the bottom-right button on the Project monitor to open another window, called the Trim view. The Trim view is similar to other windows and has some of the same controls, but it shows two clips—one to the left and one to the right of an edit point. Its tools are used for precise editing on a frame-by-frame basis.

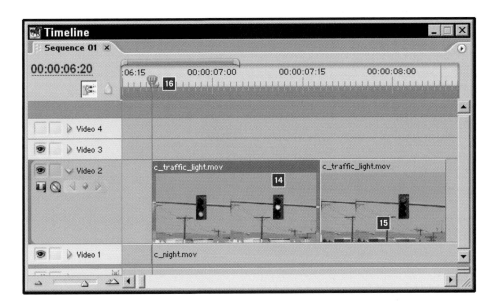

14. **Select the first clip segment of** c_traffic_light.mov **on the Timeline.**
Check its length in the Info window. It is 00:28.

15. **Select the second clip segment of** c_traffic_light.mov **on the Timeline.**
Check its length in the Info window. It is 00:21. The combined time for the two segments is 01:19.

16. **Right-click the Timeline, and choose Clear Sequence Marker→All Markers from the shortcut menu.**
The markers are removed from the Timeline.

17. **Choose File→Save, or press Ctrl+S to save the project.**
You have completed some difficult edits. You worked with the Program view monitor and Timeline windows, adding In and Out points to the Timeline to isolate the segment for editing. You then completed an Extraction edit. What started as a long clip slowly showing a traffic light changing color is now a short pair of clips showing the color change segments.

Tutorial

» Completing Some Beach Segment Edits

In the final tutorial for this session, you edit four clips at the end of the project in preparation for the next session. Three of the four clips are already present in the Timeline. You adjust these clips and then add one more from the Program view monitor. Because your level of editing expertise is developing, you get to choose your own method for editing. You can edit in the Timeline or the Source view monitor. Experiment to see which method you prefer. It is simpler to set precise times in the Source view monitor, but it's quick and easy on the Timeline.

1. **Move the zoom slider on the Timeline to approximately 1/2 magnification.**
   Scroll through the project to display the last few clips on the Timeline in Video 1.

2. **Collapse all Video and Audio tracks except for Video 1.**
   You don't need content from any other track for this tutorial.

Table 3-1: Settings for Timeline Edits

Clip Name	Original Length	Set In point to	Set Out point to	Final Duration
v_gardens.mpg	07:13	00:19	02:08	01:20
v_drink.mpg	08:11	05:24	07:13	01:20
v_palms_night.mpg	07:29	04:06	06:20	02:15

3. **Adjust the last three clips in the project according to the values listed in Table 3-1.**

   Set the In and Out points and the start times as described in the table.

<NOTE>

The final location for the three clips isn't critical at this point. You adjust them in the next session.

4. **Click Video 1 in the headings section of the Timeline.**

   You add a clip directly to the track in the following steps, and it must be selected or targeted.

<NOTE>

Only one track is the targeted track at one time. You can see that it is a darker gray in the Timeline.

5. **Move the CTI to the open space following** v_garden.mpg.

   The location isn't critical, as long as it is at or beyond the right margin of the v_garden.mpg clip. In the example, the CTI is at 01:08:15.

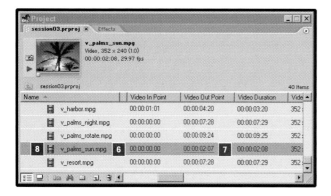

6. **Open the Project window. Click the** v_palms_sun.mpg **clip to activate it.**

You insert the clip into the project at a targeted location.

7. **Scroll right through the values headings to the Video In and Video Out points. Leave the In point at 00:00. Click the Video Out Point, and type** 207.

8. **Right-click over the filmstrip icon to the left of the clip's name.**

The shortcut menu opens.

9. **Click Overlay.**

The shortcut menu closes, and the clip is added to Video 1 at the CTI location.

10. **Select the** v_palms_sun.mpg **clip on the Timeline in Video 1.**

Check its values in the Info window. The clip has a duration of 02:08.

11. **Choose File→Save, or press Ctrl+S to save the project.**

You edited three more clips on the Timeline and added one clip from the Project window using an Overlay edit.

Tip for Editing in the Source View Monitor

Sometimes you know the length of clip you need, but you aren't sure of the precise In or Out points. Set the In and Out points; the selected duration is a blue gradient over the time ruler. Look closely at the center of the duration. You see a set of four vertical bars. As you move the cursor over the duration bar, it turns into a hand; click the vertical bars, and it becomes a dragging hand. Now you can reposition the clip duration and test the results anywhere along the clip's Timeline using the Play In to Out command.

» Session Review

In this session, you learned several ways to edit your projects' clips. First, you learned how to organize and manipulate the Timeline to show the working area more clearly. You learned how to unlink audio and video tracks from a movie clip. You learned how to do various types of edits such as extractions, overlay edits, and rolling edits. You edited clips in the Timeline, the Source Monitor view, and the Project window. You learned how to work with markers, adding them to the Timeline for reference and transferring them to the Project view for editing.

The clips are edited to display the segment that best contributes to the overall movie that you are building. Certain clips required a great deal of editing, while others needed little or no editing. The first image in this session shows one of the first clips with which you worked in this session; the final image shows one of the last clips with which you worked. That's quite a variety of material.

Here are some questions to help you review the information in this session. You can find the answer to each question in the tutorial noted in parentheses.

1. How do you lock a track on the Timeline? Is it always necessary? (See Tutorial: Configuring the Timeline Layout.)

2. How do you determine the length of a blank area on the Timeline? (See Tutorial: Unlinking and Modifying a Movie Clip.)

3. How do you tell whether a video and audio track of a movie is linked? How is it different to work with than a linked movie? (See Tutorial: Unlinking and Modifying a Movie Clip.)

4. How do you add a marker to a Timeline? How are they used? (See Tutorial: Using a Rolling Edit on the Timeline.)

5. How can you tell whether a clip on the Timeline is displaying the first frame? The last frame? (See Tutorial: Using a Rolling Edit on the Timeline.)

6. What does the Rolling Edit tool do? How does it affect the clips on both sides of an edit? (See Tutorial: Using a Rolling Edit on the Timeline.)

7. What happens to the underlying clip if you drag one clip over another on the Timeline? (See Tutorial: Adjusting Clips on the Timeline.)

8. Where do markers added to a clip in the Source view monitor display? (See Tutorial: Editing a Clip Using Multiple Windows.)

9. When you add a marker to the Timeline's time ruler, where else in the program is the marker visible? (See Tutorial: Extracting a Clip Segment in the Program View Monitor.)

10. What is an Extract edit? How is it performed? (See Tutorial: Extracting a Clip Segment in the Program View Monitor.)

11. What is a Lift edit? How are Extract and Lift edits different? (See Tutorial: Extracting a Clip Segment in the Program View Monitor.)

12. What is an Overlay edit? How is it performed? (See Tutorial: Completing Some Beach Segment Edits.)

» Other Projects

Save an extra copy of the project. As in the Other Projects in Session 2, practice working with different edits. This time, in addition to editing in different windows, experiment with some of the advanced edits you used in this session or read about in the discussion.

Using Transitions

Tutorial: **Inserting Transitions**

Tutorial: **Using a Transition to Show Two Clips**

Tutorial: **Using Another Push Transition**

Tutorial: **Adding an Iris Transition**

Tutorial: **Organizing Clips and Applying Dissolves**

Tutorial: **Freezing a Video Frame**

Tutorial: **Adding a Pair of Iris Transitions**

Session Introduction

In the first few sessions, you've come a long way in understanding how to organize and assemble a project, as well as how to edit video.

If you have worked with presentation software such as PowerPoint, you've had an introduction to transitions, which is a method of graphically changing from one image to another. Unlike those found in presentation software, the Premiere transitions are highly customizable. You can vary their start times, end times, positions, and length; use them in combination; and even program some of them to create your own transitions.

Transitions are used to transition a pair of clips in any track (or a clip and a blank space). In this session, you add transitions to the beginning and ending portions of the project. You use a variety of transitions both at the start and the end of the project; you start at the beginning and work your way to the end. All transitions are managed in the Effect Controls window (ECW). You can control some aspects of all transitions, and some have complex controls. Along with learning how to apply, adjust, and set transitions, you also learn how to use freeze frames to correct clip length problems.

On the CD-ROM, in the Bonus Discussion, More Premiere Pro Features, read the discussion named *Design Considerations for Using Transitions* for information on how to choose transitions depending on the message or tone you are trying to set in your project. In this project, the city segment has an agitated, hurried tone, while the beach segment is more laid back and fun.

Before you start working on this session, preview the sample file, session04.wmv to see how different types of transitions look in action. Then start the session with the discussion on choosing and using transitions.

TOOLS YOU'LL USE
Additive Dissolve transition, Effect Controls window, Effects tab, Iris Round transition, Iris Square transition, Push transition, Rate Expand tool, Ripple Trim edit tool, Transition settings, Video Transitions folder, Zoom level control

MATERIALS REQUIRED
Session03 project file that you created, or the session03.prproj file, session04.wmv preview file (samples folder)

TIME REQUIRED
90 minutes

Tutorial
» Inserting Transitions

You use a number of different types of transitions in the project. In this tutorial, you reconfigure the program layout and define the default transition; you also apply your first transition. The tutorial explains how to use a program workspace to organize the screen, so you may want to modify the layout further to make different windows easier to see. Transitions are applied based on the CTI location or the location between two clips. This location is referred to as the cut point.

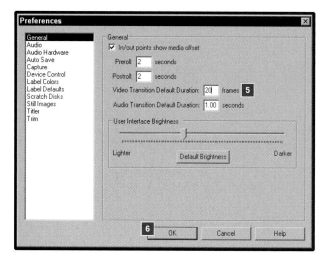

<NOTE>
You may want to rearrange the layout further. For example, click+ drag the Effect Controls window to separate it from the Monitor window. Then you can resize the dialog box more easily without affecting the size of the Project Monitor window. This configuration is used in the figures throughout the session to show you the contents of the ECW more clearly.

1. **Open Premiere Pro. When the Welcome window opens, choose** session03.prproj.
   The Welcome window closes, and the project is loaded into the program.

2. **Choose File→Save As, and resave the project file as** session04.prproj.
   The name of the new project version displays at the top of the program window.

3. **Choose Window→Workspace→Effects.**
   The program layout changes. The Effects tab is now visible in the project file in the Project window.

<NOTE>
If you didn't do the tutorials in Session 3, copy the session03.prproj file from the CD to your hard drive. In the Welcome window, choose Open Project. Browse to the location where you stored the copied project file, and select Open. Then resave the project in Premiere Pro as session04.prproj (or use another filenaming convention).

4. **Choose Edit→Preferences, and click General when the Preferences dialog box opens.**

5. **Click the Video Transition Default Duration field, and type** 20 **frames.**
   The default length of time is 30 frames, or one second; for most of the project, you use a slightly shorter transition time. Changing the default time saves time as you add transitions to the clips; instead of applying the transition and then changing its length, the default is already at the length you use most often.

6. **Click OK to close the dialog box.**
   The default transition time is reset. The duration remains at 20 frames until you reset the preference.

7. **In the Effects tab, type** dissolve **in the Contains field.**
   One folder in the Video Transitions folder opens and displays four dissolve transitions. The icon before the Cross-Dissolve transition is framed in red. This means that the Cross-Dissolve transition is the default transition set in the project. Leave the folder open and the transition displayed.

<**NOTE**>
The Cross-Dissolve transition is the program default transition. You can set a different default transition. Click the desired transition, and then click the flyout menu at the top right of the Effects tab to open a short menu. Click Set Default Transition. Also from the flyout menu, you can reset the default transition duration, which opens the Preferences dialog box that you adjusted in Steps 4 through 6.

8. **Adjust the layout of the Timeline to view the Video 1 track more clearly:**
   Drag the height of Video 1 to a larger size.
   Drag the audio tracks lower to make more space for the video tracks.
   You add the first transition to a clip on Video 1.

9. **Click** c_night.mov **in Video 1 starting at 00:20.**
   You add the first transition to the clip.

10. **Click the time indicator to make it active, and type** 20.
    The CTI jumps to 00:20. The transition is added based on the CTI location.

<**TIP**>
You can also use shortcut keys to move the CTI between edits. Press Page Up to move to the edit before the CTI's current position; press Page Down to move to the edit following the CTI's current position.

11. **Drag the Cross-Dissolve transition from the Effects tab to the CTI location, also known as the cut point or edit line on the** `c_night.mov` **clip. Do not release the mouse yet.**

The first segment of the clip (equivalent in length to the transition's duration) reverses color when the transition is positioned correctly.

<NOTE>

Transitions snap to the cut point in one of three ways—either they overlay the cut point with an equal number of frames of the transition applied to the clips on either side of the cut point; the transition ends at the cut point (applied only to the clip prior to the cut point); or the transition starts at the cut point, and is applied only to the clip following the cut point.

12. **Release the mouse to apply the transition.**

The transition starts at the first frame of the clip and extends 20 frames into the clip.

13. **Click the transition on the** `c_night.mov` **clip.**

The transition opens in the Effect Controls window (ECW). The ECW is tabbed with the Source view monitor in the Monitor window.

14. Click Show Actual Sources.

The black space at the start of the project and the
c_night.mov clip show in the A and B preview areas
respectively.

**15. Click the Play/Stop button in the Effects Controls window to pre-
view the transition.**

The button toggles from an arrow (Play) to a square (Stop).
The transition plays in the preview area.

<NOTE>

In the ECW, you see a grayed-out option named Alignment, with
"Start at Cut" next to the term. The option is unavailable for this
transition because you are applying it to one clip only. In later tutorials, you see that the transition can be applied at various locations
related to the cut point between clips.

16. Save the project.

You configured the program's layout and added the first transition to your project.

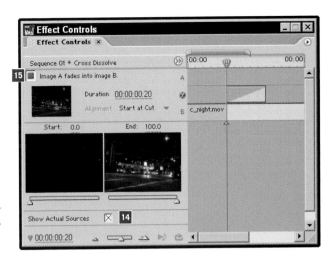

Finding Transitions

Can't remember where a transition is located? Type the name of
the transition in the Contains field at the top of the Effects tab in
the Project window. The transition and its folder scroll into view.
Use the same find process to locate audio and video effects and
audio transitions.

Tutorial
» Using a Transition to Show Two Clips

The next location for a transition is between the c_night.mov clip and the c_subway2.mov clip on Video 1. The transition that you apply in this tutorial doesn't change the view from one clip to another; instead you use it as a way to position the contents of the two clips to play at the same time. This is a split-screen effect. You apply the same transition to two pairs of clips. Additional elements are added to the split screens starting in Session 8.

1. **In the Effects tab, type** push **in the Contains field.**

   The Slide folder in the Video Transitions folder opens, and the Push transition is displayed.

   <NOTE>

   If you want to browse through the Effects folders, delete the content from the Contains field first. Otherwise, all you see are the filters and effects that contain the search term.

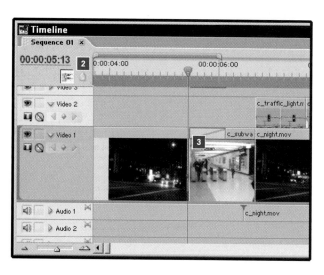

2. **On the Timeline, move the CTI to the start of the** c_subway2.mov **on Video 1 starting at 05:13.**

   Press Page Up or Page Down to move the CTI to the cut point at 05:13.

3. **Drag the Push transition from the Effects tab to the Timeline, and drop it just to the right of the CTI.**

   The transition is applied to the right of the CTI. The transition extends for 20 frames, as that is the length you reset as the default in the previous tutorial.

4. **On the Source view monitor, click the Set In Point button.**
   The In point for the transition is set at 05:13.

<NOTE>

If you set In and Out points on the Timeline, you can quickly and easily view the transitions as you apply and modify them.

5. **Move the CTI to 08:09. Click the Set Out Point button to set the Out point for the transition.**

6. **Click the Loop button.**
   The selected Timeline segment loops when you preview.

7. **On the Timeline, click the Push transition that you added in Step 3 to the** c_subway2.mov **clip to open it in the ECW.**
   You modify the transition's settings. The default layout of the ECW shows the before and after clips as A and B in the preview area.

8. **Click the Duration value, and type** 107.
   You lengthen the transition to the length of the entire c_subway2.mov clip. The Alignment option changes to Custom Start automatically.

<NOTE>

The hatched area at the right edge of the purple transition bar indicates that the transition extends beyond the end of the c_night.mov clip. Now look at the c_night.mov clip in green above the purple transition track. A vertical bar at the same location at which the hatched area starts on the transition track shows the end point of the c_night.mov clip.

9. **Click Show Actual Sources.**
   The default A and B images are replaced by the two clips.

10. **Click the edge selector arrow at the right of the sample.**
    This sets the orientation for the transition—that is, the direction displayed on the screen. The default option uses an edge selector arrow on the top of the sample, which splits the screen horizontally.

<TIP>

This transition is frozen—that is, the start and end positions are the same. In a moving transition, you choose the side from which you want the transition to start and where you want it to end.

11. **Type** 50 **in both the Start and End fields above the A and B preview areas.**
    You set the start and end points to 50%. Rather than one clip replacing the other, both are displayed over half the screen—this is a split-screen effect.

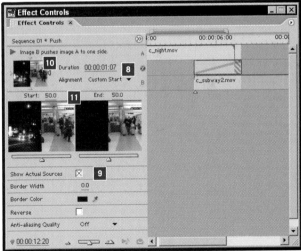

<NOTE>

Some transitions are directional, that is, they can be applied from several directions. For example, a wipe can start from the left and proceed to the right, or vice versa. At the edges of the sample area you see small arrows for directional transitions. Click an arrow to define the direction the transition is applied.

> **117**

12. On the Program view monitor, click the Play In to Out button.

The segment of the Timeline defined by In and Out points earlier in the tutorial play, showing the transition. Click the Play In to Out button again to stop the playback.

< N O T E >

When you are previewing transitions, you can only view them in the Program view monitor. The Source view monitor shows the clip, but doesn't show applied effects.

13. Click on the eye icon for Video 2 to toggle it off.

You work with the clips in Video 1, and the traffic light clips are visible overlaying the Video 1 content.

14. Press the Page Down key to move the CTI to the next cut point at the start of the second copy of the c_night.mov clip at 06:14.

You add another copy of the Push transition.

15. Drag the Push transition listing from the Effects tab, and drop it on the cut point at 06:14.

The transition is added to the clip and extends for the 20 frames right of the cut point.

16. Drag the right margin of the Push transition right until its length is 01:25.

You can see the duration, start time, and end time for transitions in the Info window. The extra length used for the transition is the segment of the c_subway2.mov beyond the Out point that you set in an earlier session.

17. Click the transition to display it in the ECW. Repeat Steps 9 through 11 to modify the settings. Repeat Step 12 to preview the clip in the Program view monitor.

18. **Save the project.**

You added a Push transition to two pairs of clips and configured the transitions to create a split-screen effect. The split screens are an interesting way of showing more than one clip on the screen at a time. Showing two scenes at once contributes to the tone of the city segment of the project, which is quite rushed and hurried.

Tutorial
» Using Another Push Transition

Moving along the Timeline, you add transitions to another pair of clips. The first is another Push transition, and the second is a simple dissolve. The clips you work with in this tutorial are the drivethrough traffic clips. As described in the preceding tutorial, preview the segment of the Timeline in the Program view monitor. On the Timeline or in the Program view monitor's timeline, move the cursor over the set of four vertical bars at the center of the bracketed In to Out area. Drag the bracketed area right along the Timeline as you work with different parts of the project.

1. Move the CTI to the start of the `c_drive1.mov` on Video 1 starting at 11:08. Press the Page Up or Page Down key to move the CTI to the cut point at 11:08.

2. Drag the Push transition from the Effects window to the Timeline, and drop it over the CTI.
   The transition is applied at its default length of 20 frames.

3. Drag the right margin of the transition to extend it the full length of the `c_drive1.mov` clip.
   The clip is 00:21 in length; dragging the margin of the transition increases its length to 00:21 as well.

4. Click the transition to display it in the ECW.
   You modify the settings as in the preceding tutorial.

5. In the ECW, set these options:
   Set the Start and End points at 50%.
   Click the edge selector arrow at the left of the sample.
   Click Show Actual Sources to see the clips in the ECW.

6. Preview the transition segment in the Project view monitor.
   You see the drivethrough traffic on the left side of the screen.

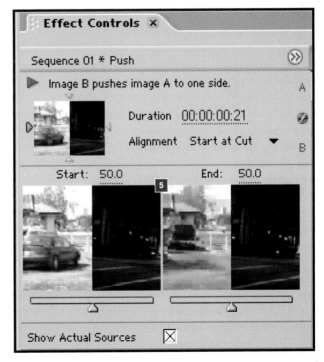

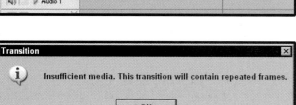

Transition Handles

You see in some of the transitions you apply in this session that the transition bar shows hatch marks, or displays a warning about repeating frames. In some cases, there are extra frames before and/or after the In and Out points on a clip. At other times, no extra frames exist, and you see the warning. The transition is applied to the content before or after the In or Out point, and the actual footage that you designate with the In and Out points is seen clearly. This method of applying transitions preserves the action in your clip.

7. **Press the Page Down key to jump to the next cut point at 11:29.**
   The `c_drive2.mov` clip starts at this cut point.

8. **Press Ctrl+D, the shortcut key for applying the default transition.**
   A dialog box opens stating that there is insufficient media and that frames will be repeated.

9. **Click OK to close the warning dialog box and apply the transition.**

10. **Preview the transition area in the Project view monitor.**
    Look at the first segment of the transition starting at 12:00. You see that the first clip remains static as it fades out, while the second clip is in motion. The effect complements the look of the pair of clips.

11. **Save the project.**
    You added another pair of transitions. You added one final Push transition and applied the default transition using a shortcut key. You have now added three split screen segments to the project. The split screen areas are used as the foundation for more clips and effects applied over the rest of the sessions.

Tutorial
» Adding an Iris Transition

If you watch old-fashioned cartoons or silent movies, you have seen the Iris Round transition in action in which a circle expands or shrinks to gradually show underlying action. You use the Iris Round transition later in the session. In this tutorial, you use the Iris Square transition, which is very similar in effect—only the shape is different.

1. Move the CTI to the next cut point at 12:23.
The Iris Square transition is used to transition from the second drivethrough clip to the man throwing paper in the air at the end of the city segment of the movie.

2. In the Effects tab, select Video Transitions→Iris→Iris Square.
You apply the transition to the clip. You can also search for the clip by typing the name in the Contains field.

3. Drag the Iris Square transition to the cut point at the c_man_papers.mov clip on Video 1.
The transition is applied to the clip to the right of the cut point.

4. Click the transition on the Timeline to open the Iris Square settings in the ECW.
You customize the settings for the transition.

< T I P >
Leave the default A and B preview views so you can see the center point more clearly.

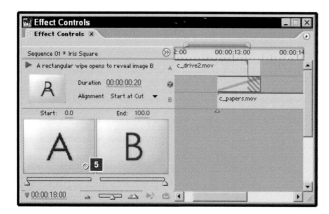

5. **Move the transition's center point to the bottom right of preview area A.**

   The center point is the small white circle at the center of the Start preview. It defines the location on the screen where the transition opens.

   < N O T E >

   The center point of the transition is at the center of the screen by default. You can move the center point to any location on the screen.

6. **Click the Play In to Out button in the Program view monitor to preview the transition. Click Stop or press the spacebar to stop the playback.**

   You see the video of the man gradually open to replace the drivethrough clip.

   < T I P >

   You can also preview the transition area using the CTI in the ECW. Click+drag the CTI across the clips and watch the transition in the Project view monitor.

7. **Save the project.**

   You added an Iris Square transition to transition the drive-through traffic clip to the man throwing paper. The square iris is a linear transition. The sharp angles of the transition are in keeping with the tone of the city segment of the project.

Tutorial
» Organizing Clips and Applying Dissolves

Now it's time to return to the end of the project and work with the last few clips again. In this tutorial, you align the clips that you edited in the preceding session. The exact location of your clips on the Timeline depends on whether you moved them after setting In and Out points in the last session; the final placements on the Timeline weren't important. In this tutorial, you move clips to specified locations, adjust the rate of one clip using a tool, and apply the first transitions for this segment of the project. You use a different transition placement than you have used previously.

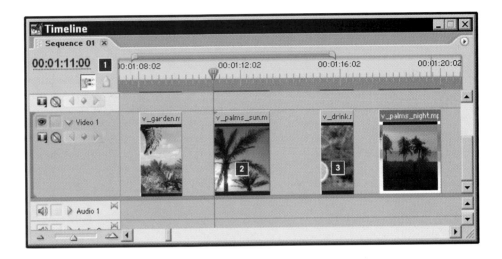

1. **In the time indicator on the Timeline, type** 11100.
   The CTI jumps to 01:11:00. You start working with a set of clips from this location.

<NOTE>
In case you were wondering, you ARE going to do something with the clips added to the first minute or so of the beach segment. Starting in Session 8, you work with a variety of animation and effects tools, which are featured in the beach segment. The material in that segment of the movie does use a few transitions, but you apply them as you work with other effects.

2. **Click** v_palms_sun.mpg **on Video 1; drag the clip to snap to the CTI.**
   The clip starts at 01:11:00. It's duration is 02:08; the clip ends at 01:13:08.

3. **Click the** v_drink.mpg **clip to the right of** v_palms_sun.mpg. **Press Alt+left arrow on the keyboard to nudge the clip left until the start time is at 01:15:08.**

<TIP>
Press Alt+left arrow to nudge the clip left frame by frame; press Alt+right arrow to nudge the clip right one frame at a time. Press the Shift+Alt+left or right arrow key to nudge the clip five frames at a time in either direction.

> **123**

4. **Using the method of your choice, move the**
   v_palms_night.mpg **clip to a start time of 01:17:20.**
   The clip ends at 01:20:03.

5. **Press the Page Down key to move the CTI to the next cut point.**
   The CTI moves to the end of the v_palms_sun.mpg clip
   ending at 01:20:03.

6. **Drag the** v_garden.mpg **clip located to the left of the**
   v_palms_sun.mpg **clip on Video 1 to snap to the CTI at**
   01:13:08 (at the right edge of the v_palms_sun.mpg **clip).**
   The clip's duration is 01:20, and it ends at 01:14:28. There
   is a gap of 00:10 following the clip.

7. **Press Ctrl+D.**
   The default transition, Additive Dissolve, is added to the clips.
   The transition is centered over the cut point and extends
   for 00:20.

8. **Click the Additive Dissolve transition on the Timeline to display it**
   in the ECW. Click the Duration value of 00:20 to activate the field,
   and type 100.
   You increase the length of the transition to one second.

< T I P >

You can type **30** instead of **100**. The program converts the number
of frames automatically—that is, 30 frames is the same as 1 second based on your frame rate of 30 frames/second.

9. **Click Show Actual Sources.**
   The two clips display in the preview areas replacing the
   default A and B images.

10. **Click the Play/Stop button to preview the clip in the preview area.**
    You see the palm trees fade out and the garden fade in.

11. **Press the Page Up key.**

    In the Source view monitor, you see that the CTI jumps to the starting frame of the `v_palms_sun.mpg` clip at 01:11:00. The Source view monitor and Timeline display the same information at the same time and use the same shortcut keys.

12. **Click the Set In Point button on the Source view monitor toolbar.**

    The In point is set.

13. **Press the Page Down key several times to move the CTI to the end of the `v_palms_night.mpg` clip at 01:20:03. Click the Set Out Point button on the Source view monitor toolbar.**

    You set an In to Out point range on the project to use for previewing the transitions, as you did in an earlier tutorial for the first segment of the Timeline.

<TIP>

Instead of using the Page Down key, you can type **12003** in the time indicator in either the Timeline or the Program view monitor to move the CTI into position.

14. **Click Play In to Out on the Program view monitor to play the specified segment of the Timeline.**

15. **Click the Rate Stretch tool on the toolbar to select it.**

    You adjust the rate of a clip.

16. **Move the Rate Stretch tool over the right margin of the `v_garden.mpg` clip ending at 01:14:28.**

    The tool becomes active; you see that the vertical bracket turns red.

17. **Drag the right margin of the `v_garden.mpg` clip right with the Rate Stretch tool until the gap is filled.**

    The clip extends to 02:00, and its rate decreases to a speed of 83.33%.

<CAUTION>

Don't simply click+drag the right margin of the clip with the default Selection tool. You want to use the current In and Out points; if you click+drag the margin, you add extra frames to the end of the clip. You can also right-click the clip, choose Speed/Duration, and reset the duration in the dialog box.

18. **Click the Selection tool on the toolbar to deselect the Rate Stretch tool.**

19. **Save the project.**

    You organized a set of four clips that are shown at the end of the beach segment of the movie. You added one transition centered over the cut point to change the scene from palm trees to a garden, and extended the rate of one clip using the Rate Stretch tool.

Tutorial
» Freezing a Video Frame

Isn't this interesting? This is a session about using transitions and I want you to freeze frames. One way you can control how transitions look and work is by combining video and still images. Rather than exporting a frame of a clip and then importing it as a still image, you can freeze the video frame. A freeze frame extends the length of a single frame to use for transitioning when you don't want to use any action during the transition. In this tutorial, you learn how to freeze a clip so that only one frame displays for the duration of the clip. You use the Out point in the project.

1. **Click** v_drink.mpg **in Video 1 starting at 01:15:08. Choose Edit →Copy, or press Ctrl+C, to copy the clip.**

2. **Move the CTI to the end of the** v_palms_night.mpg **clip at 01:20:03. Choose Edit→Paste, or press Ctrl+V.**
   You paste a copy of the clip following the last clip in the sequence.

< N O T E >

The copy of the v_drink.mpg clip is moved later in the tutorial to its final location. If you paste the clip to its final location at its present length, you shuffle other clips on the Timeline. It takes more steps to correct the layout than pasting to a blank area and then moving after the clip is resized.

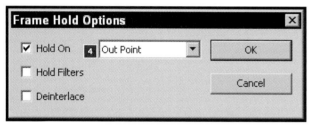

3. **Choose Clip→Video Options→Frame Hold.**
   The Frame Hold Options dialog box opens.

4. **Click the drop-down arrow, and choose Out Point. Click Hold On, and then click OK to close the dialog box.**

< N O T E >

Using the Frame Hold option is the same as using a single frame of a clip as a still image. You can choose the clip's In point, its Out point, or add a marker numbered 0 to the clip and use that location as the Frame Hold location. You can choose from three different types of holds. You can choose the default Hold On (you use this option) or define a location to hold effects called Hold Filters, or modify the characteristics of the video clip, called Deinterlace.

5. **On the Timeline, drag the right edge of the** v_drink.mpg **copy until the length is 01:00.**
   Check the length in the Info window as you drag the edge. You shorten the clip before moving it.

6. **Drag** v_drink.mpg **from its position following the**
   v_palms_night.mpg **clip at 01:20:04. Drop it in the blank**
   space starting at 01:16:18.

7. **Preview the sequence in the Program view monitor.**
   You see that the v_drink.mpg clip plays and then the Out
   point displays for the duration of the second copy of the clip.

8. **Save the project.**
   You added a shortened copy of the tropical drink clip and
   applied a Frame Hold to display the Out point of the clip. The
   frozen copy of the clip showing the tropical drink is used along
   with other clips in the project to create some interesting transitions at the end of the beach segment. In the next tutorial,
   you use the new clip in two transitions.

Tutorial
» Adding a Pair of Iris Transitions

In the preceding tutorial, you created a shortened copy of the v_drink.mpg clip and applied a freeze frame to hold the Out point. This tutorial uses two copies of the Iris Round transition in conjunction with the two copies of the v_drink.mpg clip. Like the Iris Square transition that you applied earlier in the session, one clip is replaced by another through an expanding display, in this case a circle. You also learn a way to precisely place the center point of a transition. When you have finished applying the transitions, move the CTI to the start of the clip sequence you work with in this tutorial (at about 01:10:00) and view the Timeline in the Program view monitor.

1. **Move the CTI to the start of the first copy of the** v_drink.mpg **clip at 01:15:08.**

   Press the Page Up or Page Down key to jump between cut points, or type the value in the time indicator.

2. **In the Effects tab, choose Video Transitions→Iris→Iris Round.**
   You select the first transition.

3. **Drag the Iris Round transition from the Effects tab to the cut point that you set in Step 1.**
   The transition is added to the clips, centered on the cut point. Click the transition to open it in the ECW.

4. **Click the default duration, 00:20, and type** 105.
   You increase the length of the transition to 01:05.

5. **Click Show Actual Sources.**
   The garden clip displays in the preview A area, and the drink displays in the preview B area.

6. **Click Reverse to swap the views.**

   Now the garden displays in the preview B area, and the drink is in the preview A area. You can't control the direction of the transition, that is, whether it starts in B and ends in A or starts in A and ends in B; the transition always moves in the same direction. If you swap the views, you can control which clip is seen as going "into" or coming "out" of the other.

7. **Drag the center point down and to the right to center it over the center of the orange slice.**

   The transition opens at the center of the orange slice, rather than from the general center of the screen.

8. **Click Reverse again to swap the views back to their original locations.**

   You precisely placed the center for the transition.

9. **Preview the transition in the ECW or in the Program view monitor.**

   You see the garden gradually replaced by the drink from the orange slice outward.

10. **Move the CTI to the next cut point of 1:17:18 using the method of your choice.**

    The next cut point follows the copy of the v_drink.mpg clip.

11. **Drag the Iris Round transition from the Effects tab to the cut point.**

    This time, release the transition to the left of the CTI.

< T I P >

If you slowly move the transition over the CTI location, you see little icons that indicate whether the transition is at the left, at the right, or centered over the cut point.

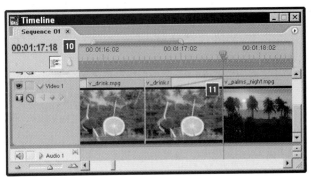

12. **Click the transition on the Timeline to open it in the ECW.**

    You customize the transition the same way as you did for the first copy of the Iris Round transition.

< N O T E >

In the ECW, you see that the transition is at its default duration of 00:20, and its Alignment is shown as End at Cut.

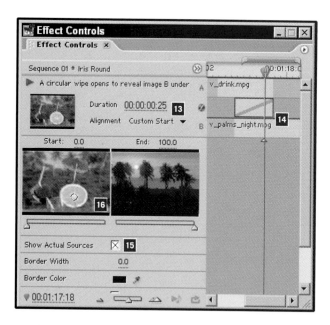

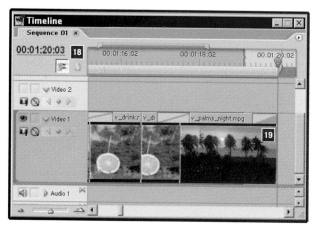

13. **In the ECW, click the duration to activate the field and type** 25.

    You increase the length of the transition to 00:25.

14. **Move the mouse over the transition; you see the cursor change to the Ripple Trim tool. Drag the transition right several frames to end at 01:17:25.**

    You can check the exact location in the Info window as you move the transition in the ECW.

15. **Click Show Actual Sources.**

    The two clips display in the preview A and B areas.

16. **Drag the center point down and to the right.**

    You align the center of the transition over the center of the orange, which means the palm trees clip gradually appears from the location of the orange's center outward, rather than from the center of the screen outward.

17. **Preview the segment in the Program view monitor.**

    You see the first Iris Round open to the drink clip and then close again to the palm trees.

18. **Move the CTI to the last cut point in the project at 01:20:03.**

    You add one final transition.

19. **Press Ctrl+D to add the default transition.**

    A 20-frame Additive Dissolve transition is added to the v_palms_night.mpg clip. The program allows the transition to be added only before the cut point because no clips follow the cut point.

20. **Save the project.**

    You added two Iris transitions to a pair of clips and added a final transition for the project. Using the same transition and the frozen copy of the tropical drink clip, you can see the garden transitioning to the center of the orange and then expanding outward again to show the next scene, the palm trees at night.

» Session Review

This session covered working with transitions. You learned how to add different types of transitions to your project—from simple to customized to specialized. You learned how to freeze a clip to use as a still image. You applied some simple transitions, such as the default Additive Dissolve, and used Push transitions to create a split-screen effect. You added the transitions to your project, and you learned to make attractive visual changes between clips, such as what is shown in the final figure in this session. This is one of the frames using an Additive Dissolve transition. Compare it to the same frame shown at the beginning of this session. Doesn't this final image look more interesting?

Here are questions to help you review the information in this session. You can find the answer to each question in the tutorial noted in parentheses.

1. How do you set a default transition? How is it identified in the Video Transitions listing? (See Tutorial: Inserting Transitions.)

2. How do you control the start and end points of a transition? (See Tutorial: Using a Transition to Show Two Clips.)

3. Can you preview the actual clips being used in a transition in the ECW? (See Tutorial: Using a Transition to Show Two Clips.)

4. What keyboard shortcut keys can you use to apply the default transition? (See Tutorial: Using Another Push Transition.)

5. What happens if there aren't enough frames before or after a clip to use for a transition? (See Tutorial: Using Another Push Transition.)

6. How do you adjust the center point for an Iris transition? (See Tutorial: Adding an Iris Transition.)

7. What keyboard shortcuts do you use to move the CTI to the next cut point? To the previous cut point? (See Tutorial: Organizing Clips and Applying Dissolves.)

8. What is the Rate Extend tool and how do you use it? (See Tutorial: Organizing Clips and Applying Dissolves.)

9. What options can you use to define a freeze frame? (Tutorial: Freezing a Video Frame.)

10. How do you use the Slide tool with a transition in the ECW? (See Tutorial: Adding a Pair of Iris Transitions.)

» Other Projects

You used a limited number of transitions in this project. Spend time experimenting with other transition options. Open a copy of the project. Using two clips, try different transitions. Preview the transitions in the Transitions dialog box, or set In and Out points for a segment of the Timeline and preview in the Project view monitor. Do you find any that are particularly interesting, particularly attractive, unattractive, or downright ugly? Think of projects in which different types of transitions would be appropriate.

Part IV

Working with Audio

Session 5 **Editing Audio Clips**   p 134

Session 6 **Mixing Audio and
        Adding Effects**   p 164

Editing Audio Clips

Discussion: **How and Why to Use Audio**

Tutorial: **Organizing the Timeline for Audio**

Tutorial: **Preparing Audio Files**

Discussion: **Understanding Audio Characteristics**

Tutorial: **Adding Trimmed Audio Clips to the Timeline**

Tutorial: **Editing Audio Clips in the Timeline**

Tutorial: **Adjusting Audio Signal**

Tutorial: **Editing a Group of Clips in the Timeline**

Tutorial: **Applying Sound Transitions**

Session Introduction

In this session, you start working with the audio in your project. You add numerous sound effect clips to the first segment, learn how to edit the clips, and learn how to use more than one copy of an audio track. You can put your newly gained video editing skills into practice with the audio clips, because many of the processes are the same. You also add new audio tracks to the project and manage the Timeline display in this session.

All the clips that you need for the first section of the project were imported into your project in Session 1. Aside from the sound of the ocean, you work only with the clips in the city segment of the project in this session.

You can work with audio in two ways in Premiere: in the Timeline and Source view monitor and in the Audio Mixer window. You work in the Timeline and Source view monitor in this session. The Audio Mixer window is a feature first introduced in Premiere 6.0, and it is designed for working in real time; you work with the Audio Mixer in Session 6. This session has an audio-only sample named `session05.wma`. You can hear the raw audio for the first segment of the project after it is trimmed and fades are applied.

TOOLS YOU'LL USE
Add Tracks command, Audio Transitions, Clip Gain dialog box, Constant Power transition, CTI, ECW, Effects tab, Group command, Loop, Play In to Out, Program view monitor, Project window, Render Work Area command, Set In Point button, Set Out Point button, Source view monitor, Time indicator, Timeline, Toggle track output, Ungroup command, Unnumbered markers, Work area bar

MATERIALS NEEDED
Session 4 project file that you created, or the `session4.prproj` file from the CD-ROM

TIME REQUIRED
90 minutes

Discussion

How and Why to Use Audio

Think about the last scary movie you watched, or the last science fiction or space epic. Now think what that movie would be like with the sound turned off. You can still see the door slowly open to allow the bad guy to enter, or a star going super-nova in a blaze of fiery glory. But so much is missing.

That missing ingredient is sound. Sound has three primary functions in a movie. The first is to provide aural cues for events and activities, such as the ominous creaking of an opening door. The second function is to provide an overall mood for the movie. This is the role of the score. Imagine the scary movie with a light-pop soundtrack or a military march. It doesn't have quite the same impact, does it? Of course, there are exceptions to the rule. The evil villain may accomplish his nefarious deeds with a particular musical accompaniment. In that case, the music becomes a cue rather than a basic score.

The final sound function is to provide voices or narration. Since the advent of the "talkies" in the 1920s, you expect to hear actors say something when you see their lips move. Many applications use voiceovers as well, also known as narrations. Sometimes you see text on the screen accompanying the voiceover. Textual cues and voiceovers are often used together in training videos. In other types of videos, such as documentaries and movies in which a narrator is used as a tool for developing the plot or back story, the voice is rarely accompanied by text.

So how does this information apply to the task at hand? Your project has two very distinct elements—the city sequence at the start of the project, followed by the beach sequence. The opening sequence illustrates your prospective client's hurried and harried lifestyle. The sound for this segment should not be calm and tranquil. For this segment, the score is several loops and segments of a drum track. The drum score is strident enough to contribute to the overall sense of irritation and anxiety conveyed by the video in the first segment of the project (without being annoying).

The segue to the second vacation sequence begins with the sound of the ocean. This works as a trigger in the mind of the viewer and makes him begin to think about beaches and oceans before the first video even begins. A clever device, if I do say so myself.

Now consider the beach footage. What kind of music do you consider for the types of video you have assembled for the second half of the project? It can be energetic, because many videos of active water sports and activities are included. It can be light because this is a vacation. It also can be age-appropriate and current as well.

Match your movie's audio message to the overall message of the movie. Choose music and voices that appeal to the audience you are trying to reach, and make sure that the audio and video content match. Accompany soft images with soft music; use heavy drum-laden music for car chases and exploding planets.

Tutorial
» Organizing the Timeline for Audio

In the first session, you imported a folder of audio files into your project. In this tutorial, you configure the Timeline to work with the audio clips. You change the layout, move clips, and change the types of tracks used.

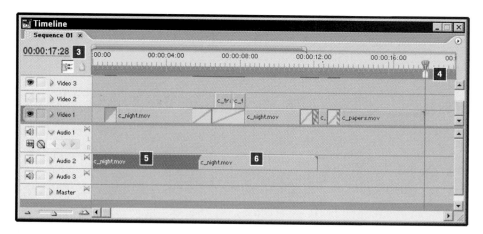

1. **Open Premiere Pro. When the Welcome window opens, choose** `session04.prproj`.
   The Welcome window closes, and the project is loaded into the program.

<NOTE>

If you didn't do the tutorials in Session 4, copy the `session04.prproj` file from the CD to your hard drive. In the Welcome window, choose Open Project. Browse to the location where you stored the copied project file, and select Open. Then resave the project in Premiere Pro as `session05.prproj` (or use another filenaming convention).

2. **Choose File→Save As, and resave the project file as** `session05.prproj`.
   The name of the new project version displays at the top of the program window.

3. **Click the time indicator to make it active, and type** `1728`.
   The CTI jumps to 17:28.

4. **Press * (asterisk) on the number pad to add an unnumbered marker to the Timeline.**
   You use the marker as a frame of reference because it identifies the end of the `c_paper.mov` clip, the last video element in the city segment of the project.

5. **Drag the audio track of the first copy of the** `c_night.mov` **movie from its position starting at 00:20 in Audio 1 to start at 00:00 in Audio 2.**
   You clear out Audio track 1 to use it for the city drum score.

<NOTE>

The positioning you use in Step 5 is a split edit, in which a clip's video and audio components start or end at different times. The clips in the project play the audio before the video starts. This is called a J-cut. If the positioning is reversed, that is, if the audio Out point is later than the video Out point, the edit is called an L-cut.

6. **Drag the audio track from the second copy of the** `c_night.mov` **movie from its position at 06:14 in Audio 1 to follow the first copy in Audio 2.**
   The clip starts at 05:24.

<TIP>

The Audio 1 track is used for the musical scores in the project. Content in the score is marked to correlate with video content in the video tracks. Using Audio 1 allows you to quickly see the markers when you are working with the video tracks.

7. **Click Audio 2 to make it the target track.**
   The background for the head information turns dark gray, and the left edge of the track is bracketed.

8. **Right-click Audio 2 to open a shortcut menu, and choose Add Tracks to open the Add Tracks dialog box.**
   You add one more audio track to the project.

9. **Type 0 in the Add Video Tracks field.**
   The default setting is 1 track; if you don't change the value to 0, you add an additional video track as well.

10. **Type 1 in the Add Audio Tracks field.**
    You add one more track to the project.

11. **Click the Placement drop-down arrow, and choose After Target Track from the options.**
    You want the new track to follow Audio 2.

12. **Click the Track Type drop-down arrow, and choose Mono from the options.**
    You currently have stereo tracks in the project; several of the sound effects are mono clips and require placement on a mono track.

<TIP>
You can see in a track's header area whether it is stereo or mono. A stereo track has a pair of speakers; a mono track shows a single speaker.

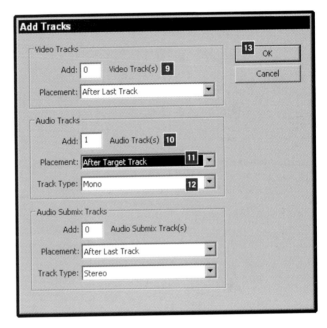

13. **Click OK to close the dialog box.**
    An additional Audio track is added to the project.

14. **Right-click Audio 1, and choose Rename from the shortcut menu. When the track name becomes an active field, type** score.

15. **Repeat Step 14 for Audio 2, Audio 3, and Audio 4. Rename the tracks** fx 1, fx 2, **and** fx 3.

16. **Save the project to save the setting changes.**

You moved the audio segments of two movie clips and added a new track. You named the tracks and added a marker to the Timeline.

Tutorial
» Preparing Audio Files

In the first session, you imported a folder of audio clips into the project. In this tutorial, you trim the clips to length from the Project window, using the Source view monitor.

1. **Click the car.wav clip in the audio folder in the Project window to select it.**
   Basic information about the clip is displayed at the top of the Program window, including sound characteristics and file length.

2. **Double-click car.wav to open it in the Source view monitor.**
   You adjust the In and Out points visually.

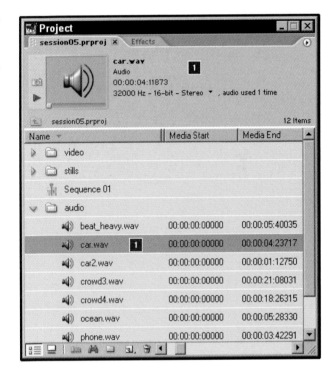

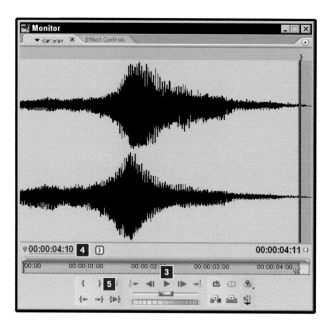

3. **Click the Play button to run the clip.**
   Play the clip several times until you are familiar with the sound.

4. **Click the time indicator to make it active, and type** 410.
   The CTI jumps to 04:10.

5. **Click the Set Out Point button.**
   The clip's Out point is set to 04:10. You see a line through the waveform showing the location of the Out point. When you add the clip to the Timeline later in the session, you see that it loads only the portion between the In and Out points.

6. **Trim the other audio clips using the same process for each.**
   The clip name and the frame at which to set the In and Out points are listed in Table 5.1.

<NOTE>
The beat_heavy.wav and ocean.wav clips are used later in the session and are edited in their respective tutorials.

7. **Save the project.**
   You listened to the audio effects used in the project and trimmed six clips to length. You have prepared all the sound effect clips you need for the city segment of the project. In the next tutorial you add the sound effects to the audio tracks.

Table 5.1: Data for Trimming Audio Clips

Clip	Set Point at...
car2.wav	00:20 (Out point)
crowd3.wav	04:25 (Out point)
crowd4.wav	04:25 (In point) 7:15 (Out point)
phone.wav	01:00 (Out point)
truck_horn.wav	02:00 (Out point)

Discussion
Understanding Audio Characteristics

The same type of information always exists for every audio clip. Along with the file name and format, you see the rate, format, and bit depth settings. Rate (also known as sample rate) ranges from 5000 Hz (hertz) to 48000 Hz. A Hertz is a unit of frequency (or cycle) in a sound wave of one cycle per second.

The audio in the project is conformed to a sample rate of 44100 Hz. When you first import audio clips or movie clips containing audio, Premiere Pro conforms, or adjusts, the audio according to the settings that you apply when the project is created. After audio is brought into the project and conformed, copies of the clips are stored in a folder with your other Premiere Pro files and folders; the folder is named Conformed Audio Files.

In the image of the Project window, you can see the basic information for the sounds used in the project. If you look at the times, however, the numbers look much different than what you have seen previously. The times for audio are displayed in samples. For example, the `car.wav` clip is 04:11 in length (using frames). Using samples, its rate is 04:23717. By the way, in the image, the Audio Info column has been dragged left through the Project window information columns to display the content you see.

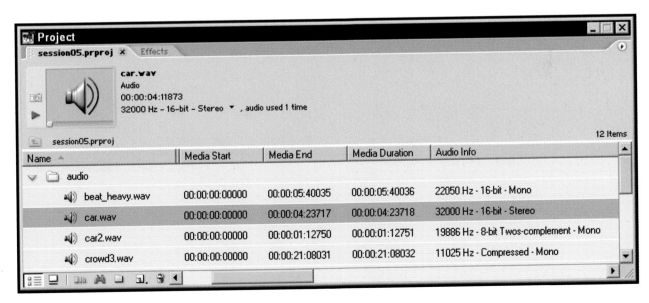

The Master Audio Track

Every sequence you create includes a Master audio track. The Master track can be designated as Mono, Stereo, or 5.1 (Surround Sound) when you create a new sequence. The default option is a Stereo master track. Use the Master track to control output from all the other tracks, such as the volume or balance. For example, you can add audio clips to several tracks, add effects to individual tracks, or to individual clips, and then adjust the entire audio output for your project using the Master track.

Common formats for audio include mono and stereo. Music sounds best in stereo, while voiceovers work well in mono sound. Sound is recorded in two channels—left and right. Monophonic sound (commonly referred to as mono sound) processes each channel separately, and stereo sound processes both channels simultaneously. Bit depth is either 8-bit or 16-bit and refers to the number of bits of data processed in a second. Voices have good quality with 8-bit sound, and music usually sounds better at 16-bit depth. For the most part, there is no advantage to reducing sound to an 8-bit depth as you don't realize much saving in terms of file size, and only degrade the quality. You use both mono and stereo sound in the project.

Premiere Pro includes surround sound, called 5.1 sound. Unlike stereo, which has two channels, the surround sound format contains three front channels (left, center, and right), two rear channels (left and right), and a low-frequency effects (LFE) subwoofer speaker channel.

One final audio format available is called Submix. When you create a submix, you output the signals of any and all channels that you designate. Submixes can be used for applying the same effects or settings to a number of channels at one time.

Tutorial
» Adding Trimmed Audio Clips to the Timeline

You have a total of four audio tracks at this point. Audio 1, which you renamed score in the preceding tutorial, is empty. You go back to that later to add the music score. In this tutorial, you work with fx 1 and fx 2. You have already moved the audio tracks from the c_night.mov clips into fx 1. In this tutorial, you add the audio clips that you trimmed in an earlier tutorial.

1. **Collapse the audio tracks, and shuffle the structure of the Timeline to show all audio tracks plus Video 1.**
   You don't need to see the waveforms, but you do need to see all the tracks.

2. **Drag the** car.wav **clip from the Project window to fx 3. Position the stereo clip on the stereo track to start at 00:00.**

3. **Drag the** car2.wav **clip from the Project window to fx 2, the mono track. Position the clip to start at 01:10.**

4. **Select the** car2.wav **clip that you placed in Step 3. Choose Edit→Copy, or press Ctrl+C.**

5. **Move the CTI to the end of the** car2.wav **clip at 02:01. Choose Edit→Paste, or press Ctrl+V, to paste a second copy of the clip at the CTI.**

<NOTE>

Instead of copying and pasting clips in the Timeline, you can drag new copies from the Project window. Working only in the Timeline is often quicker because you don't have to move from one window to another.

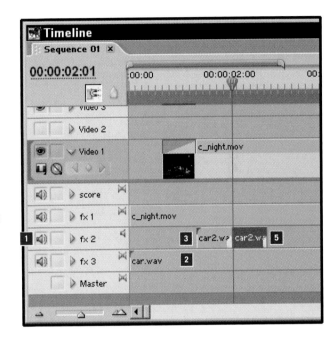

6. **Press Shift and click to select both copies of the** car2.wav **clip. Choose Clip→Group, or press Ctrl+G, to group the pair of clips.**

7. **Choose Edit→Copy, or press Ctrl+C.**
   You copy the group (pair) of clips.

8. **Click the time indicator to make it active, and type** 715.
   The CTI jumps to 07:15.

9. **Press Ctrl+V, or choose Edit→Paste.**
   A second pair of the car2.wav clips is added to the Timeline in fx 2 starting at 07:15.

10. **Choose Clip→Ungroup, or press Ctrl+Shift+G, to ungroup the pair of clips.**
    In order to see the information about each clip and to work with the clips, you have to ungroup them again.

11. **Click the first pair of** car2.wav **clips on fx 2 starting at 01:10. Choose Clip→Ungroup, or press Ctrl+Shift+G.**
    The car2.wav clips are ungrouped.

<NOTE>
You can use the grouping method of adding sequences of the same clip to the Timeline quickly. If you aren't comfortable working with shortcut keys, it may be faster for you to paste single copies to the Timeline.

12. **Add these audio clips from the Project window:**
    truck_horn.wav to fx 3 starting at 09:07
    phone.wav to fx 2 starting at 13:13
    phone.wav to fx 2 starting at 14:14 (following the first copy)

13. **Click the time indicator to make it active, and type** 513.

    The CTI jumps to 05:13, the start of the subway2.mov clip.

14. **Press * (asterisk) on the number pad to add an unnumbered marker.**

    You use the marker location to align clips in the next steps.

15. **Drag the** crowd3.wav **clip from the Project window to the Timeline over the gray area below the Master audio track.**

    A new mono audio track is added to the Timeline, Audio 5, and the crowd3.wav clip is added at the CTI location.

<NOTE>

You can't add the mono crowd3.wav to any track except for fx 2, and the truck_horn.wav clip is already on the fx 2 track in the desired location. Dragging the clip to the area at the bottom of the Timeline adds a clip and a track using the format of the clip being dragged, in this case, a mono clip. You previously added a video clip and a track to the Timeline using the same method.

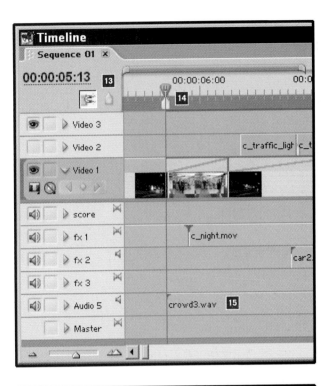

16. **Drag the** crowd4.wav **clip from the Project window to the Timeline. Place it in Audio 5 starting at 14:14.**

<NOTE>

No hard and fast requirements exist for adding sound to tracks. If you are using multi-layered sound effects, such as those in the first segment of the project, the relative strengths of the sound are managed by fade controls. For the most part, I add the master score into the first track and then start layering other sound into subsequent tracks.

17. **In the Project view monitor, click the time indicator and type** 0.

    The CTI moves to the 00:00 start of the project.

18. **Click the Play/Stop button in the Program view monitor to listen to the sound effects that you added.**

    Note the locations where the sounds are placed—for example, the crowd3.wav clip starts when the subway crowd video starts.

19. **Save the project.**

    Your project contains a collection of sound effects now; you added several different city sounds to the city segment of the project either as single clips or in multiples. You learned to group and ungroup clips to speed up the construction process. The sound effects are still in their raw state.

Tutorial
» Editing Audio Clips in the Timeline

The audio clips that you added to the Timeline were trimmed to length in the Source view monitor before you added them to the Timeline. In this tutorial, you edit a clip in the Timeline and correlate the clip with a Timeline marker.

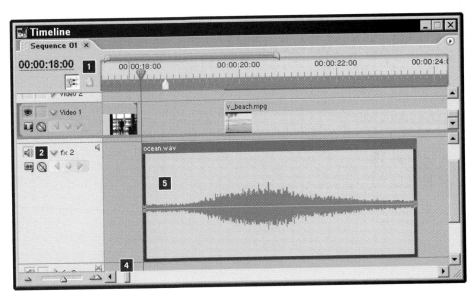

1. **Click the time indicator, and type** 1800.
   The CTI moves to 18:00.

2. **Click the spindown arrow to the left of the fx 2 track name.**
   The track display is opened.

3. **Move the cursor over the separation lines between the audio track headers.**
   You see the horizontal sizing icon display.

4. **Drag downward to increase the height of the fx 2 track.**
   The sizing process is the same as that of the video tracks, except that you drag downward in the Audio portion of the Timeline window to increase the depth of a track; in the Video portion, you drag upward.

5. **Drag the** ocean.wav **clip from the Project window to fx 2 at the CTI position.**
   The clip displays its waveform in the Timeline track.

<NOTE>

Once you are familiar with how audio waveforms look, you can easily identify locations on the audio clip that you want to synchronize with video, or locate errors such as pops or silences. Arrange the audio roughly using the waveform and then tweak it using the Source view monitor, markers, and the Timeline.

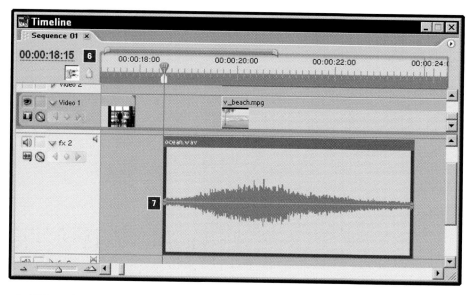

6. **Click the time indicator, and type** 1815.
   The CTI moves to 18:15.

7. **Drag the left margin of the** ocean.wav **clip to snap to the CTI.**
   The clip's length decreases to 05:04. The CTI is at the marker location that you added in an earlier session to identify the end of the city segment; the ocean wave sound builds to start the second segment of the movie.

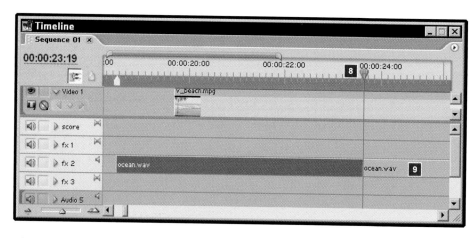

8. **Press Page Down to move the CTI to the end of the** ocean.wav **clip.**
   The first copy of the clip ends at 23:19.

9. **Copy the** ocean.wav **clip. Paste a second copy of the clip on fx 2 starting at 23:19 following the first copy.**

10. **Listen to the segment of the project in the Project view monitor.**
    You hear the sound of two repeating ocean waves.

11. **Save the project.**
    You added the sound of the ocean to your project and edited the clip from the Timeline. The sound of the ocean is used as a segue from the city to the beach segments of the project. It is also the only sound effect you use in the beach segment. In the next session you add the score (music) to the beach segment; you add the drum score to the city segment later in this session.

Tutorial
» Adjusting Audio Signal

Your project uses audio from a number of sources. Because neither you nor I recorded the clips, we have no control over the signal strength used. If you listen to the clips, you can hear differences in how loud or strong they sound. The loudness or strength of a clip is referred to as audio gain. In this tutorial, you adjust the gain of the clips so the sound strength is correct throughout the project.

1. **In the Timeline, press the Home key.**
   The CTI moves to 00:00. You can also type a value in the time indicator.

<TIP>

Use the Home key to move to the start of the Timeline; use the End key to move to the end of the project. For a selected clip, Home moves to the start of the clip, and End moves to the end of the clip.

2. **Right-click the first copy of the** c_night.mov **clip starting at 00:00 in fx 1, and choose Audio Gain from the shortcut menu.**
   The Clip Gain dialog box opens.

3. **Click Normalize.**
   The gain value increases to 6.5 dB (decibels). The normalize process adjusts the signal strength of a clip to the maximum standardized strength without clipping, or distorting.

4. **Click OK to close the Clip Gain Dialog box.**

<NOTE>

You can manually enter a Gain value. The Normalized value is standardized and produces a set of clips with an equivalent strength much more easily than experimenting with Gain settings manually.

5. **Using the Audio Gain feature, normalize the gain setting for the** ocean.wav **audio clips.**
   You added the clips in the preceding tutorial in the fx2 track starting at 18:15.

6. **On the Program view monitor, click the Play/Stop button.**
   Listen to the sounds, and pay attention to the relative loudness of the clips.

7. **Save the project.**
   The gain is adjusted for all your audio clips. The signal strength for the audio clips is consistent, which makes adjusting settings simpler and more predictable.

The Difference between Loudness and Volume

Gain adjusts the loudness of the clip, but this isn't the same as adjusting the volume. You can adjust the volume of various clips in a project to simulate clips of similar strength. However, clips that are captured at a low signal strength can distort before you can increase the volume loud enough to match other clips. If you adjust the gain, you start from a common point and can adjust volumes throughout your project more easily and predictably. The perfect example is television programs and commercials. You set the volume of your TV to a comfortable level. When the commercials begin, they seem much louder. They aren't really—their gain has been adjusted.

Tutorial
» Editing a Group of Clips in the Timeline

The last audio clip that you add from the audio folder in the Project window is the drum beat for the first section. You use five copies of this clip and edit the clips to create a single score. You add the first clip, edit it, and then use the edited clip for the remaining elements. You define the work area and render a preview in this tutorial. The work area defines a segment of the Timeline to use for rendering a preview (processing the audio and video to create a smooth playback) or exporting the movie.

1. **Click the Speaker icon to the left of the audio tracks to turn the track output off. Turn off all audio tracks except score.**
   Isolating the track you need makes editing simpler when you work with multiple tracks in a project.

2. **Drag the** beat_heavy.wav **clip from the Project window to the score track to start at 00:00.**

3. **Right-click the clip, and choose Audio Gain from the shortcut menu. When the Audio Gain dialog box opens, click Normalize.**
   The value changes to 4.1 dB.

4. **Click OK to close the Audio Gain dialog box.**

5. **Double-click the clip on the Timeline to open it in the Source view monitor. Click the time indicator, and type** 417.

The CTI jumps to 04:17.

6. **Click the Set Out Point button to set the Out point.**

A red line displays on the waveform indicating the Out point.

7. **Click the Loop button.**

You want to listen to the clip play several times; setting the clip to Loop plays it automatically.

8. **Click the Play In to Out button.**

Listen to the shortened clip. The loop should be continuous.

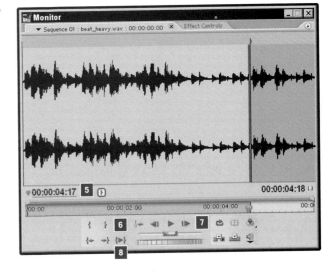

9. **In the Timeline, copy the** beat_heavy.wav **clip. Paste a copy into the score track to the right of the original clip.**

10. **Paste a second copy into the score track to the right of the first copy.**

The first two copies of the clip along with the original make a sound loop. That is, the sound repeats continuously across the three clips.

11. **Paste a third copy of the clip to the right of the second copy.**

The first portion of the third copy adds to the sound loop. You edit the end of the clip to correspond with edits that you do in later steps to a fourth copy.

12. **Double-click the third copy to open it in a Clip window.**

You edit this copy further.

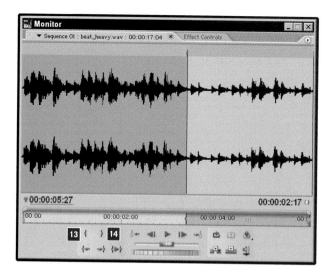

13. **Click the time indicator, and type** 310 **to move the CTI to 03:10. Click the Set In Point button to move the In point.**

The waveforms display a red line where the In point is set.

14. **Move the CTI to the end of the clip at 05:27. Click the Set Out Point button to adjust the Out point.**

You want the third copy of the clip to blend with the fourth copy of the clip. Setting the Out point stops the sound in the clip at a frame where it blends into the fourth copy's sound.

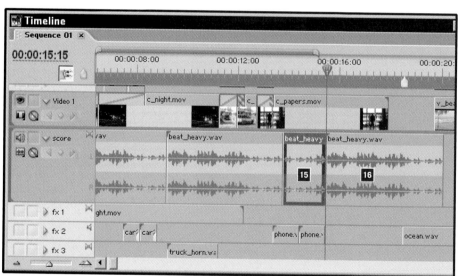

15. **On the Timeline, drag the edited clip left to butt against the second copy.**

The clip starts at 13:24, runs for 02:17, and ends at 16:11.

16. **Paste one final copy of the clip into the score track.**

You don't have to copy the clip in the Timeline first. The last copied item remains in Premiere's memory.

17. **Double-click the fourth copy to open it in the Source view monitor.**

18. **Move the time marker to 03:11. Click the Set In Point button to move the In point.**

   You move the starting frame of the audio clip to a position where its starting sound blends with the ending sound of the copy prior to it on the Timeline.

19. **Move the end point to 04:15. Click the Set Out Point button to adjust the Out point.**

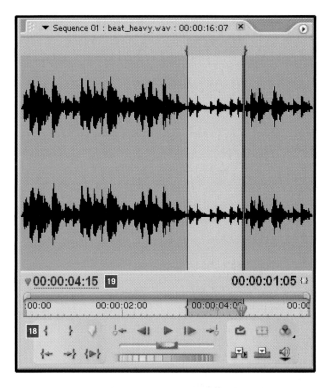

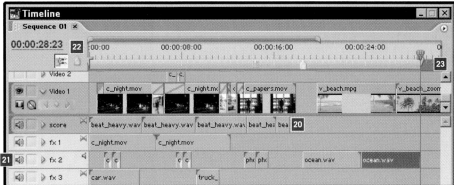

20. **On the Timeline, drag the edited clip to butt against the previous copies.**

   Check the location on the Timeline. This final clip starts at 16:07, runs for 1:05, and ends at 17:12.

21. **Toggle all audio tracks to audible, making the speaker icons visible.**

   You render a preview in the next steps and need to hear the contents of all tracks.

22. **Move the CTI to 28:23.**

   This location is the end of the second copy of the ocean.wav clip on fx 2.

23. **Click the right margin of the Work Area bar, and drag it right to snap to the CTI location.**

   The Work Area bar is the horizontal beige bar below the time ruler on the Timeline. It is used to define a segment of the Timeline for exporting or producing a preview.

< T I P >

Drag an end of the Work Area bar to change its length; drag from the center to move the entire Work Area bar. Double-click the Work Area bar to cover the visible portion of the Timeline.

24. Press Enter, or choose Sequence→Render Work Area.

The Rendering Files progress bar displays, showing the file processing. When the work area is rendered, the playback starts immediately.

< T I P >

Rendering refers to the function where Premiere Pro processes all the video, audio, and effects information in each frame of the selected area.

25. Press the spacebar when the rendering is complete to stop the playback.

Listen to the layered sound effects as the rendered segment plays. The clips need effects and transitions applied, but you get the general idea of the sound.

26. Save the project.

You completed a complex audio edit sequence, building a score from one short drum clip. You also rendered a preview of a Timeline segment. You have assembled all the audio content for the city segment of the project. In the next tutorial you add some transitions.

< N O T E >

You can press the spacebar to start the playback. You can also open the Program view monitor and press Play. To save time, set In and Out points on the Timeline and use the Loop function to control the segment of the Timeline that plays, just as you did for testing video transitions in Session 4.

Tutorial
» Applying Sound Transitions

In the preceding session, you added transitions to video clips, fading one image out and replacing it with another. Just as the video faded in and out, the audio fades in and out when using transitions. Premiere Pro has only two audio transitions, so you don't need to use the search feature to find them. The Constant Power transition is the default, and it uses a default time of one second. In this tutorial, you add transitions to several clips starting in the fx 1 track. Toggle the other tracks' output to off to hear the transitions as you apply and test them.

1. **Choose Window→Effects to open the Effects tab.**

2. **Choose Audio Transitions→Crossfade→Constant Power.**
   The Constant Power transition is highlighted with a red frame, identifying it as the default transition.

3. **In the Timeline, click the time indicator to make it active and type** 0.
   The CTI jumps to the start frame of the project.

4. **Drag the Constant Power transition from the Effects tab and drop it at the CTI position on the Timeline on fx 1 over** c_night.mov.
   The transition overlays the clip for one second starting at 00:00.

<NOTE>
You can also view and edit transitions in the ECW.

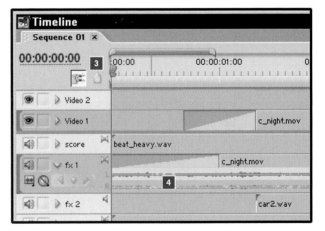

5. **Drag the right margin of the transition left on the Timeline until the duration is 00:20.**
   You shorten the duration of the transition.

<TIP>
You can use the CTI as a guide for adjusting the length. On the Timeline, press the Page Down key to move the CTI to 00:20, or drag it manually to the start of the c_night.mov clip in Video 1.

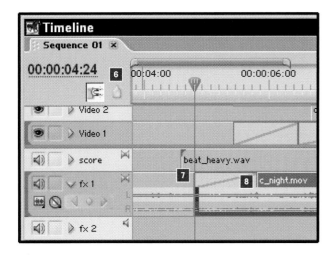

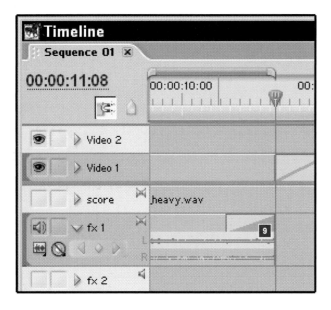

6. **Move the CTI to 04:24.**

   You overlap the two city clips, so you need a reference point.

7. **Click the copy of the** c_night.mov **audio clip starting at 05:24 in fx 1. Drag the clip left to snap to the CTI at 04:24.**

   You create a tail segment for the first copy of the c_night.mov clip (from 04:24 to 05:24) and a head segment for the second copy of the c_night.mov clip (from 04:24 to 05:24).

< N O T E >

In order to create a crossfade between two clips, material must be available at the tail of the first clip and the head of the next clip. Unlike video transitions, which can hold a frame, you can't do that practically with audio.

8. **Drag the Constant Power transition from the Audio Transitions folder in the Effects tab to the CTI.**

   The transition snaps into place starting at the cut point.

9. **Move the CTI to 11:08, the new end time for the first copy of the** c_night.mov **clip on fx 1. Drag the Constant Power transition to the clip.**

   The transition snaps to the left of the cut point. Adjust the length to 00:20.

10. **Move the CTI to 00:00, and listen to the edits that you made in fx 1.**

    Save the project.

11. **Scroll down the Timeline window or resize it to display all the audio tracks.**

    You work with the Audio 5 track.

12. **Right-click Audio 5, and choose Rename to activate the name field. Type** fx 4.

    Name the track fx 4 to correspond with the other audio tracks.

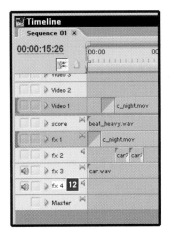

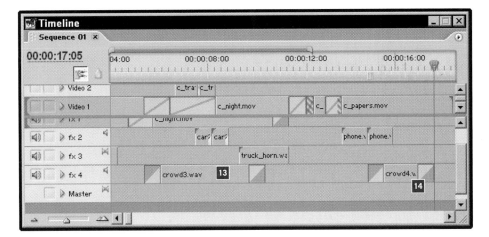

13. **Apply the Constant Power audio transition to the** crowd3.wav **clip in fx 4.**

    Apply the transition to both the start and end of the clip. Decrease the duration to 00:20.

14. **Repeat Step 13 with the** crowd4.wav **clip starting at 14:14 in fx 4.**

    You add another pair of fades.

<TIP>

To quickly move the CTI to the start or end of a clip, select the clip on the Timeline. Then press Home to move the CTI to the first frame, or press End to move the CTI to the last frame of the clip.

15. **Preview the transitions that you added to fx 4.**

    You hear the two crowd clips fade in and out.

16. **Right-click the Timeline time ruler, and choose Clear Sequence Marker→All Markers.**

    The markers that you added as you were working with different clips are removed.

17. **Save the project.**

    You added a number of audio transition fades to clips in two tracks. You applied transitions to fade in and fade out the sounds of the city and crowds in the city segment of the project.

Audio Fades

A crossfade fades one clip's volume out as another clip's volume fades in. The default crossfade is the Constant Power transition, tuned to how our ears hear sound. The other transition is the Constant Gain audio transition. This transition is more mathematically based. Try the two transitions with the same pair of clips—it is usually difficult to tell the difference between the two transitions.

You can adjust the lengths of transitions in the Timeline, as you did in the tutorial, or in the ECW, as shown in the figure. Just as

with the video transitions, you can move the transition in the ECW Timeline, and adjust duration. Alignment can be reset for some transitions depending on the material available.

Add audio transitions at any point (over a cut point, before a cut point, or after a cut point) as you did with video transitions. To control the volume and transition more precisely, you can use a keyframing process and adjust sound precisely from the Timeline or Audio Mixer. You work with those methods in the next session.

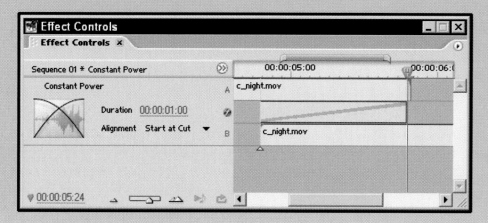

» Session Review

You finally have audio in your project, which certainly makes a difference, doesn't it? This session introduced you to working with audio. You learned how and why to use audio, and how to work with audio in Premiere Pro. You learned how to edit audio clips in the Source view monitor and in the Timeline, and how to use multiple copies of a clip. You adjusted signal strength of your clips to make further editing and effects easier to apply, and you made a Work Area rendered preview.

You added some audio transitions to clips on both existing tracks and additional audio tracks. The image at the start of the session shows the location in the video where you add the first clip in a new track; the final image in the session shows the location in the video where you added a clip of crowd noise.

This session contains lots of information. Answer the following questions to review the information in this session. Answers to the questions are in the tutorial or discussion noted in parentheses.

1. What roles does sound play in a movie project? (See Discussion: How and Why to Use Audio.)

2. What is a split edit? What types of split edits can you perform on a movie clip? (See Tutorial: Organizing the Timeline for Audio.)

3. How do you target a track? How do you identify the targeted track on the Timeline? (See Tutorial: Organizing the Timeline for Audio.)

4. What window do you use to edit an audio clip visually? (See Tutorial: Preparing Audio Files.)

5. What does it mean to conform audio? Why is it done? (See Discussion: Understanding Audio Characteristics.)

6. What are the different audio formats, and how are they used in Premiere Pro? (See Discussion: Understanding Audio Characteristics.)

7. Why do you group clips in the Timeline? Can you work with clips individually if they are grouped? (See Tutorial: Adding Trimmed Audio Clips to the Timeline.)

8. How can you add a clip and an audio track simultaneously? (See Tutorial: Adding Trimmed Audio Clips to the Timeline.)

9. How do you resize audio tracks to see the content more clearly? (See Tutorial: Editing Audio Clips in the Timeline.)

10. Why must your clips have similar signal strengths? (See Tutorial: Adjusting Audio Signal.)

11. Must all the audio tracks in a project be active? How do you isolate an audio track in the Timeline? (See Tutorial: Editing a Group of Clips in the Timeline.)

12. Do you need to have head and tail material in both clips to use a crossfade between a pair of clips? (See Tutorial: Applying Sound Transitions.)

13. What shortcut keys can you use to move the CTI to the start or end of a selected clip on the Timeline? (See Tutorial: Applying Sound Transitions.)

» Other Projects

Investigate the process of voiceover recording in Premiere Pro. Record a voiceover to use with the project. Place it in a separate audio track. The script for the voiceover should describe or enhance what the viewer sees on the screen.

Mixing Audio and Adding Effects

Tutorial: **Adjusting Track Volumes Using the Audio Mixer**

Discussion: **Using Keyframes to Control Settings**

Tutorial: **Fading Volume over Multiple Clips**

Tutorial: **Adding Audio Effects to Tracks in the Audio Mixer**

Tutorial: **Panning Clips**

Tutorial: **Adding Music Clips to the Project**

Tutorial: **Editing the Music Clips**

Tutorial: **Fine-Tuning the Music Tracks**

Session Introduction

In Premiere Pro, you can work with audio two ways. In this session, you finish editing the sound files that you added to your project in Session 5, construct the score for the beach segment of the project, and add effects to some of your project's clips.

You learn to work with the Audio Mixer window, which uses an audio editing deck analogy. In this session, you perform some of the project audio edits in the Audio Mixer. Whether you work mostly in the Audio Mixer or in the Timeline is a matter of personal preference.

In your project, you use the Audio Mixer window to adjust tracks and add track effects. You adjust audio settings as you watch your video. The adjustments that you make to a track transfer to the clips in the Timeline. The Audio Mixer window contains a set of controls that correspond to each track in your project, just like a big audio mixing deck.

At this point, the soundtrack for the city segment of your project has been added to the Timeline, trimmed, and adjusted for gain. The soundtrack is still quite rough. The sound on some tracks is too loud, some clips contain lots of background noise, and so on. At the end of this session, your soundtrack will be nearly finished, aside from some touch-ups in the final session. You can listen to the soundtrack for your project in the audio-only `session06A.wma` and `session06B.wma` sample clips.

TOOLS YOU'LL USE
Audio Mixer controls, Audio Mixer window, Audio workspace, Clip Keyframes, Clip Volume graph, CTI, Easy Curve In keyframe interpolation, Easy Curve Out keyframe interpolation, ECW, Editing workspace, Effects tab, keyframe graph line, keyframes, Level slider, Loop, Lowpass audio effect, Numbered Markers, Pan effect, Pan/Balance dial, Pen tool, Play In to Out, Program view monitor, Read Automation mode, Selection tool, Set In Point button, Set Out Point button, Show/Hide tracks dialog box, Source view monitor, time indicator, Timeline, Track Keyframes, Unnumbered markers, VU meters, Work Area bar, Write Automation mode

CD-ROM FILES NEEDED
Session 5 project file that you created, or the `session05.prproj` file from the CD-ROM, contents of the music folder

TIME REQUIRED
90 minutes

Tutorial

» Adjusting Track Volumes Using the Audio Mixer

The clips in the first section of the project are in place, and you have done some editing—adding transitions, trimming the clips, and adjusting gain. In this tutorial, you start working with the Audio Mixer to adjust tracks and add some track effects. The Audio Mixer allows you to make adjustments to your audio track content in real time—as you are listening to it. You adjust volumes in your project. All audio effects include another option, called a bypass option, that allows you to turn the effect on or off specified by keyframes that you set for the track or clip. In this session you use the Audio workspace, which is an arrangement of the program's windows specifically for editing audio.

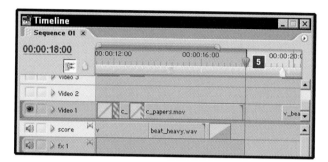

<NOTE>

The Show/Hide Effects and Sends arrow on the Audio Mixer window is similar to the Collapse/Expand track arrow on the Timeline. Click the spindown arrow to display the content; click the spindown arrow again to hide the content. As you see later in the session, the Effects and Sends can use a lot of space on the screen.

1. **Open Premiere Pro. When the Welcome window opens, choose** `session05.prproj`.
   The Welcome window closes, and the project is loaded into the program.

<NOTE>

If you didn't do the tutorials in Session 5, copy the `session05.prproj` file from the CD to your hard drive. In the Welcome window, choose Open Project. Browse to the location where you stored the copied project file, and select Open. Then resave the project in Premiere Pro as `session06.prproj` (or use another filenaming convention).

2. **Choose File→Save As, and resave the project file as** session06.prproj.
   The name of the new project version displays at the top of the program window.

3. **Choose Window→Workspace→Audio.**
   The Premiere Pro interface rearranges the windows and displays the Audio Mixer at the left of the screen.

4. **On the Timeline, press the Home key to set the CTI to 00:00. Right-click the Timeline time ruler, and choose Set Sequence Marker→In to set the In point on the Timeline.**

5. **Click the Timeline's time indicator, and type** 1800 **to move the CTI to 18:00. Right-click the Timeline time ruler, and choose Set Sequence Marker→Out to set the Out point on the Timeline.**
   You have defined a segment of the Timeline for editing.

6. **Choose Window→Workspace→Audio.**
   The program's windows rearrange, and the Audio Mixer displays on the screen.

<NOTE>

To see the entire set of audio tracks in your project, drag the bottom-right corner to resize the Audio Mixer.

7. **Click the Show/Hide Effects and Sends arrow to collapse the tracks.**
   You work with the effects area in the next tutorial; collapse the tracks to save space.

8. **On the Audio Mixer, click the Loop button.**
   Only the portion of the Timeline defined in Steps 4 and 5 plays; you don't have to reposition the playback location manually.

<NOTE>
If you look at the top right of the Audio Mixer window, you see the In to Out segment identified.

9. **Click the Audio Mixer's Play In to Out button; click the Stop button to stop playback.**
   The portion of the Timeline that you selected in Steps 4 and 5 plays. You can hear all audio tracks. You can see the values for the sound volume display in each track's VU meter, and see the values for the entire set of tracks display in the Master VU Meter.

<NOTE>
The Master track shows one or two VU meters, depending on project settings. Your project uses stereo sound, and will output stereo sound, so the Master track displays two VU meters. You can see two VU meters for the individual stereo tracks. As fx 2 and fx 4 are mono tracks, each has only one meter. A VU, or Volume Unit, meter shows relative volumes of the audio clips as they play. Most car, home, and computer sound systems have VU meter display options.

10. **Click the Solo button above the VU meter for the score track.**
    The remaining tracks are muted, indicated by the mute track icon.

<TIP>
You can play more than one track at a time; click the Solo icon for each track you want to hear; or click the Mute icon for each track you want to mute.

11. **Click the Play In to Out button to listen to the track play.**

12. **Repeat Steps 10 and 11 with the other tracks.**
    Now you are familiar with the sound of the clips. In the next tutorial, you edit tracks from the Audio Mixer.

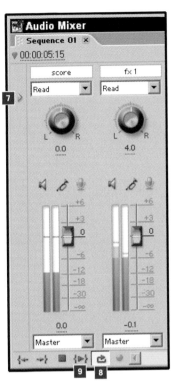

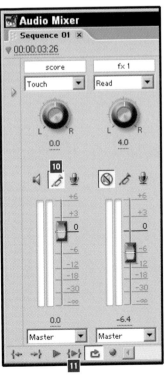

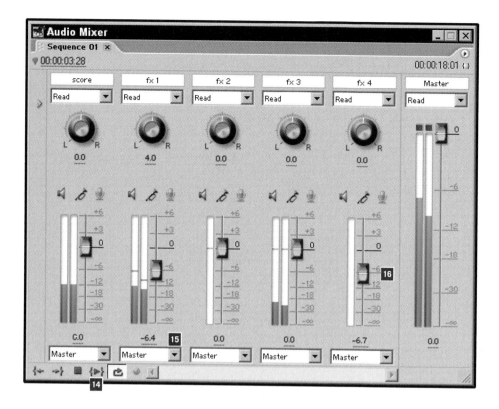

13. **After you have listened to the individual tracks, deselect any solo track.**
    You want to hear all tracks together to adjust the overall sound.

14. **Click the Audio Mixer's Play In to Out button to hear the entire sequence again. Watch the VU meter in the Master track.**
    You see that at some points the meter displays red, indicating that the sound is too loud and will start to distort. This distortion is called clipping.

<NOTE>
If the audio level is set too low, you hear excessive noise.

15. **Drag the volume thumb control for the fx 1 track downward to -6.4 dB, or click the text below the VU meter and type** -6.4.
    You decrease the volume for the entire track; the background traffic sound in fx 1 is decreased.

<NOTE>
A decibel is a value for measuring the intensity of sound. Decibels (abbreviated dB) measure sound pressure level on a logarithmic scale. A ten-decibel (dB) increase represents a doubling of sound level; a ten-decibel decrease represents a halving of sound level.

16. **Drag the volume thumb control for the fx 4 track downward to -7 dB; the closest dB value, -6.7, is displayed.**
    You adjust the overall volume for the track containing the crowd noises.

17. **Save the project.**
    You started working with the Audio Mixer and learned how to use its controls and adjust track volumes. You adjusted the volume for the drum score in the city segment of the project.

Discussion
Using Keyframes to Control Settings

Premiere Pro uses keyframes in both the Timeline and the ECW's Timeline to control settings. A video or audio clip plays over time, which is represented on the Timeline as a horizontal gold graph line. You can specify locations as the clip plays where you want to make changes to the clip's settings. These points, or nodes, are called keyframes. On the Timeline's graph line, keyframes are added with the Pen tool, and display as white dots along the graph line, as you can see in the image below.

At each keyframe, you can control the application of effects, and volume or opacity changes. You can also define how changes are made between keyframes, using a process called interpolation. Keyframes can be dragged along the graph line to reposition them in time, and can be removed by using the Pen tool.

The appearance of the keyframes in the ECW Timeline is different than the Timeline, and keyframes are applied differently. In the ECW Timeline, keyframes are added when the value of a setting changes at a particular frame; keyframes are added and removed using the keyframe navigator and stopwatch button.

You work with ECW keyframing starting in the next session.

Keyframe Interpolation

For each keyframe that you add to a clip or track's Timeline, you can adjust the speed at which the change starts and the speed at which the change ends. Keyframes use Normal interpolation by default. You see a straight line to and from the keyframe node. A convex curve means that the interpolated values accelerate to or from the keyframe. A concave curve means that interpolated values decelerate to or from the keyframe. If you change the speed leaving a node, the speed approaching the next node automatically changes.

Tutorial
» Fading Volume over Multiple Clips

In the preceding tutorial, you started working with the Audio Mixer. You learned how to listen to your project's content and how to manipulate the Timeline to play a segment in the Audio Mixer. In this tutorial, you make adjustments to the volume of a track in real time, writing the changes to the track in the Timeline.

1. **Click the flyout arrow in the upper-right corner of the Audio Mixer window to open a shortcut menu. Click Show/Hide Tracks to open a dialog box.**

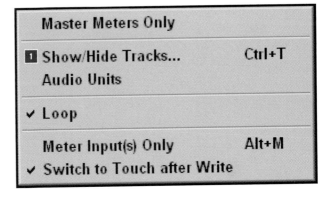

2. **In the Show/Hide Tracks dialog box, deselect all tracks except the score track. Click OK to close the dialog box.**
   The Audio Mixer collapses and displays only the score and master tracks.

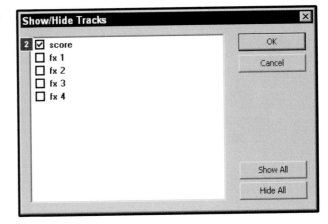

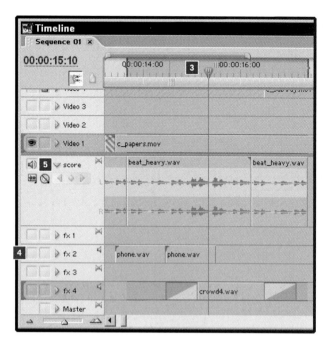

3. **On the Timeline, adjust the In point to 13:15 and the Out point to 17:15.**

   You are going to adjust the volume of the last two copies of the beat_heavy.wav clip starting at 13:20 and ending at 17:12. Resetting the In and Out points creates a shorter loop for you to use as you adjust the volumes.

<TIP>

If you want, you can set the In and Out points at the first and last frames of the clips; adding several frames of blank track lets you clearly hear when one loop ends and the next one starts.

4. **Turn off all audio tracks except for the score track.**

   You want to hear only the drum beats to make the adjustments.

5. **Click the spindown arrow to open the score track.**

   You work with the track's keyframes in this tutorial.

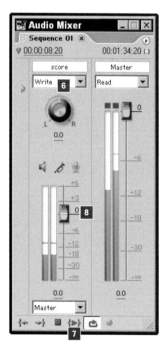

6. **In the Audio Mixer, click the drop-down arrow below the score track's name and select Write from the Automation modes, which writes all adjustments that you make with Audio Mixer controls to the clip on the Timeline.**

   The Automation modes determine *how* your settings are transferred to the Timeline. Automation can be written only while controls are being dragged (Touch), during and after a control is moved (Latch), or a combination of Write and Touch. You can select the Write option, meaning that animation is written as you adjust controls; the option then switches back to a Touch status when playback is stopped (Write/Touch). Off is the default mode, which allows you to use the Audio Mixer's controls without stored automation settings; the Read mode reads the track's stored settings and plays them as you play the track.

7. **Click the Play In to Out button.**

   The Audio Mixer plays the segment of the Timeline between the In and Out points. You set the Loop option earlier.

8. **As the clip plays, slowly drag the thumb slider for the score downward from the start of the clip to the end.**

   The volume of the clips decreases over the course of the two clips until it fades out completely.

9. **In the Timeline, click the Show Keyframes icon to open a menu and choose Show Track Volume.**

   A gold graph line and a number of white nodes display over the clips on the track. The individual clips on the track become inactive because you have activated the entire track.

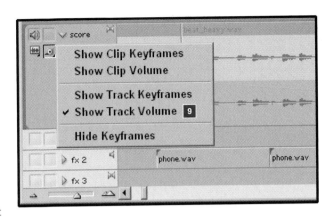

<TIP>

If you have been working with Timeline keyframes and find that you can't select a clip, check to see that the keyframes aren't turned on.

<NOTE>

When you write audio changes to the tracks or a clip in real time, it is virtually impossible for you to duplicate results. You will always have some discrepancy in the numbers of keyframes as well as the settings for each keyframe, both volume and location.

10. **Choose the Pen tool from the toolbox.**

    You need only three nodes over the two clips (at the start of the first clip, end of the first clip, and end of the second clip), plus one where the sound returns to full volume; use the Pen tool to select extra nodes for deletion.

<NOTE>

If you hold the Pen tool over a keyframe node, you see a tooltip describing the time location on the Timeline as well as the strength of the clip at that location in decibels.

11. **Click an extra keyframe node on the gold graph line to select it; the node turns gold.**

    Press Delete on the keyboard to remove the extra keyframe.

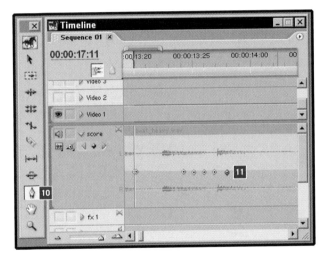

<TIP>

To add a keyframe to the keyframe line, Ctrl+click the line with the Pen tool where you want the keyframe. You can move a keyframe along the line as well. Click it with the Pen tool, and drag left or right.

12. **Repeat Step 11 until you have the final set of four keyframes. The keyframe locations and their volumes are:**
    13:00 0 dB
    16:06 -6.45 dB
    17:11 -oo dB
    18:00 0.02 dB

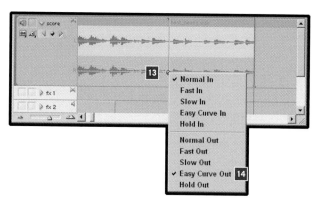

13. **Right-click the keyframe between the fourth and fifth copies of the** beat_heavy.wav **clip at 16:06.**
    A menu opens displaying In and Out speed options.

14. **Click Easy Curve Out.**
    You smooth out the change in volume from the location of the keyframe. The options in the menu are *keyframe interpolation* options, which define how fast or how slow a change is made. You chose an option that eases out the keyframe speed. After adding the interpolation, you see that the keyframe's line no longer has a sharp point at the node's location; instead it curves out from the node and into the subsequent node.

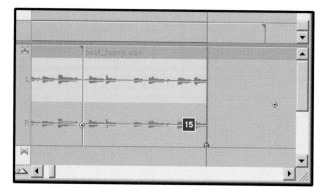

15. **Look at the node at 17:11.**
    You see that its incoming path smooths automatically.

<NOTE>
If you right-click the node at 17:11 to open the keyframe interpolation menu, you see that its incoming speed changed from Normal to Easy Curve In automatically.

16. Click the Selection tool on the toolbar to deselect the Pen tool.

You removed extra keyframes.

<TIP>

You can move the cursor over the keyframes to see the volumes and location, but you can't adjust the keyframes with the Selection tool.

17. Click the Keyframe icon on the score track to open the menu again. Click Hide Keyframes.

The keyframes are hidden, and the clips on the track are active.

18. Save the project.

You set the volume for multiple clips in real time working from the Audio Mixer and adjusted the keyframes on the Timeline. Because you use five copies of the clip to make the complete score for the city segment of the project, the sound is gradually decreased over the length of the last two of the five clips and finally fades out (gets quieter in volume or disappears completely).

Processing Audio

Audio is processed in a specific sequence. From first to last:

>> Gain adjustment

>> Audio effects

>> Track settings (also in a specific order: prefade effects, prefade sends, mute, fader, meter, postfader effects, postfader sends, pan/balance)

>> Track output volume from left to right in the Audio Mixer window, from audio tracks to submix tracks, to the Master track

Tutorial
» Adding Audio Effects to Tracks in the Audio Mixer

You made some track adjustments in the Audio Mixer and then fine-tuned the changes. In this tutorial, you make final edits to the clips in the city segment of the project for this session, adding audio effects to two tracks. Effects can be added to either an entire track or to individual clips. Track effects are added only in the Audio Mixer window. In this tutorial, you add effects to the night traffic clips and to the crowd clips to make them less noisy and more useful as a background layer of sound.

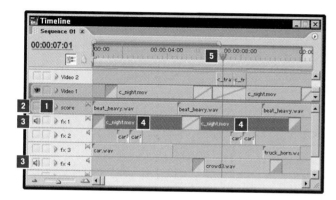

1. Click the spindown arrow next to the `score` track's name to close the track.
   You are finished working with the track.

2. Toggle the score track's output to off (the speaker icon is hidden).
   You don't need to hear the track.

3. Toggle the fx 1 track's and fx 4 track's output to on (the speaker icon is visible).
   You work with these two tracks in this tutorial.

4. Click the `c_night.mov` clip in fx 1 starting at 00:00, and hold the Shift key while you click the second copy of the clip starting at 04:24.
   You define an area to use for In and Out points in Step 5.

5. Right-click the time ruler on the Timeline, and choose Set Sequence Marker→In and Out Around Selection.
   The In and Out markers start and end at the margins of the clips that you selected in Step 4.

6. Click the flyout menu on the Audio Mixer, and choose Show/Hide Tracks to open the Show/Hide Tracks dialog box.

7. Click the fx 1 and fx 4 tracks, and deselect the score track. Click OK to close the dialog box and modify the visible tracks in the Audio Mixer.

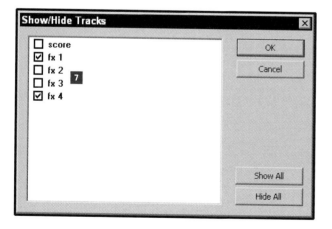

8. Click the Solo icon on the fx 1 track.

The fx 4 track is set to mute. You work with the fx 1 track first.

9. Click the spindown arrow at the upper left of the Audio Mixer to display the effects and submix areas of the Audio Mixer.

You select track effects in this area of the window.

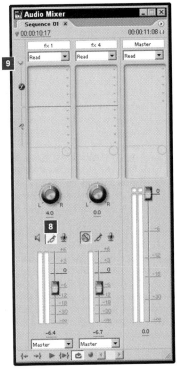

10. Click the top arrow under the Automation mode list to display an effects menu.

The list includes effects that you can apply to an entire track.

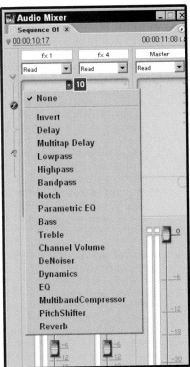

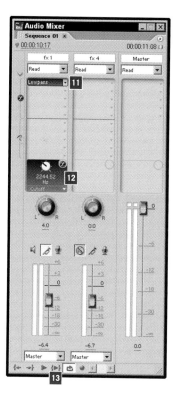

11. Click the Lowpass effect.

The menu closes, and the effect is listed on the Audio Mixer window track. The Lowpass effect eliminates frequencies above the specified Cutoff frequency.

< T I P >

If you add an effect and then want to remove it, click the drop-down arrow to open the effects menu again and click None.

12. In the effect controls, rotate the dial slightly to the 2200 to 2300 Hz range.

You adjust the setting using the mouse; because there is no field in which to type a value, use an approximate value.

13. Click the Play In to Out button, and listen to the clip.

You hear that the hissing sound of the traffic is removed.

< T I P >

To hear the result of the effect, listen to the clip as you rotate the effect's dial. If the Cutoff is set too high, you don't hear much difference in the clip between the raw audio and that using the effect. If the Cutoff is set too low, you don't hear much sound at all.

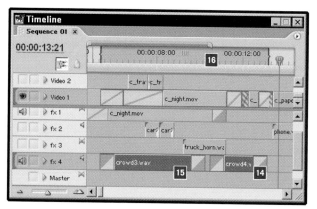

14. On the Timeline, drag the `crowd4.wav` **clip starting at 14:14 in fx 4 to the left until it is at approximately 10:15, following the** `crowd3.wav` **clip ending at 10:09.**

Moving the two clips together temporarily makes creating a loop simpler. Leave a few frames between the two clips to separate them.

15. Select both the `crowd3.wav` **clip in fx 4 starting at 05:13 and the** `crowd4.wav` **clip following.**

16. Right-click the time ruler on the Timeline, and choose Set Sequence Marker→In and Out Around Selection.

The In and Out markers start and end at the margins of the clips that you selected in Step 5.

17. **In the Audio Mixer window, repeat Steps 10 through 13 for the fx 4 track. Set the Cutoff in the 1900 to 2100 Hz range.**

<**NOTE**>

You can hear how your effect impacts the clip by toggling the effect on and off in the Effect Controls area (identified in the figure accompanying Step 17).

18. **In the Timeline, move the** `crowd4.wav` **clip back to its original location starting at 14:14.**

You set the second track's effects.

19. **Save the project**

You defined specific In and Out points on the Timeline by defining groups of clips. You added effects to two tracks in the project.

20. **Turn all audio tracks back on in the Audio Mixer and Timeline, and listen to the city segment of the project.**

The traffic and crowd noises are now deeper and more in the background of the soundtrack. Smoothing the sound effects allows the drum track to be more prominent.

Click to toggle
effect on and off

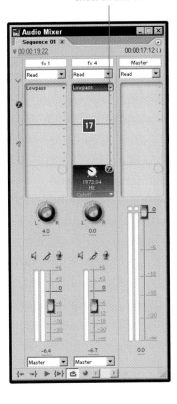

Tutorial
» Panning Clips

Think of how a car sounds as it passes in front of you. First, you hear the sound in one ear as the vehicle approaches. It increases in volume as it passes in front of you, at which time you hear it in both ears. It then gradually decreases in volume via your other ear, and then finally disappears. The car clip in fx 3 sounds like a car passing from right to left. You can achieve this effect using the Pan/Balance controls in the Audio Mixer and using keyframes on the Timeline. In this tutorial, you learn to set pan/balance. After isolating a portion of the Timeline, you work with keyframes in the Timeline and then view the action in the Audio Mixer.

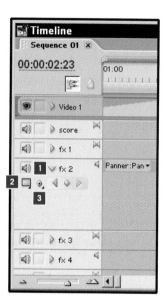

1. **Click the spindown arrow to open fx 2; close all other audio tracks.**
   You don't need to see content on any other track.

2. **Click the Set Display Style icon, and select Show Name Only.**
   You have been working with the audio waveforms displayed, and it is difficult to see the keyframes over the waveform.

3. **Click the Show Keyframes icon, and choose Show Track Keyframes from the menu.**
   The keyframe layout for the track displays; you see that the menu at the top left of the track and the individual clips' names are faded.

<TIP>

Remember that you can't select an individual clip when the track keyframes are active.

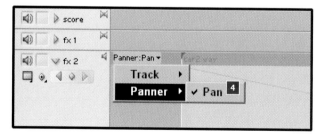

4. **Click the track's menu at the top left of the track. Choose Panner→Pan.**
   You set keyframes to adjust which ear hears the sound in a pair of clips by assigning the sound to different (left and right) channels.

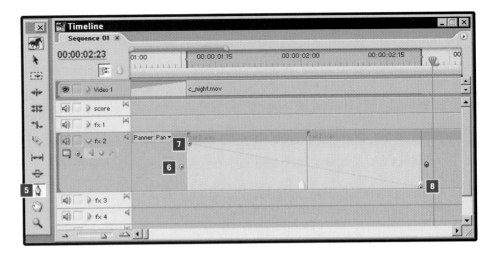

5. **Click the Pen tool in the toolbar to select it.**
   You add keyframes to the gold pan/balance graph line. The
   fx 2 track is a mono track, meaning that it uses one channel.
   You pan a monophonic audio track to set its position between
   the left and right stereo channels in the project's master track.

6. **Ctrl+click with the Pen tool on the line to the left of the first copy
   of the car2.wav clip, the start of the car2.wav clip at 01:10,
   the end of the second copy of the car2.wav clip at 02:21, and
   to the right of the second copy of the car2.wav clip.**
   This adds four keyframes to the pan/balance graph line on
   fx 2. The precise frame locations for the outside keyframes
   aren't critical.

<TIP>
Pan/balance is applied to a track, not to a clip. In order to prevent
changes to the other clips on the track, you can add keyframes and
set bypass options for each clip, which can be time consuming; or
you can add two extra keyframes to isolate the location that you
want to modify from the default setting.

7. **Drag the second keyframe node, at the start of the first
   car2.wav clip at 01:10, upward as far as you can drag it.**
   The value displays at -100, meaning that the sound is completely moved to the left channel and that you hear it only in
   your left ear.

8. **Drag the third keyframe node, at the end of the second
   car2.wav clip at 02:21, downward as far as you can drag it.**
   The value displays at -100, meaning that the sound is completely moved to the right channel and that you hear it only in
   your right ear. The fourth keyframe node stays at its default
   location, and you don't adjust its location above or below
   the default.

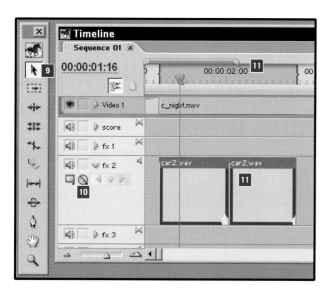

9. **Click the Selection tool on the toolbar to deselect the Pen tool.**
   You have completed the adjustments to the Timeline.

10. **Click the Show Keyframes icon, and select Hide Keyframes from the menu.**
    The track's keyframes are hidden, and the clips are active.

11. **Select the two** car2.wav **clips starting at 01:10 and ending at 02:21. Right-click the time ruler on the Timeline, and choose Set Sequence Marker→In and Out Around Selection.**
    The In and Out points for the Timeline are added for the duration of the pair of clips.

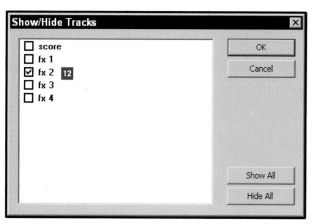

12. **In the Audio Mixer, click the menu arrow and choose Show/Hide Tracks to open the Show/Hide Tracks dialog box. Select the fx 2 track, and hide all other tracks.**
    You view the pan effect in fx 2.

The Difference between Pan and Balance

These two terms refer to the type of channel content. Sound comes in two channels—right and left. A mono audio clip uses one channel, either left or right. Stereo sound uses both channels (which is why stereo is a fuller sound). You pan a mono clip from one channel to another, while you adjust the balance of the channels in a stereo clip. Similarly, in a surround sound clip, you balance the sound among the 5.1 channels.

13. **Click the Loop button, and then click the Play In to Out button.**

The pair of clips plays. Listen to the pan effect.

14. **Watch the Pan/Balance dial on the Audio Mixer as the clips play.**

You can also see the pan change from left to right as the clips play.

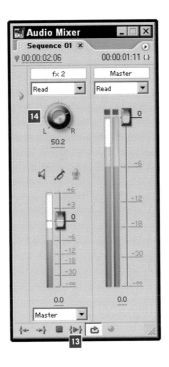

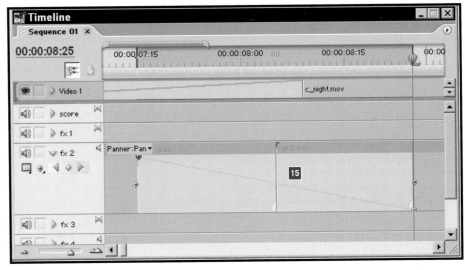

15. **Repeat Steps 3 to 10 with the second pair of** `car2.wav` **clips on fx 2 starting at 07:15 and ending at 08:25. Add the keyframe nodes on the line to the left of the first copy of the** `car2.wav` **clip, the start of the** `car2.wav` **clip at 07:15, the end of the second copy of the** `car2.wav` **clip at 08:25, and to the right of the second copy of the** `car2.wav` **clip.**

The precise frame locations for the outside keyframes aren't critical.

16. **Save the project.**

You added some track effects to four clips in the project. You adjusted the pan setting to make the sound shift. Now it sounds like the car horns and noises are passing from one ear to the other, creating a sense of motion and making the sound effects more interesting. You have finished adjusting the sound effects in the city segment of the project.

Tutorial
» Adding Music Clips to the Project

So far you have been working primarily with the clips at the start of the movie. You have done a considerable amount of editing and adding effects and transitions to the clips in the five audio tracks. In this tutorial, you start working with the final section of the movie. The beach segment of the project contains only the sound of the ocean so far. Now you add music clips that you edit to create a soundtrack for the beach segment. You use clips from two different pieces of music. You can edit the music for the project quite well in Premiere Pro. However, if you would like to experiment further or with more options and control, try Adobe Audition, the audio editing component of Adobe's video editing suite. A demo copy of Adobe Audition is on the CD-ROM.

1. **Choose Window→Workspace→Editing.**
   You are working with a new set of clips, and need to see the Project window and Timeline rather than the Audio Mixer window.

2. **Choose File→Import. Browse to the location where you stored the project files, or open the footage folder on the Premiere Pro Complete Course CD.**
   Select the music folder, and click Import Folder to import the folder and its contents into the project in a new bin.

3. **Preview the clips in the Project window. Select a clip, and click Play in the preview area.**
   Listen to all the clip segments.

4. **On the Timeline, right-click the time ruler and choose Clear Sequence Marker→All Markers.**
   Any markers you have placed on the Timeline are removed.

About the Premiere Pro Complete Course Music

The Studio Cutz Music Library is a collection of music specifically composed and produced to enhance visual and audio production such as Video Production, Television, Radio, Advertising, Film, Multimedia, On Hold Service, and more. Songs and CDs are licensed as a 'Lifetime Synchronization License' (this is not how all libraries work), which means that you pay a one-time licensing fee and use the music forever. Studio Cutz has a catalog of many

different styles for many different moods and applications. Listen to the Studio Cutz demo on the CD.

The music used in the project is taken from two pieces of music provided by Studio Cutz from two of their collections. A third song is on the CD, which you can use for experimentation. Refer to the Other Projects at the end of this session.

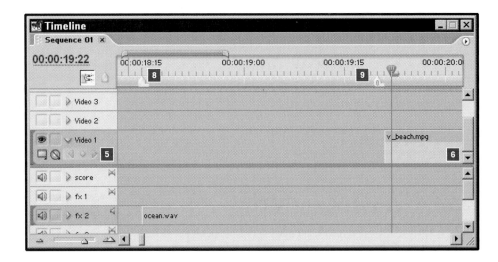

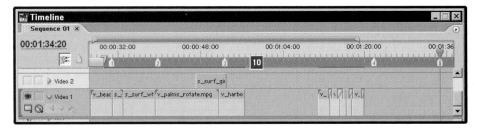

5. **Collapse the audio tracks, and open Video 1.**
   You need to see the video track to adjust clips, but you're finished with the lower audio tracks.

6. **Resize the Video/Audio segments of the Timeline. Move the cursor over the resize bar at the right of the Timeline, and drag downward.**
   You work with audio and video tracks and need to see the video more clearly.

7. **Click the current time indicator to activate the field, and type** 1815.
   The CTI jumps to 18:15.

8. **Press * (asterisk) on the number pad to add an unnumbered marker.**

9. **Move the CTI to 19:20. Right-click the time ruler on the Timeline, and choose Set Sequence Marker→Next Available Number.**
   A marker numbered 0 is added to the Timeline at the CTI location, which is the start of the opening scenery segment of the movie.

<NOTE>
In the figure, the CTI is moved to show you the marker.

10. **Repeat Step 9 adding numbered markers at these locations:**
    1 at 30:26 (start of first sports segment)
    2 at 39:20 (start of second scenery segment)
    3 at 52:15 (start of second sports segment)
    4 at 01:21:25 (start of third scenery segment)
    5 at 01:34:20 (approximate end of the movie)
    The markers identify areas on the Timeline where the music changes to coordinate with the video.

<TIP>
In the tutorials, the locations are referred to by their numbered markers.

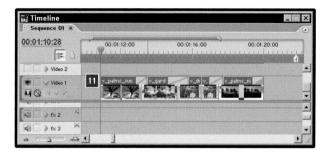

11. **On Video 1, select the final group of five clips starting with the** v_palms_sun.mpg **clip at 01:10:28, ending with the** v_palms_rotate.mpg **clip, which ends at 01:20:01.**
You move the clips to their marker locations. Positioning clips starting from the end of the Timeline and working backward is simpler. That way, you don't have to worry about overlaying any clips on the Timeline and accidentally causing errors in clip length or position.

12. **Drag the selection right until it snaps to the right of Marker 4 at 01:21:25.**
You adjusted the final set of scenery clips on the Timeline.

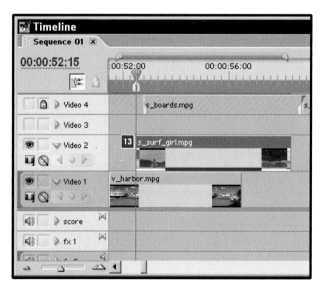

13. **In Video 2, drag the** s_surf_girl.mpg **clip right to snap to the Marker 3 location at 52:15.**
The clip is the start of the second sports segment, which runs from Marker 3 to Marker 4.

< N O T E >
You have several other sports clips sitting in Video 4; you start working with those clips in the next session.

14. **Save the project.**
You added several numbered markers to the Timeline to use as guides for positioning music clips. You imported the folder of music segments. In the next tutorial you add the music to the beach segment of the project.

Tutorial
» Editing the Music Clips

In the preceding tutorial, you created the set of five music clip segments that together make up the soundtrack for the beach segment of the project. These are portions of two pieces of music from Studio Cutz Music Library. In this tutorial, you add the segments to the Timeline, adjust them for length, and add transitions. Make sure to preview the music as you add it to the Timeline and apply transitions. The caliente segments are smooth, rhythmic pieces of music; the latinotek music contains a very strong beat as well as voice. The latinotek music is used to introduce the sections of the beach segment showing different water activities; the caliente segments are used for segments showing scenery, as well as the ending of the project.

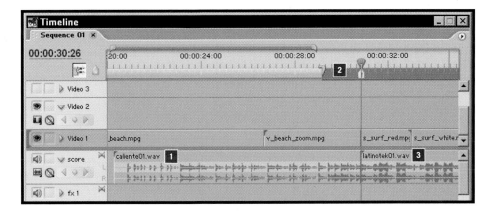

1. **Drag** caliente01.wav **from the music folder in the Project window to the score track, and place it to start at 20:10.**
   The first music segment starts a few frames after the beach video first displays starting at 19:20.

2. **Move the CTI to the Marker 1 position at 30:26.**
   You add the next clip at this location.

3. **Drag** latinotek01.wav **from the music folder in the Project window to the score track at the CTI position.**
   The clip starts at 30:26 and crops the end of the caliente01.wav clip. This is the location where the first set of sports clips will be placed in upcoming sessions.

4. **Open the Effects tab. Choose Audio Transitions→Crossfade→ Constant Power, and drag the transition from the Effects tab to the** latinotek01.wav **clip on the** score **track at the CTI position.**
   The transition snaps to the CTI overlaying the latinotek01.wav clip on the score track.

5. **Click the transition to open it in the Effect Controls window (ECW).**
   You adjust and test the transition in the ECW.

6. **Click the Duration setting in the ECW to activate the field, and type** 15.
   You shorten the transition length to 15 frames.

> **187**

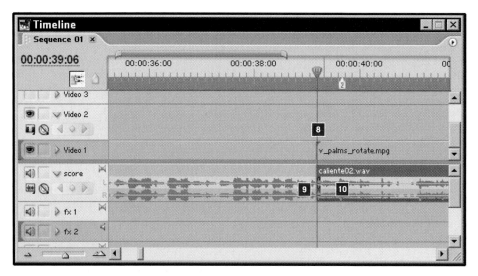

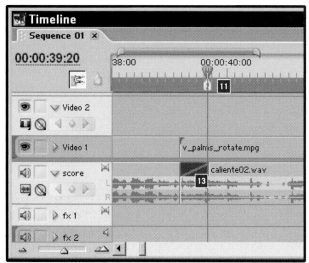

7. **Press the spacebar, and listen to the transition play.**
   You can work from the ECW or the Timeline; the CTI moves as the clip plays.

8. **On the Timeline, move the CTI to 39:06, the start frame of the v_palms_rotate.mpg clip in Video 1.**
   You use the position for shortening the clip in the next step.

9. **Drag the right edge of the latinotek01.wav clip left to snap to the start of the CTI position at 39:06.**
   You reset the Out point of the clip.

10. **Drag caliente02.wav to snap to the CTI in the score track starting at 39:06.**
    You add the third music segment to the Timeline, following the caliente01.wav and latinotek01.wav segments. The second scenery-type music segment starts at the location of the palm tree scenery clip.

11. **Move the CTI to the Marker 2 position at 39:20.**
    You use the CTI location for placing the next transition.

12. **Open the Effects tab. Choose Audio Transitions→Crossfade→ Constant Power. Drop the transition over the cut point between the two clips on the score track.**

13. **Drag the transition's right end to snap to the CTI location at Marker 2.**
    The transition starts at the cut point. The duration is 00:15. Preview the transition.

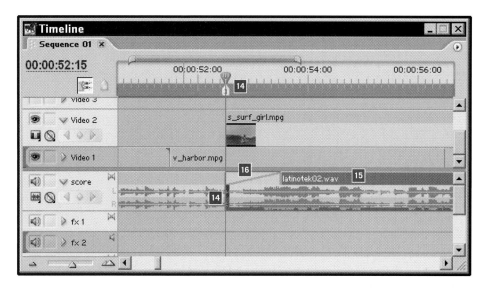

14. **Move the CTI to the Marker 3 position at 52:15, and drag the right edge of the** `caliente02.wav` **clip left until it snaps to the CTI position.**
    You reset the Out point for the `caliente02.wav` clip.

15. **Drag the** `latinotek02.wav` **clip from the Project window to the score track to snap to the right of the CTI location at Marker 3.**
    You add the fourth music segment to the Timeline, which will be the start of another group of water sports clips.

16. **Open the Effects tab again. Choose Audio Transitions→ Crossfade→Constant Power. Place the transition at the cut point.**
    Leave the default length of 30 frames.

17. **Move the CTI to 01:16:03.**
    You position another clip starting at this frame.

18. **Drag another copy of** `caliente01.wav` **from the Project window to the score track. Snap the clip to the CTI starting at 01:16:03.**
    The clip overlays the `latinotek02.wav` clip that you added in Step 14.

19. **Drag the Constant Power transition used several times in this tutorial to the cut point at the CTI.**
    The transition snaps to the right of the cut point.

20. **Drag** `caliente03.wav` **to the Timeline, and drop it in the score track. Drop the clip to follow the second copy of the** `caliente01.wav` **clip that you added in Step 18.**
    You combine two segments of the same type of music. In order to make the two clips flow seamlessly, you must edit the In point of the `caliente03.wav` clip.

21. **Double-click the clip to open it in the Source view monitor.**
    You edit the clip's In and Out points.

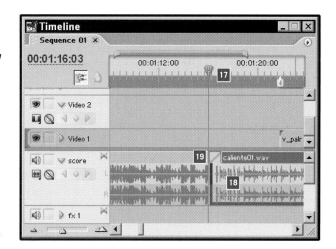

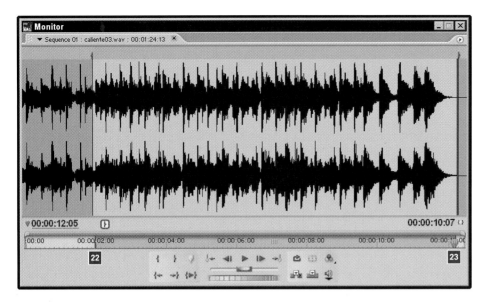

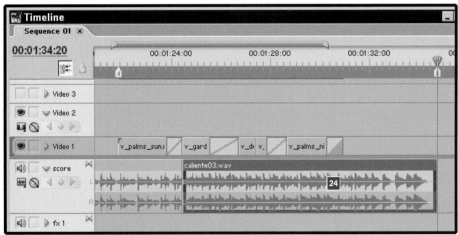

22. **Move the CTI to 01:29. Click the Set In Point button to set the In point for the clip.**

    The caliente03.wav clip now sounds seamless when you listen to it on the Timeline; it should be difficult to determine where the caliente01.wav clip ends and the caliente03.wav clip starts unless you watch the CTI on the Timeline.

23. **Move the CTI to 12:05. Click the Set Out Point button to set the Out point for the clip.**

    You set the end of the music for the entire project.

24. **On the Timeline, move the** caliente03.wav **clip to start at 01:24:13 and end at Marker 5 at 01:34:20.**

    This is its final position.

25. **Save the project.**

    You completed a series of complex edits. You added six music clips to the Timeline and trimmed them for length. You added several transitions to make one cohesive soundtrack. Listen to the soundtrack for the beach segment of the movie. The beat of the latinotek clips picks up from the smoother beat of the caliente clips, and vice versa.

Tutorial
» Fine-Tuning the Music Tracks

In this final tutorial of the Session, you finish the audio editing for your project. You adjust the volumes of the ocean wave clips on the Timeline and learn how to adjust keyframes for volume in the ECW. The ECW is attached to the Monitor window as a tab behind the Source view monitor in the editing workspace.

1. **On the Timeline, collapse the score track and open the fx 2 track.**
   You adjust two clips from the Timeline.

2. **Move the CTI to the start of the first copy of the** ocean.wav **clip on fx 2.**
   The clip starts at 18:15.

3. **Click the Show Keyframes icon, and choose Show Clip Volume from the menu.**
   A horizontal gold graph line displays across the clip.

4. **Click the Pen tool in the toolbox to select it.**
   You use the tool to adjust the volume level of the clip.

5. **Move the tool over the gold graph line. Drag downward.**
   You see a dB value display; drag the graph line downward until the display reads approximately -2.47 dB. (The value cannot be exactly -2.5 due to the logarithmic scale used to define dB values.)

6. **Click the Selection tool to deselect the Pen tool.**
   You adjust the second clip in the ECW and no longer need the Pen tool.

7. **Click the second copy of the** ocean.wav **clip in fx 2 starting at 23:19.**
   You adjust its volume in the ECW.

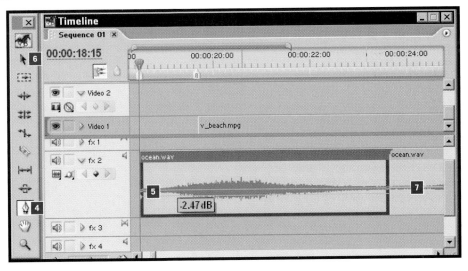

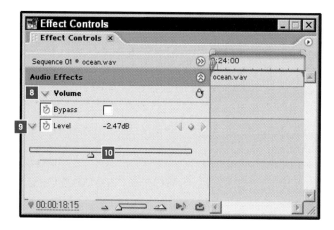

8. **Open the ECW. Click the spindown arrow to the left of the Volume heading.**

   Bypass and Level options display.

9. **Click the spindown arrow to the left of the Level heading.**

   You open a slider.

10. **Drag the slider left to read -2.47 dB.**

    You set the volume for the second copy of the clip to match that of the first copy of the ocean.wav clip. Check the two clips in the Timeline. You see that the volume graph lines are at the same level.

11. **Preview the clip segment from approximately 18:15 to 30:00 on the Timeline.**

    The ocean waves are audible, but not as loud, allowing the music to be heard more clearly.

12. **Save the project.**

    You adjusted volumes for two clips from the Timeline using different techniques. The audio component of the beach segment is finished. You built a musical score and adjusted the introductory sound effect for a smoother start to the segment.

» Session Review

This second session on audio editing showed you how to handle, modify, and manage the clips in a project. You learned how to adjust volumes for single clips or groups of clips. You had an introduction to the Audio Mixer and learned how it is used for adjusting volume and adding effects to tracks. You adjusted the pan settings for a number of sound clips on the Timeline and ECW, and you viewed the results in the Audio Mixer. You learned how to work with numbered markers on the Timeline. Finally, you learned how to adjust and edit tracks to coincide with specific components of your project, building a music score for the beach segment of the project from a set of five music clips that you trimmed both on the Timeline and in the Source view monitor. The first image in this session shows the area where you transitioned the first pair of music clips. The final image in this session shows the area where you transitioned from the final sports section of the Timeline.

Here are questions to help you review the information in this session. You can find the answers in the tutorial noted in parentheses.

1. Can you apply changes in volume to only some of the contents of a track? How is it done? (See Tutorial: Adjusting Track Volumes Using the Audio Mixer.)

2. What is a VU meter? What does it show? (See Tutorial: Adjusting Track Volumes Using the Audio Mixer.)

3. What are decibels? What do they measure? (See Tutorial: Adjusting Track Volumes Using the Audio Mixer.)

4. How do you write changes to a track from the Audio Mixer? What are the options? (See Tutorial: Fading Volume over Multiple Clips.)

5. When you adjust volumes in the Audio Mixer, can you work with the results on the Timeline? Is the reverse true as well? (See Tutorial: Fading Volume over Multiple Clips.)

6. What is keyframe interpolation? What does it do? (See Tutorial: Fading Volume over Multiple Clips.)

7. Where do you add track effects? (See Tutorial: Adding Audio Effects to Tracks in the Audio Mixer.)

8. How do you pan or balance a clip? What is the difference between pan and balance? (See Tutorial: Panning Clips.)

9. Can you move more than one clip at a time on the Timeline? (See Tutorial: Adding Music Clips to the Project.)

10. Can you use a clip more than one time in a project? (See Tutorial: Editing the Music Clips.)

11. Can you adjust the volume for a clip in the Timeline? (See Tutorial: Fine-Tuning the Music Tracks.)

» Other Projects

The audio clips are arranged and edited a specific way in the project. Experiment with different clip arrangements and edits. Use a separate copy of the project, or add extra audio tracks for experimentation.

An additional piece of music is available on the CD in the `extra music` folder named `irie mon_full.wav`. Experiment with segments of the song in your project.

Part V

Adding Transparency
Effects

Session 7 **Controlling Clips with Fixed and Transparency Effects**   p 196

Controlling Clips with Fixed and Transparency Effects

Tutorial: **Resizing Clips Using Fixed Effects**

Tutorial: **Changing Clip Opacity and Stacking Order**

Tutorial: **Adding More Beach Segment Clips**

Tutorial: **Adjusting Transparency Using Luminance and Screen Keys**

Tutorial: **Using a Garbage Matte Effect**

Tutorial: **Using a Color Keying Effect**

Session Introduction

You work with a number of simple effects in this session. First, you work with Fixed effects. If you select a clip on the Timeline and check in the ECW, you see a listing named Fixed Effects. Regardless of the video or visual clip (movies, video, stills, or titles), you can apply Fixed effects. The Fixed effects include two categories—Motion effects composed of Position, Scale, Rotation, and Anchor Point settings; and Opacity. In this session, you adjust some settings numerically. You can also change the values visually using handles on the clip; you use the visual technique with three clips in this session.

In this session, you also work with a group of effects called Keying effects. You can key out or remove specific color from clips based on color ranges that you choose. A key identifies pixels in an image that matches color or brightness levels and makes those pixels transparent or semitransparent.

Video and certain image formats are composed of three image channels, one each of red, green, and blue. These are referred to as RGB color. An alpha channel is a fourth type of channel and defines transparent or opaque areas of an image or frame—the image channels are referred to as RGBA color. Programs like Premiere Pro, Photoshop, and After Effects use this fourth channel to superimpose contents of one clip over another clip. You can base keying on luminance of an image rather than transparency. Luminance is another common type of key where darker and lighter values are used for defining transparency. Darker values are transparent; brighter areas are opaque. A number of color keys designate specific colors or color ranges as transparent. Layering clips one on top of another, and blending them using different keys and fades, is called superimposition.

As you can imagine, experimentation is required to achieve the perfect effect. You can preview the work that you complete in this session in the sample files, session07A.wmv and session07B.wmv.

TOOLS YOU'LL USE
anchor point, Blue Screen Key effect, clip resize handles, Cross Dissolve transition, Cutoff value, ECW, Fixed effects, Garbage Matte Key effect, Hide Keyframes command, Keyframe, Keyframe stopwatch, Luma Key effect, Motion fixed effects, Opacity effect, opacity graph, opacity slider, opacity value setting, Paste Attributes command, Pen tool, Program view monitor, scale value setting, Screen Key effect, Speed/Duration settings, Threshold value, Timeline, Track visibility toggle, Uniform Scale setting, x-axis and y-axis value settings

MATERIALS NEEDED
Session 06 project file that you created, or the session06.ppj file from the CD-ROM

TIME REQUIRED
90 minutes

Tutorial
» Resizing Clips Using Fixed Effects

In this tutorial, you work with some Fixed effects for three clips in the city segment of the project. The default setting for all clips is to display at 100 percent of their original size in the center of the screen. You can change the position, scale, and rotation of a clip by adjusting the values. All values are based on the anchor point position, which is at the center of the clip; in your project, the center is at 160x120 pixels.

< N O T E >

If you didn't do the tutorials in Session 6, copy the session06. prproj file from the CD to your hard drive. In the Welcome window, choose Open Project. Browse to the location where you stored the copied project file, and select Open. Then resave the project in Premiere Pro as session07.prproj (or use another file-naming convention).

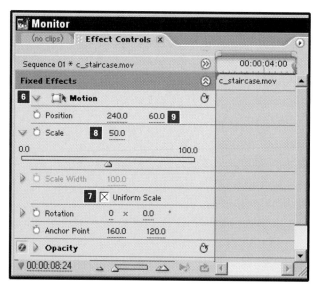

1. **Open Premiere Pro. When the Welcome window opens, choose** session06.prproj.
   The Welcome window closes, and the project is loaded into the program.

2. **Choose File→Save As, and resave the project file as** session07.prproj.
   The name of the new project version displays at the top of the program window.

3. **Choose Window→Workspace→Effects.**
   You work with the ECW in this tutorial.

4. **On the Timeline, toggle the track lock for Video 4 to off.**
   You work with the two clips that you added to this track in an earlier session.

5. **Toggle the track visibility for Video 4 to on.**
   You need to see the track contents over the contents of lower tracks.

6. **In the ECW, click the spindown arrow to the left of the Motion effects heading to display the contents.**
   Fixed effects are available in the ECW for every clip; you adjust the size and location of the entire clip.

7. **Click Uniform Scale.**
   You resize the clip the same amount vertically and horizontally.

8. **Click the Scale value (100.0), and type 50.**
   The clip is resized to 50 percent of its original height and width.

< N O T E >

In the figure, the Scale spindown arrow is opened to show you the slider. You can also adjust the scale by dragging the slider value.

9. **Click the first value, the x-value, and type 240; click the second value, the y-value, and type 60.**
   The resized clip moves to the upper right of the screen.

10. **Drag the** c_staircase.mov **clip down to Video 2 starting at 02:27.**

    You placed the clip on Video 4 for storage in Session 3 when you were first organizing the Timeline and editing. The clip ends at 06:14.

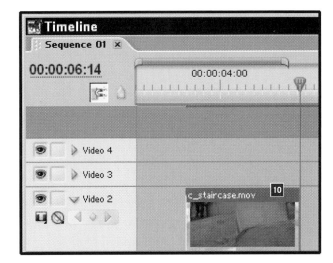

11. **Preview the segment in the Program view monitor.**

    You see the c_staircase.mov clip in the upper-left quarter of the screen. The city traffic and subway riders are also visible; the screen view was split using a transition in Session 4.

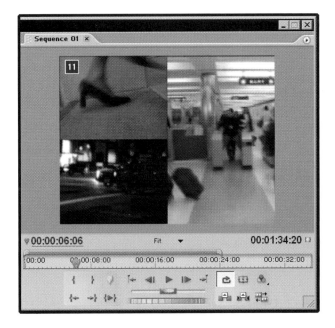

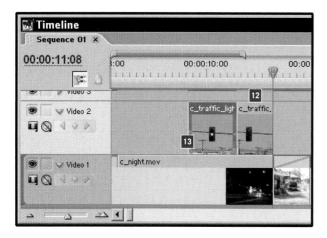

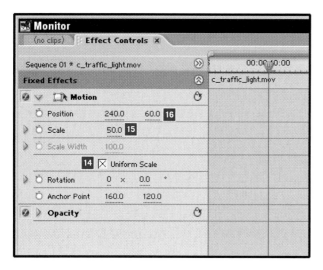

12. **Drag the two** c_traffic_light.mov **clips, starting at 06:20, along Video 2 to start at 09:19 and end at 11:08.**
The light sequence ends at the same time as the c_night.mov clip ends in Video 1.

13. **Click the first copy of the** c_traffic_light.mov **clip starting at 09:19 to select it.**
You set position and scale for the clip.

14. **In the ECW, open the Motion effects. Click Uniform Scale.**
You want the clip to resize equally; the Scale Width value is grayed out, leaving one Scale value setting.

15. **Click the Scale value, and type** 50.
The clip decreases to 50 percent of its original size.

16. **Click the x-value, and type** 240; **click the y-value, and type** 60.
The clip moves to the upper right of the screen.

17. **In the Timeline, click the second copy of the** c_traffic_light.mov **clip starting at 10:17.**
You apply the same settings to this copy.

18. **Repeat Steps 14 through 16.**
The second copy of the traffic lights clip moves to the upper right of the screen.

19. Preview the clip segment.

You see the different clips display in different locations on the screen, both those to which you applied Motion effects, as well as the clips to which you applied transitions in Session 4.

<NOTE>

All the edges of the clips, both horizontal and vertical, use a graphic bar to finish the edges and add some impact. You apply these bars in a later session.

20. Save the project.

You used fixed effects to transform three clips in the project. You resized the clips and placed them in different locations on the screen.

How to Define a Location on the Screen

The location of content on a frame is defined by basic geometry. The horizontal axis is the x-axis, and the vertical axis is the y-axis. The number of pixels along each axis depends on the size of the project. You are working with a frame size of 320x240. Therefore, there are 320 pixels along the x-axis and 240 pixels along the y-axis. If the center of your frame is at the top left of the screen, the x- and y-values are 0,0 as shown in the figure below. All values are based on the anchor point position, which is at the center of the clip; in your project, the center is located 160 pixels from the left (or right) and 120 pixels from the top (or bottom).

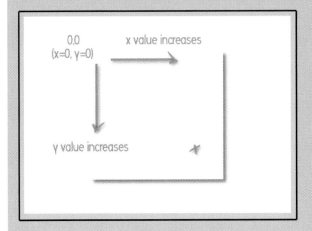

You can use negative values to describe a location OUTSIDE the frame. For example, a location having x-value of -200 and y-value of -200 means the center of the frame is 200 pixels to the left and 200 pixels above the frame.

The simplest way to understand how coordinates work is to experiment. Follow these steps:

>> Click any clip on the Timeline to display it in the ECW.

>> Click the spindown arrow to open the Motion effects.

>> Click the Motion label in the Fixed Effects list in the ECW to display handles around the clip and its center, or anchor point.

>> Click the View Zoom Level setting below the monitor in the Program view monitor and choose a low value such as 50%; you want to see the gray area surrounding the monitor.

>> Click the clip and drag it to different locations.

>> Watch the two Position coordinates' values as you move the clip.

Tutorial
» Changing Clip Opacity and Stacking Order

In this tutorial, you work with another Fixed effect—Opacity. You change the opacity of one clip already added to the project, and you add a still image to the Timeline and adjust its opacity as well as its position. You can precisely control the transparency of a clip using the Opacity effect. The higher the number of the Video track, the higher the content is in the visual stacking order. That is, clips on Video 1 are seen only if there is no content on Video 2 or if special transparency effects are used. A track is said to be superimposed if it overlays another track. Several terms are used when talking about basic transparency edits. Fade levels refer to the opacity level of the entire clip, which can range from 0 to 100 percent. A fade refers to changing the opacity for a specific segment of a clip between two keyframe nodes.

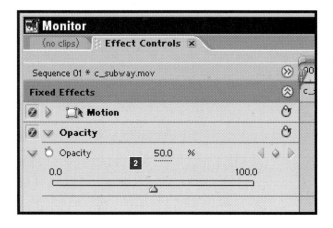

1. **Drag the** c_subway.mov **from its location in Video 4 starting at 16:15 to Video 3 starting at 07:21.**
   You originally added the clip to the Timeline in Session 1.

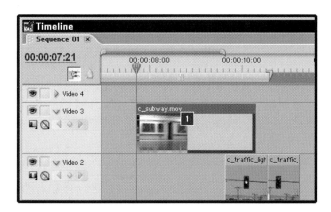

2. **Open the ECW. Click the Opacity value (100.0), and type** 50.
   You decrease the opacity of the clip to 50 percent.

<NOTE>
In the figure, the Opacity setting is expanded to show you the slider. You can drag the slider to reset the value instead of typing or dragging the blue active text value.

3. **Preview the segment of the Timeline.**

   You see the subway train overlay the underlying clips. Watch the area where the traffic light first appears. You see the subway train overlay for a short portion of the clip. You need to see the traffic lights clearly because you add effects to them later in the project.

4. **Drag the two** c_traffic_light.mov **clips upward from Video 3 to Video 4; drag the** c_subway.mov **clip from Video 3 downward to Video 2, and then move the two** c_traffic_light.mov **clips down to Video 3 from Video 4.**

   You reorder the content on two tracks. In the Timeline, the higher the track, the higher the content is in the stacking order. In order to see the traffic lights clearly, you must move the clips to a higher track than the subway clip.

5. **Preview the Timeline segment again.**

   Now you see that the traffic light overlays the semi-opaque subway clip.

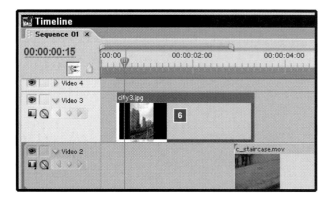

6. In the Project window, open the Stills folder and select the `city3.jpg` clip. Drag the clip to Video 3 in the Timeline starting at 00:10. Set its duration to 03:00.

7. **In the ECW, click the spindown arrow to display the Motion effects.**
   You use the settings to display the values you set in the next steps.

8. **In the ECW, click the Motion label in the Fixed Effects.**
   The still image displays resize handles around the edges of the clip and shows its anchor point as a circle at the center of the frame in the Program view monitor.

9. **Drag the image left in the Program view monitor until the position settings read 82.0 and 120.0.**
   You reset the image's screen location.

10. **Click the Opacity setting, and type** 75 **to decrease the clip's opacity to 75 percent.**

11. **On the Timeline, click the Show Keyframes icon to display the menu and select Show Keyframes.**
    You add keyframes to control the clip's opacity.

12. **Click the Pen tool on the toolbar.**
    You use the Pen tool to add keyframes to the opacity graph line.

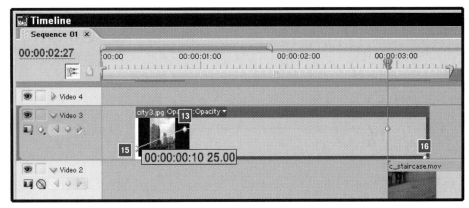

13. **Move the CTI to 00:25. Move the Pen tool over the gold graph line. Ctrl+click the graph with the tool to add a keyframe node.**

14. **Add three more keyframes at 00:10 (start of the clip), 02:27 (start of the** c_staircase.mov **clip in Video 2), and 03:10 (end of the clip).**
    You use the keyframes to adjust the opacity at both ends of the clip.

15. **With the Pen tool, drag the first keyframe at 00:10 down to 25 percent opacity.**
    As you drag the keyframe node, the opacity level displays next to the node.

16. **Drag the final keyframe at 03:10 down to 0 percent.**
    You fade the end of the clip.

<NOTE>
Look at the ECW for the city3.jpg clip. You see that the same set of four keyframes are added to the Opacity setting in the ECW.

17. **Click the Selection tool in the toolbar to deselect the Pen tool.**

18. **Click Hide Keyframes to open the menu. Choose Hide Keyframes.**

19. **Preview the segment in the Program view monitor.**
    You see the city image fade in. It is superimposed over the first city traffic movie, and then it fades out as the staircase movie starts.

20. **Save the project.**
    You adjusted opacity for clips in the ECW and Timeline. You swapped clips on the tracks to change the stacking order. You added one more clip to the Timeline. You adjusted the clip's position in the Program view monitor.

Timeline and ECW Coordination

Any changes that you make on the Timeline are reflected on the ECW and vice versa. You made changes to the opacity settings on the Timeline. If you look at the ECW, you see that the set of keyframes are present in the ECW. When keyframes are activated for a clip on the Timeline, you can click a small menu at the top of the clip next to its name and display a menu of the same Fixed effects that you can add and adjust on the Timeline, as shown in the figure.

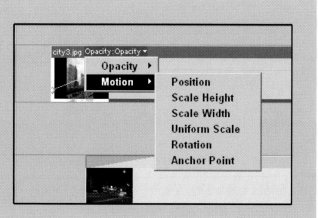

Tutorial

» Adding More Beach Segment Clips

Remember adding clips to Video 4 in Session 1? In this tutorial, you move the clips from Video 4 in the beach segment and add more clips from the Project window. Quite a few clips have no fade adjustments. Some of these clips do not have fades attached; others have fades adjusted after you apply transparency effects. Before you end the tutorial, you make scale adjustments for many of the clips based on their file format.

1. **Drag the** b_girl_running1.mov **clip from the video bin in the Project window to the Timeline to start at 24:11 in Video 2.**
   The clip overlays the beach and palm tree clips in Video 1.

2. **Drag the right edge of the clip to move the Out point.**
   The final duration is 06:15, ending at 30:26.

3. **Choose Video Transitions→Dissolve→Cross Dissolve in the Effects tab. Drag the transition to the start of the** b_girl_running1.mov **clip.**

4. **Repeat Step 3, adding the Cross Dissolve transition to the end of the** b_girl_running1.mov **clip.**

5. **Drag the** b_woman_dog.mov **clip from the video bin in the Project window to Video 3 on the Timeline to start at 37:19.**
   You add an effect to the clip in a later session that includes a color matte clip in Video 2. The matte must be placed in a lower track than the clip you apply it to, which is why you place the b_woman_dog.mov clip on Video 3.

6. **In the ECW, decrease the** b_woman_dog.mov **clip's opacity to 50 percent.**
   The underlying surf clip shows through. You make further adjustments to this clip in later sessions.

7. **Drag the** s_surf_girl.mpg **clip starting at 52:15 from Video 2 to Video 3.**
   It's exact location isn't important as you place the clip in Step 19. You need to move the clip from its original location in order to put other clips in its place.

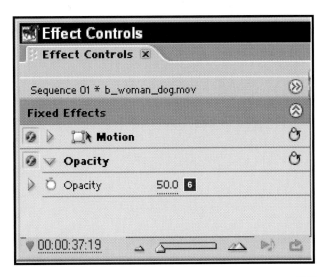

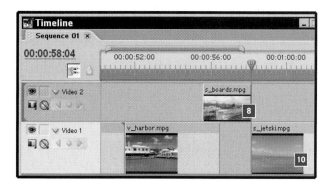

8. Move the `s_boards.mpg` clip from Video 4 (starting at 52:23) to Video 2 starting at 55:18.

9. Set the clip's In point at 01:10, and set its Out point at 03:25 for a duration of 02:16.

10. Move the `s_jetski.mpg` clip from Video 4 starting at 01:01:23 to Video 1 starting at 58:04.

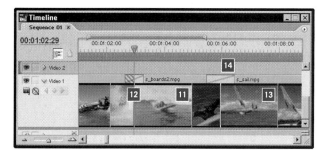

11. Move the `s_boards2.mpg` clip from Video 4 starting at 58:23 to Video 1 to follow the `s_jetski.mpg` clip starting at 01:02:29.

12. Drag the Cross Dissolve transition from the Video Transitions folder in the Effects tab to the cut point at 01:02:29.
    The two clips now have a crossfade.

13. Move the `s_sail.mpg` clip from Video 4 starting at 01:06:18 to Video 1 to follow the `s_boards2.mpg` clip starting at 01:05:29.

14. Choose Video Transitions→Dissolve→Cross Dissolve in the Effects tab. Apply the cross-dissolve transition to the cut point at 01:05:29.

15. Increase the transition's duration to 1:00 from the default 00:20.

16. Drag the `b_girl_running2.mov` clip from the video bin in the Project window to the Timeline to start at 01:12:29 on Video 1. Reset the duration to 04:20. Drag the left margin of the clip right to move the In point.

17. Drag the `s_windsurf.mpg` clip from the video bin in the Project window to the Timeline to start at 01:16:03 on Video 2. Reset the In point to 01:21; reset the Out point to 06:21.

18. Right-click the `s_windsurf.mpg` clip, and choose Speed/Duration from the menu to open the Clip Speed/Duration dialog box. Set the clip's speed to 140 percent, and click OK.
    The dialog box closes, and the duration decreases to 03:18.

19. **Move the** s_surf_girl.mpg **clip you moved to Video 3 in Step 7 to Video 2 starting at 01:10:21 following the** s_windsurf.mpg **clip.**

20. **Right-click the** s_surf_girl.mpg **clip, and choose Speed/Duration. In the Clip Speed/Duration dialog box, set the clip's speed to** 200 **percent and click OK.**
    The dialog box closes, and the duration decreases to 02:28.

21. **Apply the cross-dissolve transition to the cut point at 01:19:21. Extend the crossfade's duration to 01:00.**

22. **Apply the Cross Dissolve transition to the end of the** s_surf_girl.mpg **clip. Leave the default duration of 00:20.**

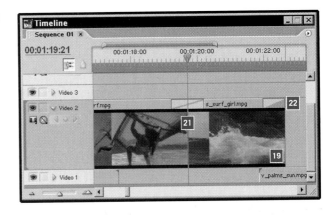

23. **Click the** v_beach.mpg **clip in Video 1 starting at 19:21 to activate the ECW for the clip.**
    Look closely—you see transparent areas (they appear black) above and below the clip's image. When you imported footage into the project, you used the Maintain Aspect Ratio command. This means that stills, video, and movies are imported at their native size. Your project uses a size of 320x240 pixels, and the .mpg file format uses a size of 352x240 pixels. The clips are resized to maintain their proportions. Now you modify the clip's scale in the ECW.

<NOTE>
You can see the margins of the clip in the Source view monitor, the Program view monitor (if you move the CTI over the clip), or by resizing the width of the track on the Timeline as shown in the figure.

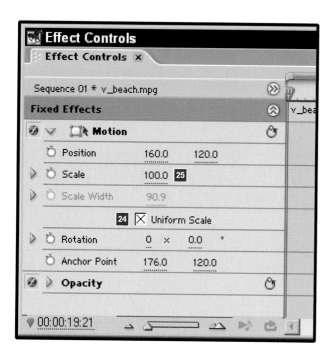

24. **In the ECW, click Uniform Scale.**

    The Scale Width setting is grayed out, leaving one active setting that is applied to both height and width.

25. **Click the scale setting (90.9), and type** 100 **to resize the clip.**

26. **Repeat Steps 23 to 25 with the remaining** .mpg **clips in the project.**

    You adjust a total of 17 clips on the Timeline for scale.

<NOTE>

This is a simple way to adjust the clips' size. You can also use cropping effects to reproportion the clip and then resize it. For the clips in this project, simple resizing is sufficient.

27. **Save the project, and preview the segment.**

    You adjusted positions for several clips, added more clips from the Project window, and modified some durations and In/Out points. You also added several transitions and adjusted a group of clips to scale. At this point, you have assembled a collection of clips that follow the opening clip in the beach segment of the project. Some of the clips are in their final positions; others are moved as you continue with the project editing.

Tutorial
» Adjusting Transparency Using Luminance and Screen Keys

The session's introduction described using keys. Keys are a type of effect that work based on a clip's pixel brightness or areas of transparency, or by specifying colors and ranges of colors to "key out" or make transparent. In this tutorial, you add two stills to the city segment and use Luma Key and Screen Key effects. When you add effects to your project, they are listed in the ECW under a separate heading named Video Effects below the Motion and Opacity headings.

1. **Right-click the** `city4.jpg` **clip in the Project window (in the stills bin) to open the menu, and click Speed/Duration. In the Clip Speed/Duration dialog box, set the duration to 00:10 and click OK.**

2. **Drag the clip to Video 4 in the Timeline starting at 02:17 and ending at 02:27.**
   The clip ends as the `c_staircase.mov` in Video 2 starts.

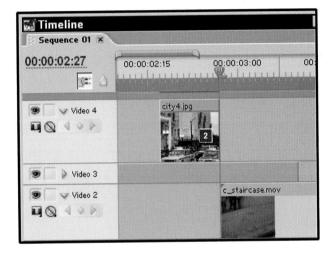

3. **In the Effects tab, choose Video Effects→Keying→Luma Key. Drag the effect to the** `city4.jpg` **clip that you added in Step 1.**
   A horizontal green line appears below the clip's name on the Timeline, indicating that an effect is applied. You use the Luma Key effect to create transparency in the clip.

<NOTE>
The Effects tab is tabbed with the Project window in the Editing workspace, which you set at the end of Session 06.

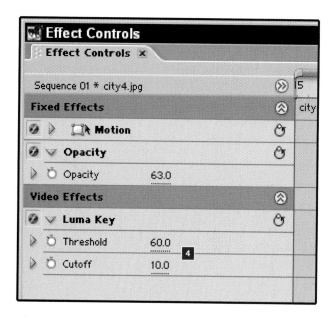

4. **In the ECW, click the spindown arrow for the Luma Key effect. Click the Threshold value (100.0), and type** 60; **click the Cutoff value (0.0), and type** 10.

   The higher the Threshold value, the greater the range of brightness values in the image that become transparent. The Cutoff, which refers to how opaque the visible areas appear, is set low at 10 percent, which means that the components in the image, such as the white cars, remain visible.

5. **In the Project window, select the** city2.jpg **clip. Reset its duration to 01:07.**

   You move the clip into a small space on the Timeline.

6. **Drag the** city2.jpg **clip to the Timeline following the** c_staircase.mov.

   The clip fits in the space between the staircase and subway movies.

7. **Drag the Additive Dissolve transition to the end of the clip starting at 07:01.**

   Leave the default 00:20 length.

8. **In the Effects tab, select Video Effects→Keying→Screen Key. Drag the effect to the** city2.jpg **clip.**

   You use the Screen Key to make the clip transparent.

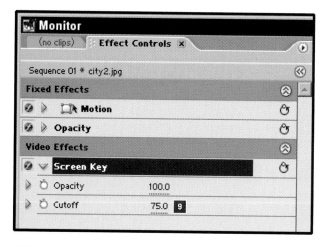

9. **In the ECW, click the spindown arrow to open the Screen Key effect. Set the Cutoff to** 75.0.

   The higher the Cutoff value, the fewer the pixels becoming transparent based on lightness. Unlike the Luma key, which is based on the darkness of a pixel, the Screen Key is based on the lightness of a pixel values.

10. **Preview the segment in the Program view monitor, and save the project.**

    You added two more clips to the project and applied two types of Keying effects. You created transparency for two still images in the city segment of the project based on the brightness or lightness of the still image clips and their underlying clips.

Tutorial
» Using a Garbage Matte Effect

In this tutorial, you work with two more still images. You edit the two clips in their entirety in this tutorial. That is, you set their durations and add them to the Timeline. Then you work with another key called a Garbage Matte. The Garbage Matte effect allows you to define an area of the image that is seen on screen. You use the effect along with two Fixed effects to create your first bit of animation, and you adjust the opacity of the clip using the Opacity effect. When you finish the first clip, you paste the same settings to the second clip.

1. Select the `sign2.jpg` clip in the stills bin in the Project window. Right-click, and open the Clip Speed/Duration dialog box. Set the duration to 01:00, and click OK.
   The dialog box closes, and the clip's length changes.

2. Repeat Step 1 with the `sign1.jpg` clip, also in the stills bin.

3. Drag the `sign2.jpg` clip from the stills bin to Video 2 to start at 13:07.

4. Drag the `sign1.jpg` clip from the stills bin to Video 3 to start at 13:17.

5. Select the `sign2.jpg` clip in Video 2. Right-click the Timeline's time ruler, and choose Set Sequence Marker→In and Out Around Selection.
   Set In and Out points to make it simpler to preview the clip as you work.

6. In the Effects tab, select Video Effects→Keying→Garbage Matte. Drag the effect to `sign2.jpg` on Video 2.
   A horizontal green effects indicator bar displays across the clip on the Timeline.

7. Click the eye icon to toggle Video 1 and Video 3 tracks' visibility to off.
   You work with the Garbage Matte and need to see the clips' background clearly.

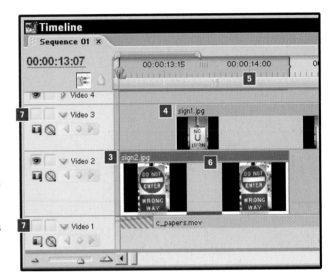

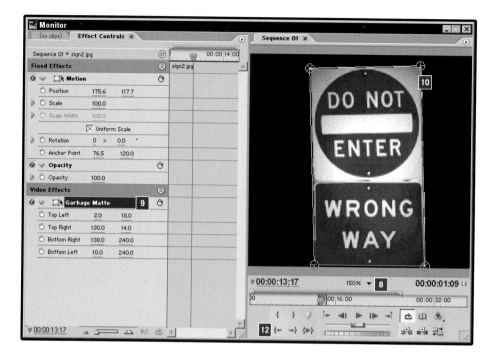

8. On the Program view monitor, click the zoom setting and choose 150%.

You want to see the margins of the street sign clearly.

9. Click the Garbage Matte effect's name in the ECW.

The resize handles are activated in the Program view monitor.

10. Slowly adjust each corner of the frame to remove the background street image that displays behind the sign.

You can see the values for each corner change in the ECW settings.

11. In the Timeline, toggle Video 1's visibility to on.

You want to see the location of the transition to move and resize the sign.

12. Click the Go to In Point button on the Program view monitor's controls to move the playback head to the start of the clip.

You start adjusting scale and position at the first frame.

13. In the Program view monitor, click the zoom level and choose 100%.

You resize the clip and need to see it clearly on the screen.

14. Click the Motion fixed effect name in the ECW to display the resize handles.

The resize handles surround the image, including the areas that you cut with the Garbage Matte, as you can see in the Program view monitor.

15. Click the Stopwatch icon for both the Position and Scale values.

The stopwatch means that keyframes are activated; when you make changes in the next steps, they are recorded on the Timeline.

16. Click the Scale setting in the ECW, and type 20.

The image is reduced to 20 percent of its original size.

17. Drag the image to the lower right of the screen at the transition's border. Drag from the anchor point location in the center of the clip.

Notice that keyframes are now added to the Timeline at the CTI position as you can see in the ECW.

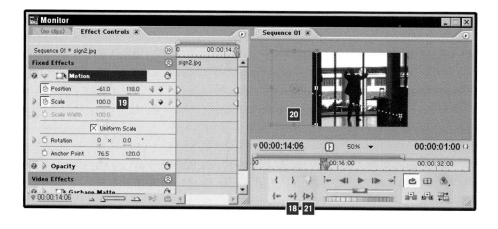

<NOTE>

The Program view monitor zoom is set to 50% in the figure to show you the full path of the clip.

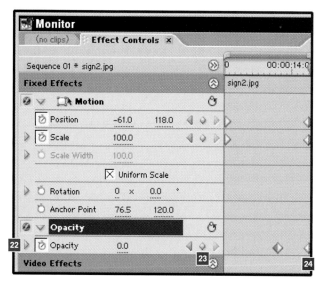

18. **Click the Go to Out Point button to move the CTI to the last frame of the clip.**
    You change size and position again.

19. **Click the Scale value in the ECW, and type** 100.
    You increase the clip's size to full size, adding another keyframe to the ECW.

20. **Drag the clip to the left of the screen.**
    You see a dotted line across the screen as you move the clip indicating a motion path. A position keyframe is added in the ECW.

21. **Click the Play In to Out button to view the clip's path and size change.**
    You see the sign gradually get larger as it moves across the screen, disappearing to the left. The Garbage Matte changes size proportionally with the clip size.

22. **Click the spindown arrow to the left of the Opacity effect to display the setting. Click the Stopwatch icon to activate the keyframes.**
    You adjust the opacity for the clip in the ECW.

23. **Move the CTI to 13:25, and click the Keyframe icon.**
    A keyframe is added to the ECW. The opacity at this keyframe's location is 100 percent; you need a starting point to fade the clip.

24. **Move the CTI to the last frame of the clip. Click the Opacity setting and type** 0 **to fade the clip.**

<TIP>

An easy way to make sure that you are at the last frame is to click Go to Out Point on the Program view monitor controls.

25. On the Timeline, select the sign2.jpg clip on Video 2 starting at 13:07. Press Ctrl+C, or choose Edit→Copy, to copy the clip.

< N O T E >

The Show Opacity keyframes setting is chosen for the sign2.jpg clip to show you the opacity settings transferred from the ECW to the Timeline.

26. Click the sign1.jpg clip on Video 3 starting at 13:17 to select it. Choose Edit→Paste Attributes.

The effects and settings that you just copied from the sign2.jpg clip are applied to the sign1.jpg clip.

27. Click the eye icon to toggle the visibility for Video 3 to on.

28. In the ECW, click the Garbage Matte effect to select it.

The handles display on the image in the Program view monitor.

29. Adjust the handles to crop the signpost from the top of the image.

The Garbage Matte size changes proportionally with the image's size.

30. Preview the Timeline segment in the Program view monitor, and save the project.

You completed a complicated set of edits. You added two clips to the Timeline. You used a Garbage Matte to crop out unwanted segments of a clip, and then you animated the clip's size and position over time. The two traffic signs appear to move across the screen and increase in size over time. You copied the clip's attributes and pasted them to a second clip.

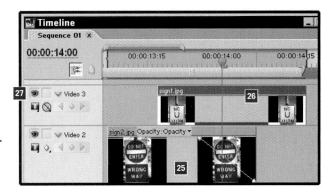

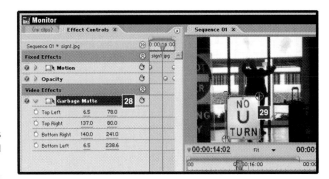

Tutorial
» Using a Color Keying Effect

In the final tutorial for this session, you work with the tropical drink clip at the end of the movie. A number of different Keying effects work with specific colors, such as blue, green, non-red, and multiple color keys. To produce the exact effect in this tutorial, making the fruit in the drink translucent, you use the Blue Screen Key effect.

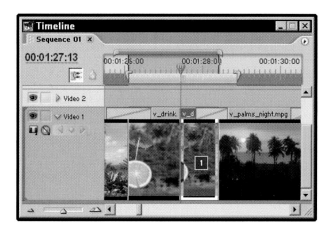

1. **From the Video Effects folder in the Effects tab, select the Blue Screen Key from the Keying effects folder. Drag the effect to the v_drink.mpg clip in Video 1 starting at 01:27:03.**

2. **In the ECW, click the spindown arrow to open the Blue Screen Key effect. Click the Stopwatch icon to the left of the Threshold value.**
   You set a keyframe to apply the effect.

3. **Move the CTI to the start of the clip at 01:27:03; click the Add Keyframe icon.**
   You add a keyframe at the start of the clip. Leave the default values.

4. **Move the CTI to the last frame of the clip at 01:28:12. Click the Threshold value, and type 25.**
   At a very low threshold, the clip gradually darkens starting from the blue colors and adding more color over time.

5. **Click the arrow to the right of the Smoothing setting, and choose High.**
   The edges of the image elements are smoothed, producing less defined boundaries and blending better with the background of the clip.

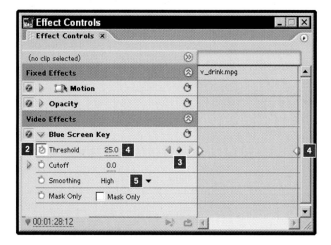

6. **Preview the Timeline segment in the Program view monitor, and save the project.**
   The Blue Screen Key effect works well for making the fruit translucent as it darkens. The Green Screen Key and Non-Red Key effects also create a similar effect. I wanted to see the orange slice and not the straw, and the Blue Screen key is the only one that produces this specific effect. You can try them all.

» Session Review

This session began a series of sessions working with effects. You worked primarily with the Fixed Effects, including Motion and Opacity. You learned to resize clips and how to work with clip attributes both numerically in the ECW and visually in the Program view monitor. You learned a method to modify a clip using settings and effects copied from another clip. You added a number of clips to the project. The first image in this session shows one of the surf clips. You adjusted opacity and added more transitions for existing and new clips, as you can see in the final image in this session.

You worked with both the city and beach segments of the project in this session. You organized several clips in the city segment and added the first animation and transparencies used to create a sense of motion. You also added specific types of transparency to the tropical drink clip in the beach segment for added impact.

The latter part of the session showed you how to work with some common types of transparency keys. You work with two more transparency keys in the next session. You also learned how to add some simple keyframes to control how an effect is applied. Notice that the tutorials are becoming more complex. That is, in addition to working with one specific process or task, you now combine different processes such as applying keys and adding motion. This is designed to reinforce the material that you learned in earlier sessions, as well as to show you common ways of working in Premiere Pro. Not only is it important for you to learn how to use the program, but it is also important for you to learn efficient ways to apply different processes to the same clip. This trend continues through the rest of the sessions.

Answer the questions below to review the information in this session. The answer for each question can be found in the tutorial noted in parentheses.

1. What do the x- and y-values of the Position fixed effect refer to? (See Tutorial: Resizing Clips Using Fixed Effects.)

2. Where can you change the opacity of a clip? Does it matter what location you use? (See Tutorial: Changing Clip Opacity and Stacking Order.)

3. What is the track stacking order? How does it work? (See Tutorial: Changing Clip Opacity and Stacking Order.)

4. Are clips resized to the project size when you import them into your project? (See Tutorial: Adding More Beach Segment Clips.)

5. When working with the Luma Keying effect, what does the Threshold value determine? (See Tutorial: Adjusting Transparency Using Luminance and Screen Keys.)

6. What effect does changing the Cutoff value have when working with a Screen Keying effect? (See Tutorial: Adjusting Transparency Using Luminance and Screen Keys.)

7. Is it better to resize or revise a clip in the Program view monitor or in the ECW? Why? (See Tutorial: Using a Garbage Matte Effect.)

8. Can you use a Garbage Matte effect if you resize the clip? (See Tutorial: Using a Garbage Matte Effect.)

9. Can you use keying effects based on specific colors or color ranges? (See Tutorial: Applying a Color Keying Effect.)

» Other Projects

In this session, you learned to work with some of the Fixed Effects added to each visual clip. Experiment with the other effects. Compare the workflow if you make and modify settings in the Timeline compared to the ECW. Do you prefer one over the other?

You worked with several Keying effects in this session. Experiment with other effects. Adjust each effect's sliders as you experiment, and see what impact changing settings has on a clip and its underlying clips.

Part VI

Working with Video Effects

Session 8 **Creating and Animating Titles**   p 222

Session 9 **Using Graphics for Special Effects**   p 250

Creating and Animating Titles

Tutorial: **Creating a Static Title**

Tutorial: **Adding Titles to the Timeline**

Tutorial: **Customizing Title Text**

Tutorial: **Adding the Beach Message**

Tutorial: **Animating a Title Using Fixed Effects**

Tutorial: **Creating More Title Animations**

Tutorial: **Using a Template for a Title**

Tutorial: **Composing a Title Sequence for the Project**

Session Introduction

What goes into the average movie or television program? Obviously, video and audio. You generally see effects aplenty as well. Have you ever seen a movie or a television program that doesn't have credits? Not likely. In fact, sometimes the credits seem to go on, and on, and on.

Aside from credits, text is used in other ways in a video project. Those of you who work with training or presentation materials are well aware of this fact. A project whose primary purpose is to provide information is usually accompanied by varying amounts of text. Titles are one element used to convey information in a project. We process visual information differently than spoken information, and we process written information in a different way again.

You use an assortment of titles in the project, but tutorials on building the entire set of titles is not included in this session. There is a Bonus Session on the CD called "Creating Project Titles and Graphics" that contains tutorials to learn how to build all the titles for the project. In this session, you learn how to build two of the project's titles.

All the titles required for the project are on the CD in the footage folder, in a subfolder called titles. As you work through this session, references are made to the tutorials in the Bonus Session. You can either create the titles using the tutorials in the Bonus Session as they are referenced in this session, or use the finished titles from the CD. If you work through both sessions simultaneously, plan on two 90-minute sessions to complete the work.

After the titles are created, you add them to the Timeline. You add two titles to the city segment and a set of five titles and one image title to the beach segment. You learn how to do more complicated animations in this session as you animate three of the beach segment's titles using fixed effects and keyframes.

There are three sample files in the samples folder: session08A.wmv shows the titles at the end of the city segment; session08B.wmv shows the three animated titles in the beach segment; and session08C.wmv shows the ending title sequence for the project.

TOOLS YOU'LL USE
Additive Dissolve transition, Cross Zoom transition, ECW, Fill properties, In and Out markers, Keyframe Interpolation options, Motion fixed effects, New Title command, Opacity fixed effect, Position commands, Program view monitor, Stroke properties, Style menu, Templates menu, Text properties, Timeline, Title Designer window, Type tool

MATERIALS NEEDED
Session 8 project file that you created, or the session07.prproj file from the CD-ROM; titles folder from the CD containing 14 title files

TIME REQUIRED
90 minutes

Tutorial
» Creating a Static Title

The first title that you create is one of the pair used in the city segment of the project. In this tutorial, you learn the basics of the Title Designer window. You create the first title and save a style. You can use the prepared file from the titles folder, `you_forgot.prtl`, or create your own following the steps in this tutorial.

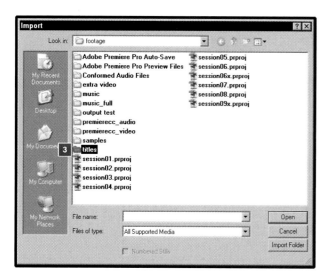

1. **Open Premiere Pro. When the Welcome window opens, choose** `session08.prproj`.
The Welcome window closes, and the project is loaded into the program.

<NOTE>
If you didn't do the tutorials in Session 7, copy the `session07.prproj` file from the CD to your hard drive. In the Welcome window, choose Open Project. Browse to the location where you stored the copied project file, and select Open. Then resave the project in Premiere Pro as `session08.prproj` (or use another filenaming convention).

2. **Choose File→Save As. Resave the project file as** session08.prproj.
The name of the new project version displays at the top of the program window.

3. **Choose File→Import. Browse to the CD or the storage location that you created on your hard drive for the project files. Select the titles folder, and click Import Folder.**
The folder is imported as a new bin and contains fourteen files; titles have the extension `.prtl`. Two of the clips in the titles folder are Photoshop files; when you import the folder, you are asked how to import them. The default option is to import as footage using Merged Layers; click OK to accept the defaults and import the files. You use the images in Session 9.

<TIP>
When you create a new title, click the titles folder in the Project window to select it. When you save the title, it is automatically added to the folder.

4. **Click the New Item icon at the bottom of the Project window. Choose Title from the menu that opens.**
The Adobe Title Designer window opens.

Templates ── Set tab stops ── Font browser

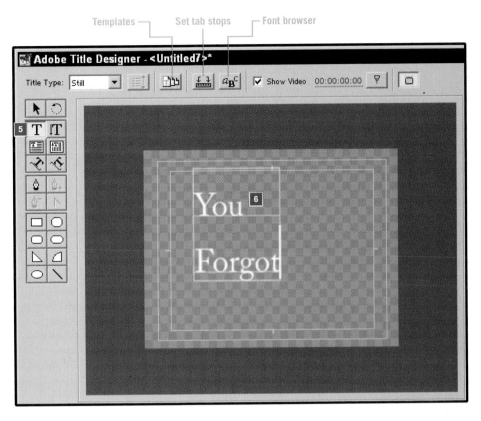

5. Click the Type tool on the layout to display the vertical I-beam.

The Type tool is the default tool selected in the toolbar when you open the Adobe Title Designer window. The location you initially click on the layout isn't important, because you adjust its size and position later.

6. Type You, **and press Enter. Type** Forgot.

This is the text for the first title. Pressing Enter between the words extends the text over two lines.

7. **Click the arrow to the left of Properties to open the Properties drop-down list.**

8. **Click the Font drop-down list, and choose Bell Gothic Standard Black.**

    The font is one of the Adobe fonts shipped with Premiere Pro; the fonts are installed automatically when you install the program.

    <TIP>

    You can visually preview fonts. Click the font name displayed in the Properties area, and choose Browser to open the Font Browser. Scroll through the list to find the font that you want to use. Click OK.

9. **Change the Font Size to** 90.0 **and the Aspect to** 125**%.**

    Click the default value to activate the text field, and type the new value. Or hold the mouse cursor over the default value shown; when it changes to a double-ended arrow, drag left (to decrease the value) or right (to increase the value).

10. **Click the check box to the left of the Fill heading to activate the settings. Click the drop-down arrow to the left of the check box to display the settings options.**

11. **Click the arrow to the right of the Fill Type setting to open a list; select Solid.**

    The text will be a solid color.

12. **Click the eyedropper next to the Color swatch and click on any white area on the Title Designer window to sample it.**

    The color swatch changes to white.

13. **Leave the default Opacity setting at 100%.**

    The title text isn't transparent.

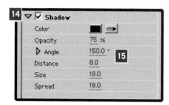

14. **Click the check box to the left of the Shadow heading to activate the settings. Click the drop-down arrow to the left of the check box to display the settings options.**

15. **Choose these Shadow settings:**
    Color Black (default color)
    Opacity: 75%
    Angle: 150.0 degrees
    Distance 8.0
    Size/Spread: 18.0

    You add a black shadow to the text. The shadow is soft, and below and to the right of the text.

16. **Right-click the title to open the shortcut menu, and choose Position→Horizontal Center; right-click again, and choose Position→Vertical Center.**
You position the title horizontally and vertically on the screen.

17. **Click the arrow at the top right of the Styles section of the window to open the Styles menu, and choose New Style to open the New Style dialog box. Name the style** city, **and click OK.**
The dialog box closes, and the new text style is added to the list.

18. **Click the Close icon at the top right of the Title Designer window.**
A dialog box opens asking if you want to save the title.

19. **Click Yes to close the dialog box and open the Save Title dialog box.**

20. **Browse to the location where you are storing the project files. Name the file** x_you_forgot, **and click Save.**
The Title Designer window closes, and the title is added to the Project window.

21. **Save the project.**
You created your first title, one of the pair of titles used at the end of the first segment of the project. The title uses large white text with a black shadow. You also created a text style.

<NOTE>
In Bonus Session 1, "Creating Project Titles and Graphics," located on the CD you will find a companion tutorial to the one you just finished. The tutorial, named *Creating a New Title from a Style,* shows you how to create a new title using a style. The tutorial describes how to create the second title used for the city segment of the project, named didn't_you.prtl. If you want to create the other half of the pair, do this before proceeding to the next tutorial.

<TIP>
You can save a title by choosing File→Save. Because you have to close the window anyway, the method described saves you one step.

<NOTE>
The first title is included in the folder from the CD with the other titles. If you prefer, you can name the title you_forgot, which overwrites the CD file and replaces the copy in your project.

Tutorial

» Adding Titles to the Timeline

In this tutorial, you add two titles to the Timeline and add transition effects. Titles are created with a transparent background behind any text or other objects that you add to the title. Use the Effects workspace. Choose Window→Workspace→Effects.

1. **On the Timeline, click the time indicator to activate the field and type** 1300.
   The CTI jumps to 13:00.

<NOTE>
Use the didnt_you.prtl and you_forgot.prtl titles from the titles folder, or the you_forgot.prtl or the x_you_forgot.prtl titles that you created in the preceding tutorial and/or the tutorial in the Bonus Session on the CD.

2. **Select the** you_forgot.prtl **file in the titles bin in the Project window. Drag the title to the Timeline to snap to the CTI on Video 4.**
   The default length for the titles was set in Session 1 and is 60 frames, or two seconds at 30 fps.

3. **Click the time indicator on the Timeline, and type** 1600.
   The CTI jumps to 16:00.

4. **Drag the right edge of the** you_forgot.prtl **clip right until it snaps to the CTI.**
   The title's duration extends to 03:00.

5. Select the `didnt_you.prt1` clip in the titles bin in the Project window. Drag the title to the Timeline to Video 4. Place the clip to start at 16:00 after the `you_forgot.prt1` title.

6. Move the CTI to the cut point at 16:00.
   You need to add a transition to the pair of clips.

7. In the Effects tab, choose Video Transitions→Dissolve→Cross Dissolve and drag the transition to overlay the cut point at 16:05.
   The first title clip gradually fades out as the second title clip gradually fades in.

8. Click the transition to open the Effect Controls window. Click the duration to activate the field, and type `105`.
   You lengthen the transition to 01:05, centered over the cut point.

9. Add three more transitions. Use the default transition, Additive Dissolve, at its default length of 20 frames. Add transitions to these locations:
   The start of the `you_forgot.prt1` title, starting at 13:00 on Video 4
   The end of the `didnt_you.prt1` title, ending at 18:15 on Video 4
   The end of the `c_papers.mov` clip, ending at 17:28 on Video 1
   The three transitions are used to fade in the first title gradually, and then to gradually fade out the second title and the man throwing papers clip.

10. Preview the Timeline segment in the Program view monitor from approximately 13:00 to 19:00.

11. Save the project.
    You have now added titles complete with dissolves to the first part of the project. The `session08A.wmv` file in the samples folder shows this segment of the Timeline.

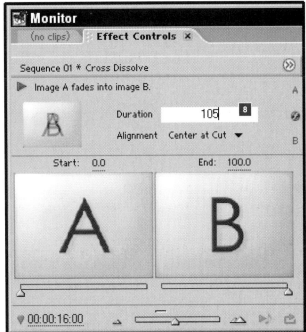

Tutorial
» Customizing Title Text

The second segment of the project also uses titles. In this tutorial, you make a new title in the Title Designer window using text features such as strokes and custom fills. This title is one of several added to the project in a later tutorial. As you work in the Title Designer window, open and close sections in the Object Style listings at the right of the window to make it easier to see the contents. For example, when you have finished selecting Properties, click the spindown arrow to collapse the section.

1. **At the bottom of the Project window, choose New→Title to open the Title Designer window.**
   You create the first title for the beach segment of the project.

2. **Click Show Video. Click the time indicator to the right of the Show Video label at the top of the Title Designer window to activate the field, and type** 3115.
   The CTI jumps to 31:15, and the s_surf_red.mpg clip on Video 1 displays as a background for the title.

< T I P >

Use frames from the project to match the color in the title. Viewing frames also helps to place titles in precise locations.

3. **Click the Type tool on the layout to display the vertical I-beam. Type the title text** LIFE. **Drag the title to the lower-right portion of the screen.**

4. Click the arrow to the left of Properties to open the Properties drop-down list. Open the Font drop-down list, and choose Lithos Pro Black (or a similar substantial font).

5. Set the font size to 62.

6. Click the check box to the left of the Fill heading. Open the Fill selection menu by clicking the arrow to the left of Fill.

7. Choose Solid from the Fill Type drop-down menu.

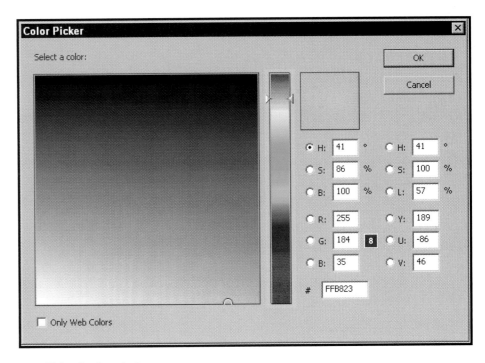

8. Click the color swatch to open the Color Picker. Set the color to RGB=255/184/35. Click OK to close the Color Picker.

   The text is now a gold color.

9. **Click the arrow to the left of the Strokes heading to open a sub-menu. Click Add to add an Inner Stroke.**

10. **Click the arrow to the left of the Inner Strokes heading to display the Inner Stroke settings.**

< N O T E >

There are no limits to the number of strokes that you can add to text. You are limited only by visual appearance.

11. **Select Edge from the Type menu.**
    You add a stroke around the edge of the text for added interest.

12. **Set the Size to** 27.0.

13. **Choose Solid from the Fill Type menu.**

14. **Click the color swatch to open the Color Picker. Set the color to RGB=255/223/72. Click OK to close the Color Picker.**
    A yellow stroke is added to the text.

15. **Click Add to add an Outer Stroke. Click the arrow to the left of the Outer Strokes heading to display the Outer Stroke settings.**
    You use the default Edge option for the Type of stroke and the default Solid Fill type. You add a stroke outside the edge of the text for contrast.

16. **Set the Size to** 20.0.

17. **Select the eyedropper tool next to the color swatch. The cursor changes to an eyedropper. Move the eyedropper over the image.**
    You can see that the color swatch changes color as the eyedropper samples different pixels in the image.

18. **When the eyedropper passes over a deep red color, click to select the color from the surfboard.**
    The sample uses RGB=175/0/40.

Using Safe Title Displays

Use the Show Safe Titles option for title layouts if you plan output to television. The two safe title areas are drawn over your title and identify the action-safe zone (outermost line) and the title-safe zone (innermost line). Television screens are not flat and do not display the entire content of a frame. Use the layout guides to prevent losing your text or motion due to the screen characteristics. Make sure that your text and graphics remain within the boundaries. If you are not using television output, you can hide the Show Safe Titles options or use the margins for placement aids.

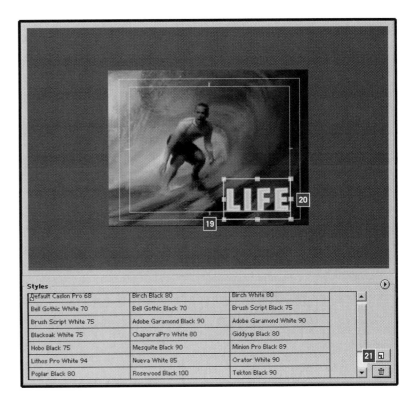

19. **Use the up- and down-arrow keys to nudge the text down to the safe title margin.**

<NOTE>
The Title Designer window shows two overlaying rectangular frames; these frames are used to define safe margins for television displays. Due to the process used to display on the curved screen on a television, the edges of the screen are cropped off. The two safe margins refer to the area that will completely display titles (the inner rectangle) and the area that will completely display action (the outer rectangle).

20. **Use the left- and right-arrow keys to nudge the text until the right margin matches the safe title margin's line.**

<TIP>
You can also move text using the x-position and y-position coordinates in the Transform section of the Title Designer window.

21. **Click the New Style icon in the Styles segment of the Title Designer window to open the New Style dialog box. Name the style** beach, **and click OK.**

22. **Click Close. In the Save dialog box that opens, name the title** life **and click Save.**
The dialog box closes, and the title is saved.

23. **Save the project.**
You created another title using strokes for added interest and font weight. You used custom colors and chose one color from the image itself. You saved the text as a new style. The title is one of the group of titles you add to the beach segment in the next tutorial.

<NOTE>
In the Bonus Session on the CD, "Creating Project Titles and Graphics," the tutorial *Duplicating Project Titles* describes how to save a style for the beach segment's text and then create the rest of the series of titles used in the beach segment of the project.

Tutorial

» Adding the Beach Message

In this tutorial, you add the five titles to the beach segment that make up the message "Life is a Beach—Find Yours" (which is very true, isn't it?). The first title was created in the previous tutorial; the four additional message titles are available in the titles folder, or you can create them yourself by working through the tutorial *Duplicating Project Titles* in the Bonus Session 1, "Creating Project Titles and Graphics" on the CD.

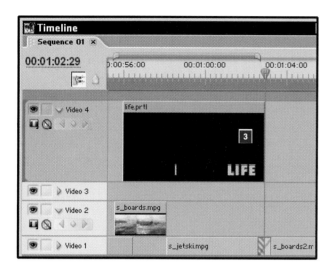

1. **In the Project window, right-click the** `life.prtl` **title and choose Speed/ Duration from the shortcut menu. In the Clip Speed/Duration dialog box, set the duration for the clip to** 07:00. Titles use the default stills length set in the program preferences.

2. **Repeat Step 1, setting the duration for the** `is_a.prtl` **title to** 04:00 **and the duration for the** `beach.prtl` **title to** 06:00.

3. **Select the** `life.prtl` **clip from the titles bin in the Project window. Drag it to Video 4 starting at 55:29 and ending at 01:02:29, the ending frame of the** `s_jetski.mpg` **clip.**

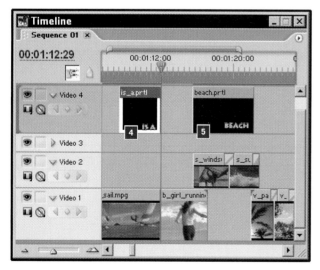

4. **Select the** `is_a.prtl` **clip from the titles bin in the Project window. Drag it to Video 4 starting at 01:08:29 and ending at 01:12:29, the end of the** `s_sail.mpg` **clip.**

5. **Select the** `beach.prtl` **clip from the titles bin in the Project window. Drag it to Video 4 starting at 01:16:02 and ending at 01:22:02, the location where the** `s_surf2.mpg` **clip fades out.**

6. Drag the `find.prtl` clip from the titles bin to Video 3 starting at 01:30:08. Set the clip's duration to 04:12, so that it ends at 01:34:20, the end of the score.

7. Drag the `yours.prtl` clip from the titles bin to Video 4 starting at 01:30:08. Set the clip's duration to 04:12, so that it ends at 01:34:20.

8. Save the project.

   You added the five message titles to the beach segment of the project, setting their durations and locations to coincide with specific video elements in the project.

9. Take a short break.

   In the next two tutorials, you animate three of the titles, so you need a clear head!

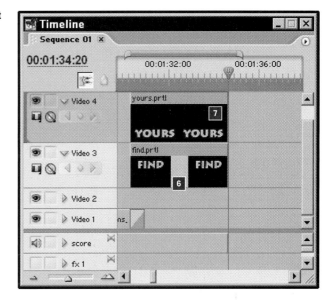

Tutorial

» Animating a Title Using Fixed Effects

In this tutorial, you animate the life.prtl title to make the title appear to move with the action. You work with many keyframes in the ECW to make this animation happen. Work carefully, and resize the ECW and Program view monitor so that you can see clearly. In addition to keyframes at the first and last frames of the title, you need an additional six keyframes throughout the clip. When working with numerous settings and keyframes, use the keyframe navigator rather than guessing at keyframe locations.

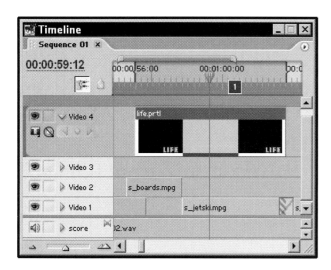

1. **Select the life.prtl clip on Video 4 starting at 55:29. Right-click the time ruler on the Timeline, and choose Set Sequence Marker→In and Out Around Selection.**

   You define the Timeline segment to make it simpler to preview in the Program view monitor as you work with the clip.

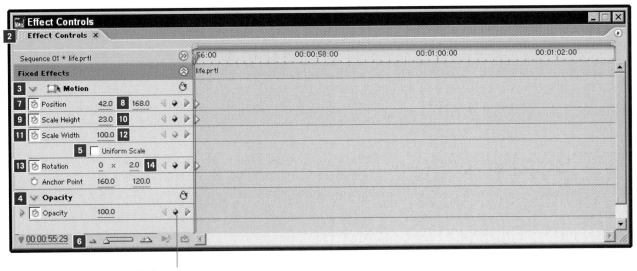

Keyframe navigator

2. **Click the ECW's tab and drag it away from the Monitor window to separate it from the rest of the window.**
   Resize the window to see the ECW Timeline clearly.

<TIP>
If you want to restore the ECW location, click the tab and drag it over the Source view monitor until you see a bold line. Release the tab and it is again attached to the Monitor window.

3. **In the ECW, click the Motion effects spindown arrow to display the settings.**

4. **Repeat Step 3 with the Opacity effect to display the settings.**

5. **Deselect Uniform Scale below the Scale Width setting in the Motion effects list.**
   You modify the height and width of the title independently.

6. **In the ECW, click the time indicator and type** 5529.
   The CTI moves to the first frame of the clip.

7. **Click the Stopwatch icon to the left of the Position effect.**
   The Stopwatch activates the keyframes.

8. **Click the x-position value to make it active (the first value) and type** 42; **click the y-position value to make it active and type** 168.
   A keyframe is added to the ECW Timeline for the Position effect.

9. **Click the Stopwatch icon for the Scale Height effect to make it active.**

10. **Click the scale height value and type** 23.
    A keyframe is added to the ECW Timeline for the Scale Height effect.

11. **Click the Stopwatch icon for the Scale Width effect to make it active.**

12. **Click the scale height value and type** 100.
    A keyframe is added to the ECW Timeline for the Scale Width effect.

13. **Click the Stopwatch icon for the Rotation effect.**

14. **Click the degrees value and type** 2.
    A keyframe is added to the ECW Timeline for the Rotation effect.

<TIP>
You don't have to type any decimal places for the values, unless you want to use a fractional value. Premiere Pro automatically adds the decimal place and two zeros to the value.

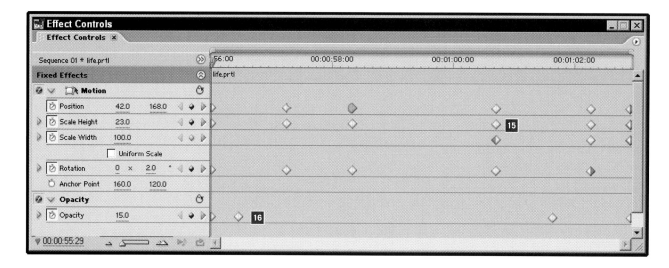

15. Repeat Steps 5 through 13 with the remaining keyframes. Add additional keyframes and settings at the time locations listed in Table 8-1.

Make sure to move the CTI to the specified time first before changing any effect values. In Table 8-1, all values are rounded off to the nearest number.

<TIP>

You can also add keyframes by clicking the Keyframe icon on the keyframe navigator.

<NOTE>

To delete any extra keyframes added by mistake, click the keyframe (it turns blue) and press Delete. Don't click the Stopwatch icon to remove a keyframe; it removes all the keyframes set for the effect instead of a single keyframe.

16. Add keyframes to change the Opacity settings at these locations, and set the values as shown:

55:29, 15%
56:13, 100%
01:01:19, 100%
01:02:28, 10%

Adding Opacity keyframes uses the same process that you followed in earlier steps to keyframe the Motion effects; the Opacity keyframes are listed separately as the keyframes are added at different time locations.

<NOTE>

The rotation value is in degrees. The setting defaults at 0 x 0.0, which is 0 revolutions and 0 degrees. You don't perform any revolutions, but you do shift degrees over the course of the animation. Make sure to change the rotation setting, the second value, and not the revolution setting, which is the first value.

Table 8-1: Motion Settings for the life.prtl Title

Keyframe	Time	Position Coordinates	Scale Height/Width	Rotation (Degrees)
0	55:29	42, 168	23, 100	2
1	57:07	179, 174	44, 100	6
2	58:10	315, 142	40, 100	0
3	01:00:21	97, 135	88, 100	-4
4	01:02:08	-157, -16	250, 250	-4
5	01:02:27	-264, -80	300, 300	-4

<NOTE>

The tables in this and following tutorials list the keyframes starting from 0 rather than from 1. The first keyframe is set at the beginning of the clip, and is used to establish a baseline value for the setting. If you break up the changes made in a clip over time according to the keyframes listed in the table, you see there are five changes between the beginning and the end of the clip, coinciding with the five keyframes following the keyframe numbered 0. That is, the first change takes place between the start of the clip (keyframe 0) and the keyframe 1 location, the next from the keyframe 1 to keyframe 2 location, and so on.

17. **Right-click the Position keyframe at 57:07 to open the keyframe interpolation menu. Click Fast Out.**

The position change from this keyframe to the next is speeded up.

<NOTE>

Interpolation refers to the way a value is changed from one keyframe to the next. You can change the speed at which a change is applied, increasing or decreasing the speed at which changes are made. You can set an interpolation method for the segment of time coming into or leaving from a keyframe.

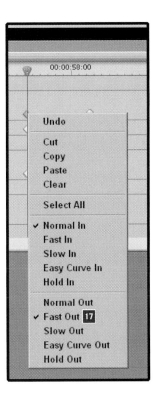

18. **Right-click the Position keyframe at 58:10, and choose Slow In.**
    The position changes slowly as the CTI moves to this keyframe's position.

19. **Click the Play In to Out button to preview the Timeline segment in the Program view monitor.**
    You set In and Out points in Step 1 that play only the segment of the Timeline you applied keyframes to. If you like, you can adjust the keyframe settings to modify the animation to your liking.

<NOTE>
Watch the ECW effect values as the CTI moves through the clip. You can see that the values for the different settings adjust as the CTI moves from keyframe to keyframe.

20. **Save the project.**
    Save your work! Animations take lots of time, and you don't want to lose any work due to unexpected computer problems. You animated the first title in the beach segment of the project. You used many motion settings to create the illusion that the title moves with the action.

Working with Keyframes

There are different ways to approach working with a large number of keyframes as in this tutorial. You can move the CTI from location to location and set a collection of keyframes for one fixed effect, or you can move the CTI and set keyframes for each effect. A simple way to reuse the same CTI location for keyframes from several effects is to work with the keyframe navigator. For example, if you have a keyframe set at 55:00 for rotation and want to

use the same keyframe location for a scale setting, click the rotation effect's keyframe navigator to move the CTI to the correct time location. Then click the scale setting and make adjustments. A new keyframe automatically displays at the correct location. Regardless of the method you use, you need to carefully coordinate the CTI location with the values for your effects.

Tutorial
» Creating More Title Animations

In this tutorial, you animate next two titles for the beach message, is_a.prtl and beach.prtl. You use different combinations of Fixed effects to create different motion paths for the titles.

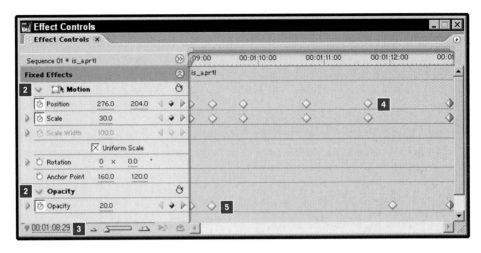

1. Select the is_a.prtl clip on Video 4 starting at 01:08:29. Right-click the time ruler on the Timeline, and choose Set Sequence Marker➔In and Out Around Selection.
   You define the Timeline segment to make it simpler to preview in the Program Monitor view as you work with the clip.

2. In the ECW, click the Motion and Opacity settings' spindown arrows to display the settings.

3. In the ECW, click the time indicator and type 10829.
   The CTI moves to the first frame of the clip.

4. Add six keyframes and settings at the time locations listed in Table 8-2.
   Leave the Uniform Scale option selected; you adjust scale height and width equally. When you type the height value, the same setting is applied to the width value.

5. Add Opacity keyframes at these locations, and set the values as shown:
   01:08:29, 20%
   01:09:08, 100%
   01:12:01, 100%
   01:12:27, 10%
   Make sure to move the CTI to the listed times first before making the opacity value changes.

Table 8-2: Motion Settings for the is_a.prtl Title

Keyframe	Time	Position Coordinates	Scale	Rotation (Degrees)
0	01:08:29	276, 204	30	2
1	01:09:09	146, 186	40	6
2	01:09:23	6, 120	100	0
3	01:10:22	0, 66	150	-4
4	01:22:01	108, 161	45	-4
5	01:12:27	139, 148	20	-4

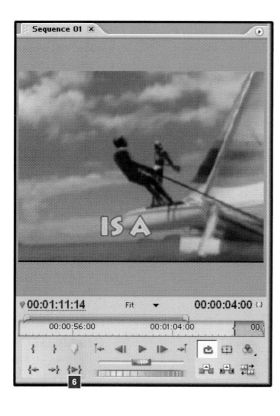

6. **In the Program view monitor, click the Play In to Out button to play the animation.**
   Preview the animation, and adjust settings to your liking.

7. **Repeat Steps 1 through 4 using the `beach.prtl` on Video 4 starting at 01:08:29. Deselect Uniform Scale on the ECW; you adjust the height and width of the clip separately.**
   You add seven keyframes and settings as listed in Table 8-3. You modify the height and width of the title independently. A value marked with "—" means that there is no keyframe at that time location.

   <NOTE>
   At any time, you can see and adjust the motion path of the title visually. Click the Motion heading on the Fixed Effects list to display the clip's margins and its motion path. If you make visual adjustments, additional keyframes are added to the ECW.

8. **Add Opacity keyframes at these locations, and set the values as shown:**
   01:16:02, 20%
   01:16:22, 100%
   01:21:06, 100%
   01:22:02, 20%
   Make sure to move the CTI to the listed times first before making the opacity value changes.

9. **Right-click the Position keyframe at 01:19:07 to open the keyframe interpolation menu. Click Easy Curve Out.**
   The position change from this keyframe to the next is smoothed.

10. **Right-click the Position keyframe at 01:21:06, and choose Easy Curve In.**
    The position changes smoothly as the CTI moves to this keyframe's position.

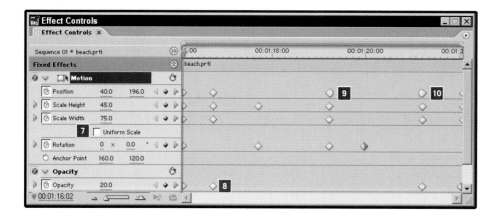

Table 8-3: Motion Settings for the `beach.prt1` **Title**

Keyframe	Time	Position Coordinates	Scale Height/Width	Rotation (Degrees)
0	01 :16 :02	40, 196	45, 75	0
1	01 :16 :22	107, 130	100, 100	—
2	01 :17 :21	—	75, 115	8
3	01 :19 :07	76, 109	140, 140	2
4	01 :19 :29	—	—	0
5	01 :21 :06	76, 100	100, 100	—
6	01 :22 :02	290, 100	50, 50	—

11. **In the Program view monitor, click the Play In to Out button to play the animation.**

    Preview the animation, and adjust settings to your liking.

12. **Save the project.**

    You animated the second and third titles in the beach segment of the project. You used a variety of Fixed effects as well as some keyframe interpolation to create the animations. You can see the three titles in the `session08B.wmv` sample file.

Tutorial
» Using a Template for a Title

The text titles are nearly complete. You have completed the phrase "Life is a Beach." In this tutorial, you use one of the templates supplied with Premiere Pro to create an image title.

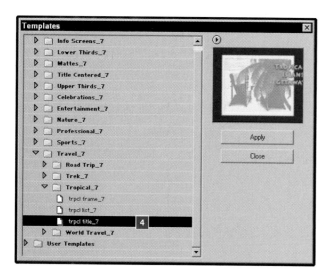

1. **On the Project window, choose New→Title to open the Title Designer window.**

2. **Deselect the Show Video option.**
   You work with the Title Designer templates, which include backgrounds.

3. **Click the Templates icon to open the Templates window.**
   Premiere Pro includes a variety of templates that you can use for different types of projects. You can also import your own template files.

4. **In the Templates window, choose Travel_7→Tropical_7→ trpcl title_7. Click Apply.**
   The Templates window closes, and the template's image and text display in the Title Designer window.

5. **In the Title Designer window, select the text block and press Delete.**
   You composite the text in the program, not in the title.

6. **Click the pink border layer behind the image, and delete it.**
   You are going to use the image from the template as a still image underlying another title clip in the project.

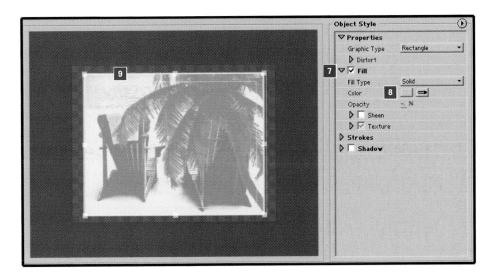

7. **Click the background dark blue layer to select it. In the Object Style palette, click the spindown arrow to display the Fill settings.**

8. **Click the Color swatch to open the Color Picker, and enter RGB=68/0/40 to change the rectangle's color to a dark maroon color. Set the Opacity to 50%.**

9. **Click the overlaying pale pink layer, and Ctrl+click to select the image layer. Resize the pair of layers by dragging the corner resize handles until they fill the safe margins area.**
   You want the title image layers to fill the screen.

10. **Click the pale pink overlaying layer to select it. Repeat Steps 7 and 8 to change the color to a dark maroon.**

11. **Save the title as** end.prtl, **and close the Title Designer window.**

12. **Save the project.**
   You made the final title for your project. You used a Premiere Pro template to create an image title to use at the end of the Timeline. You add the title in the next, and final, tutorial for this session.

<NOTE>
In the figure, most Property settings are hidden because both image layers are selected.

Tutorial
» Composing a Title Sequence for the Project

Wait until you see what happens with the titles that you built in the preceding tutorial! In this tutorial, you add the template-based title image to the project. You add several transitions to complete the ending of your movie.

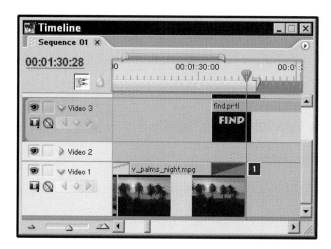

1. **Select the final transition on the** `v_palms_night.mpg` **clip ending at 01:30:28 on Video 1, and delete it.**

   You used the transition temporarily to visually end the movie as you were developing it.

2. **Click the spindown arrows to expand the Video 1, Video 3, and Video 4 tracks.**

   You add titles and transitions to the tracks.

<NOTE>

Make sure the tracks are all visible as well. The visibility icons should be toggled to on.

3. **Drag the** `end.prtl` **from the titles bin to Video 1 so that it starts at 01:30:28.** Set its duration to 03:05, ending at 01:34:03.

4. Open the Effects tab. Choose Video Transitions→Dissolve→Cross Dissolve. Add the transition to the clips using the locations and durations listed in Table 8-4.

5. Move the CTI to the cut point between the v_palms_night.mpg and end.prtl clips on Video 1 at 01:30:28.
   You add another transition.

6. In the Effects tab, choose Video Transitions→Zoom→Cross Zoom; drag the transition to overlay the cut point on Video 1.
   You add one final transition.

7. Click the transition to open the ECW. Click the Duration field, and type 0120 to extend the transition to 01:20.

8. Click Show Actual Sources.

9. Click the small circle identifying the central starting point for the transition and move the start location up and left to the location of the sun in the image.
   The zoom starts at the sun's location.

10. Preview the clip in the Program view monitor, and save the project.
    You added the text and template-based titles to the end of the project. You added a number of transitions, including a cross-zoom transition. You can view the final segment of the project that you worked with in this tutorial in the sample file session08C.wmv.

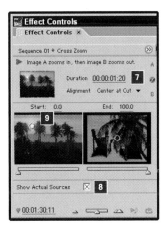

Table 8-4: Location and Duration of Cross Dissolves

Location	Duration
Start and end of the yours.prtl clip in Video 4	00:25
Start and end of the find.prtl clip in Video 3	00:25
End of the end.prtl clip in Video 1	01:00

» Session Review

In this session, you learned how to create a variety of titles using text and a template. You learned how to save a text style. You also learned how to add titles to the Timeline. You spent time animating three of the titles in the beach segment of the project to move the titles along with the action. You learned how to work with keyframes and animate numerically in the ECW and visually in the Program monitor view.

What a difference titles can make! The image at the beginning of this session shows a location on the Timeline where one of the animated titles begins. The final image in this session shows a frame from the closing sequence of the project, where you have added text titles and a title created from a template image. At this point, you have added a number of transition and transparency effects to clips throughout. The basic set of titles are added to both the city and beach segments of the project.

Answer the following questions to help you review the information in this session. You can find the answer for each question in the tutorial noted in parentheses.

1. How do you align titles in specific locations? (See Tutorial: Creating a Static Title.)

2. How do you save a text style? (See Tutorial: Creating a Static Title.)

3. Does a title clip behave the same as a still image clip in the Timeline? (See Tutorial: Adding Titles to the Timeline.)

4. Can you match text or graphic colors to colors in your project? How? (See Tutorial: Customizing Title Text.)

5. How do you add strokes to title text? How many strokes can you use? (See Tutorial: Customizing Title Text.)

6. What is the default duration for a title? (See Tutorial: Adding the Beach Message.)

7. How do you add new keyframes to the ECW Timeline? How do you remove them? (See Tutorial: Animating a Title Using Fixed Effects.)

8. Why should you add In and Out points around a clip on the Timeline when you are working on an animation? (See Tutorial: Animating a Title Using Fixed Effects.)

9. Can you work both numerically and visually to create an animation? How? (See Tutorial: Creating More Title Animations.)

10. Can you change titles based on templates supplied by Premiere Pro? (See Tutorial: Using a Template for a Title.)

11. How do you define locations for zoom transitions to start and end? (See Tutorial: Composing a Title Sequence for the Project.)

» Other Projects

The project uses a small number of Title Designer features. Experiment with the Title Designer window's functions in the project and for other projects.

The titles in the beach segment are animated using Fixed effects. Try animating a title with the Transform effect, found in the Effects window by choosing Video Effects➔Distort➔Transform.

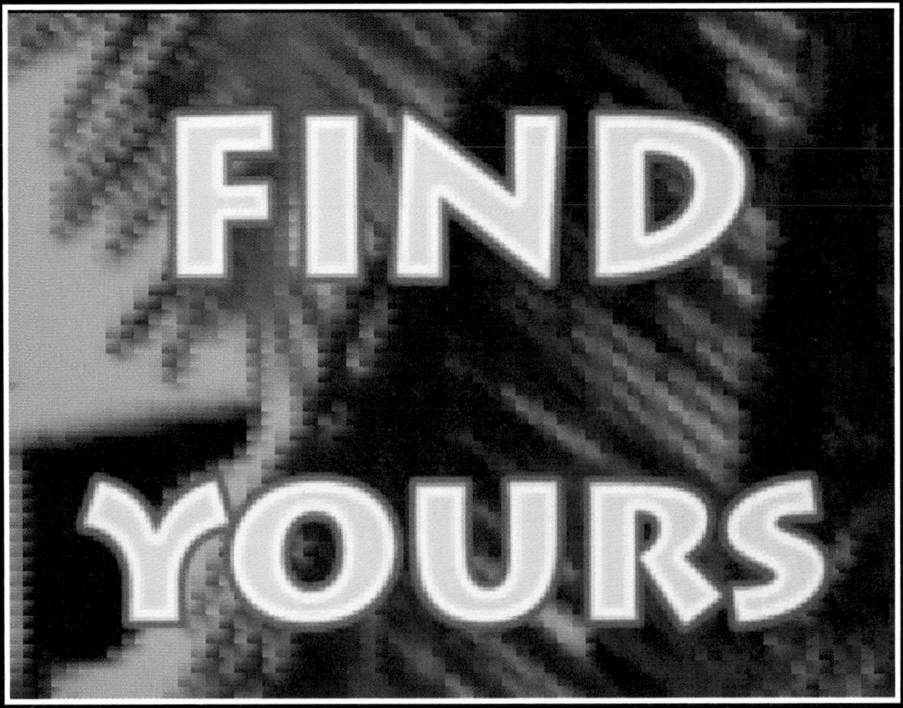
FIND
YOURS

Using Graphics for Special Effects

Tutorial: **Adding a Title Track Matte**

Tutorial: **Layering Animated Titles**

Tutorial: **Adding More Clips to the Timeline**

Tutorial: **Applying a Matte to Several Clips**

Tutorial: **Adding Graphic Frames to Split Screens**

Tutorial: **Adding Complex Transitions**

Session Introduction

In Session 7, you worked with transparency key effects to designate areas of transparency based on brightness, lightness, and color. In Session 8, you worked with titles. In this session, you work with both.

You can use the transparency of one clip to affect the transparency of another clip. This is referred to as a matte. The matte keys add lots of visual punch to a project. You can use the contents of a track as a matte for a clip in another track, which you use in the project. This is called a Track Matte. Add some motion to the clip, and you have a traveling matte, also used in the project. A matte can also be applied to a clip directly, which is called an Image Matte. You don't work with this type of matte in the project.

After the mattes are applied, you return to the first segment of the project to add some graphics there as well. You use vertical and horizontal bars to frame the split screens that you created using different techniques. The bars are graphic titles. Along with applying copies of the titles as frames for the split screens, you also animate several copies of the title. You add multiple copies of the animation in Sessions 11 and 12 when you learn how to build nested sequences.

The Bonus Session on the CD, Bonus Session 1, "Creating Project Titles and Graphics," includes three tutorials that describe how to build the two mattes and the graphic bars used in this session. Also, you should read the Discussion *Keying Effects* in Bonus Discussion 3, "The Finer Points of Premiere Pro's Effects," on the CD for more information on how the effects work. The titles created and used in this session were imported into your project with the rest of the titles folder contents in Session 8. There are three sample files for this session in the samples folder; session09A.wmv shows the frames and animations added to the city segment, session09B.wmv shows the animated track matte title in the beach segment, and session09C.wmv shows the picture-in-picture sequence from the beach segment. You start with the two sequences in the beach segment of the project and then move back to the city segment.

TOOLS YOU'LL USE
Add Tracks command, Cross Dissolve transition, Cross Zoom transition, ECW, Fill properties, In and Out markers, Motion effects, Opacity effect, Position commands, Program view monitor, Rename Clip command, Timeline, Track Matte Key effect, unnumbered markers, Zoom Trails transition

MATERIALS NEEDED
Session 8 project file that you created, or the session08.prproj file from the CD-ROM; session09A.wmv, session09B.wmv, and session09C.wmv sample files

TIME REQUIRED
90 minutes

Tutorial
» Adding a Title Track Matte

The beginning of the beach sequence is, yep, a beach. You then see a happy person running down said beach. In this tutorial, you add pizazz to your project using an animated title created as a track matte. The title is in the titles folder and is named text_matte.prtl. If you want to construct the title yourself, complete the tutorial, *Building a Track Matte*, in Bonus Session 1, "Creating Project Titles and Graphics" on the CD. The tutorial explains how to add and configure the text and how to add the crawl. If you look at the title's listing in the Project window, you see that its icon is a filmstrip (video) rather than the title icon used by other titles. The text uses a crawl animation, added in the Title Designer window, that moves the text from right to left across the screen.

<NOTE>

If you didn't do the tutorials in Session 8, copy the session08.prproj file from the CD to your hard drive. In the Welcome window, choose Open Project. Browse to the location where you stored the copied project file, and select Open. Then resave the project in Premiere Pro as session09.prproj (or use another filenaming convention).

<TIP>

Track mattes can only be used if the track visibility is toggled to off. If you add an extra track and name it, you are less likely to turn the track visibility on or add other clips to the track that aren't mattes.

1. **Open Premiere Pro. When the Welcome window opens, choose** session08.prproj.
   The Welcome window closes, and the project is loaded into the program.

2. **Choose File→Save As. Resave the project file as** session09.prproj.
   The name of the new project version displays at the top of the program window.

3. **Move the CTI on the Timeline to 24:11.**
   The track matte starts at the same time as the b_girl_running1.mov clip.

4. **Drag the** text_matte.prtl **clip from the Project window to the dark gray space below the time ruler on the Timeline.**
   The title is added to the Timeline in a new track, named Video 5.

5. **Increase the duration of the** text_matte.prtl **clip to 06:15.**
   The matte is the same length as the b_girl_running1.mov clip.

6. **Right-click the Video 5 track's name, and click Rename on the menu. In the field, type** mattes.

7. **Select the** b_girl_running1.mov **clip on Video 2 starting at 24:11.**
   You add the track matte effect to the clip.

8. **Right-click the time ruler on the Timeline, and choose Set Sequence Marker→In and Out Around Selection.**
   Select the area on which you are working to save time previewing as you test the effects.

9. **In the Effects tab, choose Video Effects→Keying→Track Matte Key. Drag the effect to the** b_girl_running1.mov **clip selected in Step 7.**

10. **In the ECW, click the spindown arrow to open the Track Matte Key settings.**

11. **Click the Matte drop-down arrow to open a small menu listing the tracks in your project. Click mattes.**
    You choose the track that you want to use for the effect. Whatever content is displayed in the selected track is displayed with the clip to which you apply the effect.

12. **Click the Composite Using drop-down arrow, and select Matte Alpha.**
    The matte uses its alpha channel by default, which is the transparency created based on the shapes of the letters.

<NOTE>
You can reverse the matte. In other words, the clip that appears inside the letters and the background clip can be reversed. Click the Reverse option. Experiment with this option to see which you prefer.

13. **In the Program view monitor, click the Play In to Out button to preview the effect.**
    You see the heavy black text scroll across the screen.

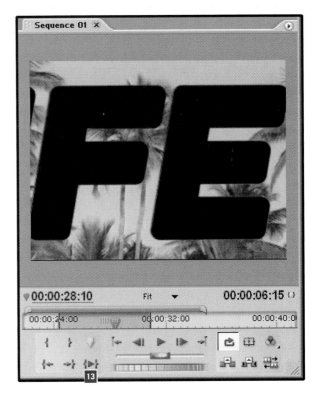

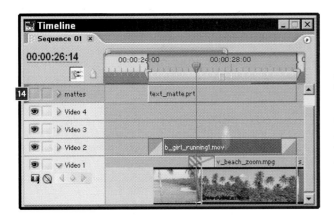

14. On the Timeline, toggle the visibility of the mattes track to off.
You don't want to see the letters; you only want to use the transparency layer as a matte for the effect.

<NOTE>
Why do you have to turn off the track's visibility? If you don't, the matte still works, but you don't see it. In the Timeline, the stacking order places the matte text above the video clips. The matte is applied to the running girl and palm trees, but the text in the fifth track is above the others. It superimposes over all other tracks and therefore is what you see.

15. In the Program view monitor, click the Play In to Out button to preview the effect again.
You see the girl running down the beach within the letters as they scroll across the screen. The speed of the crawl animation depends on the length of the scrolling text, as well as the length of the clip. If the clip were 03:00, for example, it would move at about twice the speed. Regardless of the clip's length, the clip still moves the distance that you define in the crawl.

16. Move the CTI to 26:21.

You add a transition to the beach and palm clips to blend them in the track matte background.

17. Drag the Cross Dissolve transition from the Video Transitions folder in the Effects tab to the cut point at 26:21.

Extend the duration of the transition to 01:05, centered over the cut.

18. Save the project.

You completed a complex effect. You added a Track Matte Key effect and used text as the matte. You added a transition to blend the background.

How a Matte Works

You can work with both image mattes and track mattes in Premiere Pro. The difference between the matte types is based on the source of the material. An Image Matte Key effect uses artwork in many file formats that is stored on your computer; it doesn't have to be imported into your project. A Track Matte Key effect, on the other hand, uses content assigned to a track in the project, and that content must be a piece of footage that you import into the project and add to a track. Regardless of source, mattes do the same thing—assign transparency. Both Image Matte Key and Track Matte Key effects allow you to use either alpha channel or luma transparency options. Using the alpha matte, darker colors are more transparent than lighter colors; black is totally transparent and white it totally opaque. Luma settings assign transparency based on how bright a pixel is.

Tutorial
» Layering Animated Titles

You added the crawling text to the project to use as a Track Matte. In this tutorial, you animate another layer of text in the Program view monitor. The text is added to the Timeline to overlay the transparent text. A tutorial named *Positioning a Title Using Backgrounds*, in Bonus Session 1, "Creating Project Titles and Graphics" on the CD describes how to build the title used in this tutorial. You finish the first sequence that you build in this session by adding some transitions. Preview the completed sequence in the session09B.wmv video.

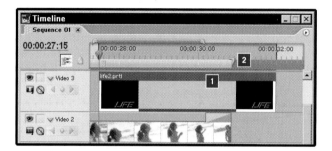

1. **Drag the** life2.prt1 **title clip from the Project window to Video 3 starting at 27:15. Extend its duration to 04:15.**
   The clip starts partway through the Track Matte sequence and ends partway through the surfer clip.

2. **Right-click the time ruler, and choose Set Sequence Marker→In and Out Around Selection.**
   You select the Timeline segment where you added the title to make it simpler to preview in the Program view monitor.

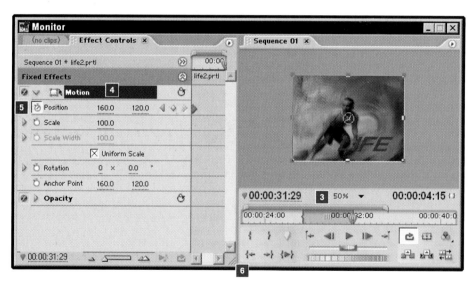

3. **In the Program view monitor, click the zoom level and choose 50%.**
   You need to see beyond the frame to animate the text.

4. **In the ECW, click the Motion heading to activate the visual outlines.**
   The clip's margins display on the Program view monitor.

5. **Click the Position Stopwatch icon.**
   You want to record keyframe values as you move the clip.

6. **On the Program view monitor, click the Go to In Point button.**
   The CTI moves to the start of the clip; you see that the text title overlays the screen.

7. **Drag the clip in the Program view monitor to the left until the letter "E" in the red text is within the lower part of the "L" of the Track Matte's text.**
If you check in the ECW, the position is at -95, 120.

8. **Click the Go to Out Point button on the Program view monitor.**
The CTI jumps to 31:29, and the surfer clip is displayed.

9. **Click the text frame, and drag right until the letter "L" is partially visible at the right margin of the screen.**
If you check in the ECW, the position is at 320, 120.

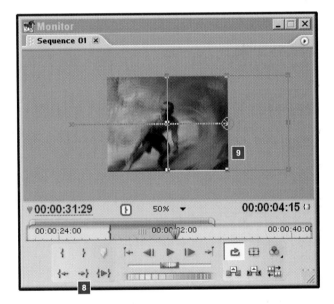

10. **In the Program view monitor, click the zoom level and choose Fit.**
    The monitor resizes itself according to the window size, giving you a better view of the layout; you don't need to see beyond the clip margins anymore.

11. **Click the Play In to Out button to preview the clip.**
    You see the red text move right. The text is well-positioned, but it needs transitions because its start and end are too abrupt.

12. **Drag the default Cross Dissolve transition from the Effect tab to the start of the life2.prtl clip at 27:15 in Video 4.**
    Leave the default length of 20 frames.

13. **Drag the default Cross Dissolve transition from the Effects tab to the end of the life2.prtl clip at 32:00 in Video 4.**
    Leave the default length of 20 frames.

14. **Move the CTI to 30:26.**
    You add a transition between the palm tree and surfer clips in Video 1.

15. **In the Effects window, choose Video Transitions→Zoom→Cross Zoom and drag the transition to Video 1 to the cut point at 30:26.**
    The transition is applied to the v_beach_zoom.mpg and s_surf_red.mpg clips.

16. **Move the CTI to 30:05.**
    You set a custom length and position for the transition based on the CTI position.

17. **Click the Cross Zoom transition that you added in Step 15 to open it in the ECW.**
    You customize the settings.

18. **Click Show Actual Sources to display the clips in the preview areas.**

19. **Click the duration value, and type** 105.
    You change the length of the transition to 01:05.

20. **Click the time indicator at the bottom of the ECW, and type** 3005.
    The CTI moves to 30:05; you use the location in the next step.

21. **Drag the left margin of the transition left to snap to the CTI.**
    You reposition the transition's start to use more of the scenery clip and less of the surfer clip, which appears to increase the zoom speed. Repositioning the transition automatically changes the Alignment from Center at Cut to Custom Start.

22. **Click the Start value (the default is 0.0), and type** 25.
    The transition starts with the palm trees zoomed in 25%, which adds to the sense of motion in the transition.

23. **Preview the Timeline segment in the Program view monitor from approximately 24:10 to 32:05, which contains the sequence that you completed in this tutorial.**
    Listen carefully to the music score change that occurs at 30:26. The end of the b_girl_running.mov clip coincides with both the transitions into the first sports clip, s_surf_red.mov and the first sporty segment of the latinotek.wav clip. This isn't a coincidence!

24. **Save the project.**
    You added and animated a title layer. You added several transitions and customized one transition to complete the Timeline sequence. You have nearly completed the titles for the beach segment of the project.

Tutorial

» Adding More Clips to the Timeline

In the previous tutorials, you completed one sequence in the project where you used text as a Track Matte. In this tutorial, you move a bit further down the Timeline. You are going to add more Keying effects, but first you need the clips. If you look in the Project window and scroll to the right to display the Video Usage column, you see three clips in the video bin that aren't used yet. You add the three clips to the Timeline and edit them in this tutorial.

1. **Click the time indicator on the Timeline to activate it, and type** 4026.
   The CTI jumps to the end of the b_woman_dog.mov clip.

2. **Drag** v_resort.mpg **from the video bin in the Project window to Video 2. Snap the clip to the CTI at 40:26. Double-click the clip to open it in the Source view monitor for trimming.**

3. **Click the time indicator, and type** 318 **to move the CTI to 03:18.** Click the Set In Point button to set the In point for the clip.

4. **Set the Out point for the clip at 06:18; the final duration is 03:00.** The clip starts at 40:26 and ends at 43:26 on Video 2.

5. **Adjust the clip's location on the Timeline to start at 40:26.** The clip shortens because you set the In point in Step 3.

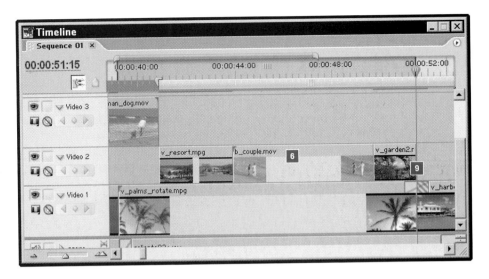

6. **Drag** b_couple.mov **from the video bin in the Project window to Video 2. Place the clip to start at 43:26 following the** v_resort.mpg **clip.**

7. **Double-click the** b_couple.mov **clip to open it in the Source view monitor. Set the In point at 03:22 and the Out point at 09:17, for a duration of 05:26.**

8. **Adjust the clip's Timeline location to start at 43:26.**
   The clip shifted when you set the In point in Step 7.

9. **Drag** v_garden2.mpg **from the video bin in the Project window to Video 2. Place the clip to start at 49:22 following the end of the** b_couple.mov **clip.**

10. **Double-click the** v_garden2.mpg **clip to open it in the Source view monitor. Set the In point to 01:00 and the Out point to 02:22, for a duration of 01:23.**

11. **Adjust the clip's location on the Timeline to start at 49:22.**

12. **Preview the Timeline segment from 39:06 to 51:15.**
    You see the start of the v_palms_rotating.mpg clip in Video 1 and then only the new clips that you added in this tutorial.

13. **Save the project.**
    You added three clips to the Timeline and trimmed them. The set of three clips overlay a clip of rotating palm trees. In the next tutorial, you add a matte to superimpose the new clips over the palm trees clip in Video 1.

Tutorial

» Applying a Matte to Several Clips

In the previous tutorials in this session, you completed one sequence in the project where you used text as a Track Matte and then layered more animated text. In this tutorial, you use the Track Matte Key effect again, but this matte is a graphic that creates a picture-in-picture effect. You also use an additional drawing superimposed over the layers to give the matte some definition. Finally, you add some transitions to finish the sequence. You can preview the completed sequence in the sample session09C.wmv clip. A tutorial named *Creating the Palm Tree Images* in Bonus Session 1, "Creating Project Titles and Graphics" on the CD shows you how the titles were constructed in Photoshop, so you can create your own.

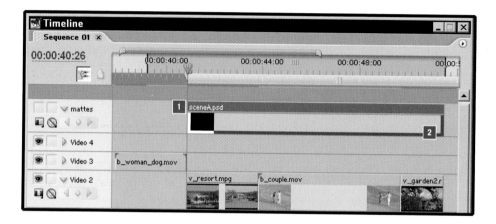

1. Drag the sceneA.psd **file from the titles bin in the Project folder to the mattes track on the Timeline. Place the clip to start at 40:26.**
   You use this clip as a matte for the segment.

2. **Drag the right edge of the clip to extend it to 51:15.**
   The clip's duration is 10:19, which spans the total length of the clips that you added in the preceding tutorial.

3. **In the Effects tab, choose Video Effects→Keying→Track Matte Key. Drag the effect to the** v_resort.mpg **clip in Video 2 starting at 40:26.**
   A magenta bar beneath the clip's name indicates that an effect is added to the clip.

4. In the ECW, click the spindown arrow to open the Track Matte Key effect's controls for the `v_resort.mpg` clip.
You assign a track for the matte.

5. Click the Matte drop-down list to display the list of tracks in the project, and select mattes.
You placed the matte clip into the mattes track, which you added to the project specifically to hold matte clips.

6. Click the spindown arrow to open the Motion effects' controls.
You adjust the clip's size.

7. Click Uniform Scale. Click the Scale value to activate the field, and type 100.

8. Preview the clip in the Program view monitor.
You see the resort clip superimposed over the rotating palm trees clip. The matte is a rounded rectangle with jagged edges at the left of the matte. The jagged edges are really the margins of a palm tree, part of the matte. Later in the tutorial, you superimpose a drawing to give the matte more definition.

9. Click the Track Matte Key title in the ECW to select it. Choose Edit➔Copy, or use Ctrl+C, to copy the effect.
You are going to copy the effect and its settings to another clip.

10. **On the Timeline, click** b_couple.mov **starting at 43:26 on Video 2 to select it. Choose Edit→Paste, or use Ctrl+V, to paste the effect.**
You see the stripe below the clip's name indicating that an effect is added.

<TIP>
Check in the ECW—you see that the effect is listed using the same settings as those you created for the original clip. You can also copy an effect from one clip and paste it directly into another clip's ECW instead of to the clip on the Timeline.

11. **On the Timeline, click** v_garden2.mpg **starting at 49:22 on Video 2 to select it. Choose Edit→Paste, or use Ctrl+V, to paste the effect.**
The effect is pasted to the third clip in the sequence.

12. **Preview the clips in the Program view monitor.**
The three clips now have a superimposed matte, showing the clip in most of the screen with the rotating palms clip in the background.

13. **In the ECW for the** v_garden2.mpg **clip, repeat Steps 6 and 7.**
You resize the v_garden2.mpg clip to 100 percent of the screen size.

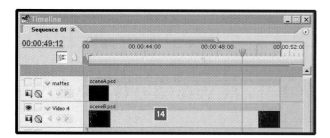

14. **Drag the** sceneB.psd **clip from the titles bin in the Project window to Video 4 starting at 40:26. Drag the right margin of the clip to extend to 51:15, with a duration of 10:19.**
The sceneB.psd clip provides some definition for the matte. The sceneB.psd clip outlines the palm tree and the matte's frame.

Table 9.1: Transition Locations and Durations

Track	Cut Point	Duration	Location
Video 1	51:15	30 frames (01:00)	centered at cut
Video 2	43:26	20 frames	centered at cut
Viceo 2	49:22	20 frames	centered at cut
Video 2	51:15	20 frames	ending at cut
Video 4	51:15	30 frames (01:00)	ending at cut

15. **Preview the segment from 40:26 to 51:15.**

You see the superimposed sketch defining areas of the matte. The sketch outlines are rough; in the next session, you add blur and shadow effects.

16. **Add the default Cross Dissolve transition to the locations and for the durations listed in Table 9.1.**

17. **Preview the segment again.**

You see the transitions applied. The start of the sequence has no transition; in the next session, you add some effects to the b_woman_dog.mov clip and then apply transitions to the sequence that you worked with in this tutorial.

18. **Save the project complete with the graphic matte and drawing.**

You used a graphic matte clip to create transparency in super-imposed clips. You also added another graphic drawing to outline objects on the matte. You added several transitions to the sequence. The completed sequence from 40:13 to 52:00 is shown in the session09C.avi clip in the samples folder.

< N O T E >

The samples folder contains another pair of images named scene1.psd and scene2.psd, similar to the images used in the tutorial, but having a slightly different matte layout. A tutorial in the Bonus Session on the CD, named *Creating the Palm Tree Images,* briefly describes how the images were created in Photoshop.

Tutorial
» Adding Graphic Frames to Split Screens

In this tutorial, you move back to the city segment of the project. You add several copies of the bar graphic titles to serve as frames for the split-screen sequences. You don't use any mattes in this tutorial. A tutorial named *Drawing Graphic Titles* in Bonus Session 1, "Creating Project Titles and Graphics" on the CD describes how the horizontal and vertical bar titles are created. In the city segment, several elements in the sequence use split screens or picture-in-picture screens.

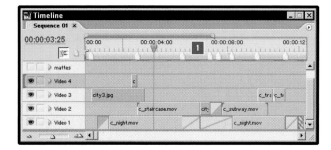

1. **For reference, set some unnumbered markers on the Timeline. Move the CTI to the listed position, and press (*) on the keyboard. Add nine markers in these locations:**
   00:09
   02:27
   05:13
   06:14
   07:01
   08:07
   09:20
   11:08
   11:28

2. **Click Video 4 to select it; right-click to open the shortcut menu, and choose Add Tracks.**
   The Add Tracks dialog box opens.

3. **Click the Video Track Add field, and type** 4. **Click the Placement drop-down arrow, and choose After Target Track.**

4. **Click the Add Audio field, and type** 0.
   The default is to add one audio track; you don't need any more audio tracks.

5. **Click OK to close the dialog box.**
   Four additional video tracks are added to the project, Video 5 through Video 8; the mattes track moves to the top of the stack.

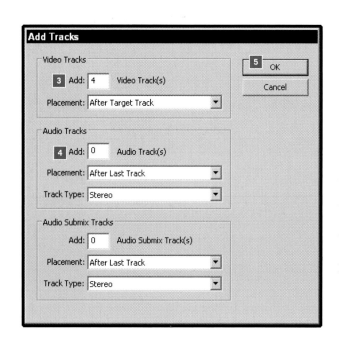

< T I P >
You can add tracks in any location in the stacking order; placing them below the mattes track in the list helps to separate "ordinary" tracks from the mattes track, which must be turned off to work correctly. Separating the tracks prevents accidentally placing clips in the mattes track and wasting time troubleshooting when your sequence doesn't display correctly.

6. **Add the** v_bar.prtl **and** h_bar.prtl **clips to the tracks at the locations and durations specified in Table 9-2.**

   You add a total of eight titles to the project in Video 5 through Video 8; six are vertical bar titles. Although spaces are reserved for clips in some areas on Video 3 and Video 4, place the clips in their own set of tracks to keep track of your project's elements. After the clips are placed, you rename them using aliases in Step 7; the alias names are also listed in Table 9-1.

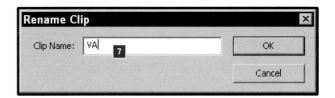

<NOTE>

For simplicity of identification, each clip has an alias assigned to it. Because there are multiple copies of the clips, using an alias makes it much simpler to identify the clip. Refer to the table to see the track and start time for the clip being referenced. For example, VA is the first vertical bar element, placed in Video 5 starting at 00:09.

7. **Right-click the first** v_bar.prtl **clip, added in Video 5 starting at 00:09. Click Rename to open the Rename Clip dialog box. Type VA. Click OK.**

   The dialog box closes, and the clip is renamed. VA indicates that it is the first vertical bar used.

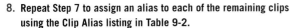

8. **Repeat Step 7 to assign an alias to each of the remaining clips using the Clip Alias listing in Table 9-2.**

   Each clip is now identified individually.

9. **Save the project.**

   You added four additional tracks and added a number of clips. You assigned aliases to the clips to identify the individual clips. Next, you animate the position and opacity of each title clip.

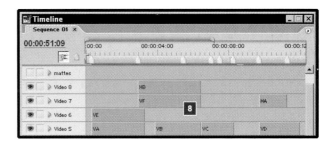

Table 9-2: Locations for Placing Graphic Bar Title Clips

Clip Alias	Track	Start Time	Duration	Clip
VA	Video 5	00:09	03:00	v_bar.prtl
VB	Video 5	03:26	02:18	v_bar.prtl
VC	Video 5	06:14	01:25	v_bar.prtl
VD	Video 5	09:21	02:08	v_bar.prtl
VE	Video 6	00:09	03:00	v_bar.prtl
VF	Video 7	02:27	03:17	v_bar.prtl
HA	Video 7	09:21	01:17	h_bar.prtl
HB	Video 8	02:27	03:17	h_bar.prtl

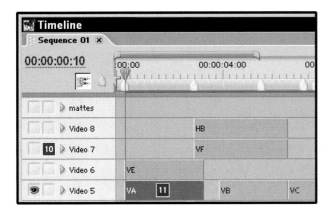

10. **Toggle the visibility for Video 6 through Video 9 to off.**

    When you are animating a single object from a group of similar objects, like the graphic bars, turn off the visibility on the other tracks. Each copy of a clip starts in the same location using the same opacity, and that can be confusing when your settings don't appear to be working.

11. **Select VA in Video 5 starting at 00:09.**

    You start animations from the lowest track containing the bars.

12. **In the ECW, click the Opacity spindown arrow to display the settings.**

    You change the opacity for the clip, but its position is already correct for the duration of the clip.

13. **Add keyframes and adjust opacity as follows:**

    00:10, 10%
    00:15, 100%
    02:01, 100%
    03:08, 10%

14. **Set the keyframes and values for the remaining graphic title clips as listed in Table 9-3.**

    As you move to subsequent tracks, toggle the track's visibility to on and leave the completed tracks visible. By the time you complete the settings for the HB clip, all the tracks from Video 1 to Video 8 are visible. In the tables, unaffected values are indicated by "—" in the column. Decimal places are not displayed in the value fields.

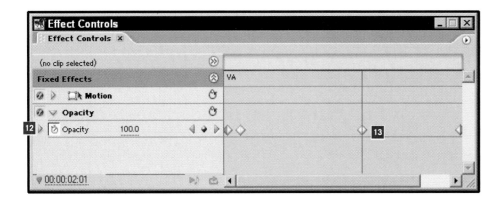

15. **Preview the Timeline segment from 00:00 to approximately 12:25.**
    You see that the split screens are framed. Some of the frames
    are further animated to slide into position over several frames.
    Most graphics have opacity settings.

16. **Right-click the Timeline time ruler, and choose Clear Sequence
    Marker→All Markers.**
    The markers that you added to aid in positioning the bar
    graphics are removed.

17. **Save the project.**
    You added several copies of the graphic bar titles to the project.
    You animated the positions and opacity of the titles to use
    them for framing split-screen segments of the project. In
    Session 11, you add more animated bars to the project.
    However, instead of animating them individually, you construct
    a set of animations in a separate sequence and then place the
    set into the current project sequence.

Table 9-3: Keyframes and Values for the Vertical and Horizontal Graphic Clips

Time	Opacity	Position
VB graphic clip		
03:26	10	310, 0
04:01	100	—
05:12	—	310, 0
05:13	—	310, 120
VC graphic clip		
07:20	100	—
07:21	50	—
08:09	10	—
VD graphic clip		
11:07	—	310, 0
11:08	—	310, 120
VE graphic clip		
00:10	10	160, 120
00:16	100	310, 120
02:17	100	—
02:26	10	—
VF graphic clip		
02:27	10	310, 240
03:04	100	310, 0
HA graphic clip		
09:21	10	160, 120
09:25	100	312, 120
HB graphic clip		
02:27	10	—
03:08	100	—

Tutorial
» Adding Complex Transitions

In the final tutorial for this session, you add transitions. You use a transition to end the c_staircase.mov clip, and you add transitions to the beginning and ending of the traffic light sequence. In order for the traffic lights to change color evenly and still use a transition, you add two copies of the clip to the Timeline and set a hold for the clip. The extra copies are used with the transition to complete the effect without impacting the flow of the traffic light color changes.

1. **On the Timeline, move the CTI to the end of the c_staircase.mov clip on Video 2, ending at 06:14.**
   You add a transition ending at the cut point.

2. **In the Effects tab, choose Video Transitions→Zoom→Zoom Trails.**
   Drag the transition to the cut line, and drop the transition to end at the cut point.

3. **Click the transition to open the ECW.**
   You customize the transition.

4. **Click the Duration time, and type 25 to extend the transition.**
   The transition should still end at the cut point.

5. **Click Show Actual Sources to display the clips in the preview areas.**
   You set a custom center location for the transition.

6. **Drag the start point to a location slightly above and left of the screen center.**
   The finished transition appears to start at the intersection of the two graphic bars on the screen.

7. **Click Custom to open the Zoom Trails Settings dialog box.**
   You change the number of zoom trails.

8. **Click the field, and type 8 to decrease the number of boxes in the zoom. Click OK to close the dialog box.**

9. **Preview the segment of the Timeline from approximately 04:15 to 06:15.**

   Watch the center point of the zoom trail boxes closely. Adjust the location if necessary as described in Step 6.

10. **Select the first** `c_traffic_light.mov` **clip in Video 3 starting at 09:21. Copy the clip.**

11. **Paste a copy of the clip to the left of the original. Drag the right margin of the copy left to shorten the clip to 15 frames, starting at 09:06.**

    Don't drag from the left side because that resets the In point, and you use the In point as a reference to hold the frames coming up in Step 13.

12. **Select the second** `c_traffic_light.mov` **clip in Video 3 starting at 10:17. Copy the clip.**

13. **Paste the copy to the right. Shorten the clip to 15 frames by dragging from the *left* margin of the clip.**

    You use the Out point as the hold frame.

14. **Right-click the first copy of the** `c_traffic_light.mov` **clip starting at 09:06. Choose Frame Hold to open the Frame Hold Options dialog box.**

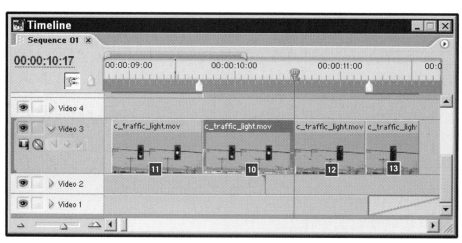

15. **Click Hold On. Choose In Point from the drop-down list. Click OK to close the dialog box.**

    You set a frame hold in order to have a copy of the clip displaying a single frame to use for a transition. The In Point is chosen as the frame. When you later apply the transition to the traffic light clips, you don't lose any of the action (the lights changing colors) as the traffic lights come into view.

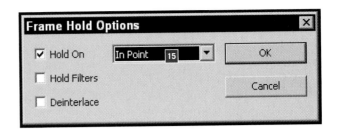

16. **Right-click the final copy of the** c_traffic_light.mov **clip starting at 11:07. Choose Frame Hold.**

    The Frame Hold Options dialog box opens again.

17. **Click Hold On. Choose Out Point in the Frame Hold Options dialog box, and click OK.**

    The dialog box closes. Again, the frame hold is used to define a single frame that is used for the transition. When the transition is applied to the copy of the clip held at the Out Point frame, the traffic light sequences aren't affected, and the transition can still be applied effectively.

18. **Select the first copy of the** c_traffic_light.mov **clip starting at 09:06. Repeat Steps 2 through 8.**

    Use the same settings, except click Reverse to reverse the direction of the transition. Move the center point over the green light.

    <NOTE>
    The default length of the transition in your project is 20 frames; when you add a transition to a clip shorter than 20 frames, as in this case, the transition resizes itself to the length of the clip.

19. **Repeat Steps 2 through 8 with the final copy of the** c_traffic_light.mov **clip starting at 11:07.**

    Use the same settings; move the center point over the red light.

20. **Preview the sequence from 11:09 to 11:22.**

    You see the transition open the first traffic light and then close the final traffic light, zooming in and out in several sequential boxes.

21. **Save the project.**

    You added some complex transitions. You used three copies of the same transition. You also added additional copies of the c_traffic_light.mov clip to use for holding the frames. This allowed the transition to be applied without affecting the animation in the clips. You can see the entire sequence of graphic bar animations and the transitions in the session09A.wmv sample file.

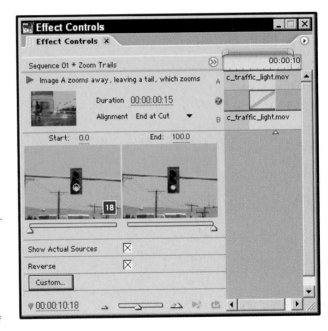

» Session Review

At the start of this session, I explained that you would work with some advanced transparency keys and produce very interesting effects. For example, the image that opens this session shows one of the palm tree clips in the beach segment. At the same frame, shown in the last image in this session, you can see how much impact transparency keys have. The couple is still walking along the beach, but this clip is playing inside another clip, also in motion.

You have completed the titles for the project, most of the transitions, and have also completed the Keying effects. Along with using keys, you also learned how to create and modify images to use as track mattes (in this case, titles). You also added several graphic titles to use for framing the split-screen sequences in the city segment and animated their Fixed effects in the Timeline. In later sessions you create additional sequences containing animations of the graphic bar titles.

The following questions are provided to help you review the information in this session. Answers for each question are found in the tutorial noted in parentheses.

1. Why do you have to hide the track used to contain a clip used for a Track Matte Key effect? (See Tutorial: Adding a Title Track Matte.)

2. What effect does reversing a Track Matte Key effect have on the visibility of the clips? (See Tutorial: Adding a Title Track Matte.)

3. When do you use a lower zoom value in the Program view monitor when working with Motion effects? (See Tutorial: Layering Animated Titles.)

4. How do you change the location of a transition's starting frame in the ECW? (See Tutorial: Layering Animated Titles.)

5. How can you tell in the Project window whether clips are used in the Timeline? (See Tutorial: Adding More Clips to the Timeline.)

6. Can you copy an effect from one clip to another? What window or windows can you use for copying an effect? (See Tutorial: Applying a Matte to Several Clips.)

7. When you apply a track matte to a clip, can you add additional layers to the clip? Does that have an effect on the matte? (See Tutorial: Applying a Matte to Several Clips.)

8. If you add a number of new video tracks to a project, do you also add audio tracks? (See Tutorial: Adding Graphic Frames to Split Screens.)

9. How do you rename a clip? Why would you use an alias for a clip? (See Tutorial: Adding Graphic Frames to Split Screens.)

10. How do you use a copy of a clip and a frame hold to apply a transition to another clip? Does it make a difference whether the transition is at the start or the end of the subject clip? (See Tutorial: Adding Complex Transitions.)

11. What happens when you apply a transition to a clip that is shorter than your default transition length? Does the transition change size, or does the clip change size? (See Tutorial: Adding Complex Transitions.)

» Other Projects

Experiment with other source materials for your image matte. The two additional clips, scene1.psd and scene2.psd, in the samples folder on the CD are similar to the sceneA.psd and sceneB.psd clips used in the session.

Experiment with other configurations and fixed effects for the graphic bar titles used in the project. Add more animation to the bars, or add more bars to the project.

Part VII

Using Video Effects and Advanced Techniques

Session 10 **Using Video Effects**   p 278

Session 11 **More Video Effects**   p 306

Session 10

Using
Video Effects

Tutorial: **Adding Color Tint Effects**

Tutorial: **Focusing the Traffic Lights**

Tutorial: **Adjusting the Drivethrough Traffic Clips**

Tutorial: **Ending the First Segment with Flair**

Tutorial: **Correcting and Modifying Color Using Effects**

Tutorial: **Brightening Palm Tree Backgrounds**

Tutorial: **Combining Transparency Types**

Tutorial: **Adding a Color Matte**

Session Introduction

In this session, you use effects that enhance the project's clips by correcting color, brightness, contrast, and other image values. As you work with Premiere Pro, you learn that you can usually achieve an effect or outcome in more than one way. You can use different effects and settings in combination to produce a similar outcome. For example, you can tint a clip using the Tint effect, or you can use the Luma Key effect and a color matte process to do much the same thing, but with more control over color.

In this and the following session, you work with a large number of effects. Rather than completing tutorials organized by effect group or category, you work basically from the start of the project to the end, with a couple of exceptions. You see your project in its near-finished state and see how an effects workflow is used. You can see the results in the three preview files for this session, `session10A.wmv`, `session10B.wmv`, and `session10C.wmv`.

Regardless of the effect that you are working with, save time in previewing by selecting the clip on the Timeline and then setting In and Out points for it, as you have done in previous sessions. When you apply effects, you often have to view the results repeatedly as you make adjustments. In this and the subsequent session, you aren't instructed to set the In and Out points on the Timeline to define a preview area; that should be a regular work habit that you are developing by now.

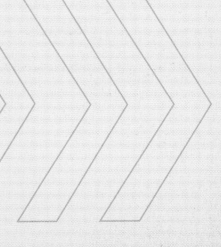

TOOLS YOU'LL USE
Additive Dissolve transition, Adjust effect, Brightness & Contrast effect, Color Balance (HLS) effect, Color Pass effect, Color Picker, Cross Dissolve transition, ECW, Gamma Correction effect, keyframes, Levels effect, Luma Key effect, Noise effect, Opacity fixed effect, Posterize effect, Radial Blur effect, Ramp effect, Scale fixed effect, Timeline window, Tint effect, Wind effect

MATERIALS NEEDED
Session 09 project file that you created, or the `session09.prproj` file from the CD-ROM; `session10A.wmv`, `session10B.wmv`, and `session10C.wmv` preview files from the samples folder

TIME REQUIRED
90 minutes

Tutorial
» Adding Color Tint Effects

The first clip that you work with is the c_staircase.mov clip in Video 2. You correct the clip's levels, meaning that you numerically manipulate the brightness and contrast in the clip. Then you color tint the clip and finish off with a transparency key. The second clip that you work with is the clip of people in a subway station in Video 1. In this clip, you strip most of the color from the clip leaving a range of red colors. None of the effects added in this tutorial uses keyframes. The Tint effect alters color information using luminance, just as transparency keys use luminance. The luminance of each pixel is mapped to selected colors.

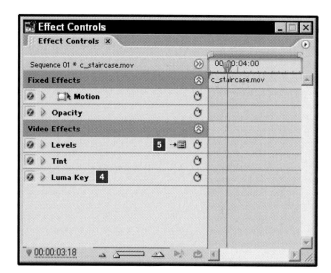

1. **Open Premiere Pro. When the Welcome window opens, choose** session09.prproj.
   The Welcome window closes, and the project is loaded into the program.

<NOTE>
If you didn't do the tutorials in Session 9, copy the session09.prproj file from the CD to your hard drive. In the Welcome window, choose Open Project. Browse to the location where you stored the copied project file, and select Open. Then resave the project in Premiere Pro as session10.prproj (or use another filenaming convention).

2. **Choose File→Save As. Resave the project file as** session10.prproj.
   The name of the new project version displays at the top of the program window.

3. **Select the** c_staircase.mov **clip in Video 2, starting at 02:27. Move the CTI to within the clip.**
   You need to see a frame to apply the effects; the exact frame isn't important.

<TIP>
When you are working with several effects, as you are in the first part of this tutorial, dragging the set of effects to the ECW and then starting the adjustments is much simpler.

4. **Select these effects in the Video Effects window, and drag them to the ECW:**
   Adjust→Levels
   Image Control→Tint
   Keying→Luma Key

5. **Click the Setup icon to open the Levels settings dialog box.**
   You adjust the brightness and contrast in the clip using the graph in the Levels dialog box. The graph, called a histogram, is a graphical representation of the amount of bright and dark areas in your image.

<NOTE>
In this tutorial, some effects have a Setup icon. The icon, a small box at the right of the effect listing in the ECW, displays whenever an effect has an additional dialog box. Click the Setup icon to open the dialog box to modify the effect's settings. Setup dialog boxes are often used with effects that include a preview area so you can see the effect of modifying settings as you work. Changes you make in the Setup dialog boxes are listed in the effect's settings in the ECW.

<NOTE>
An explanation of how the histogram and its values are used is included in the sidebar *Using the Levels Histogram*.

6. **In the Input Levels fields, type** 12, 1.00, 219.

   The x-axis of the histogram represents brightness values from darkest (0) at the far left to brightest (255) at the far right; the y-axis represents the total number of pixels with that value. Adjusting the values increases the contrast between the pixels in your clip.

7. **In the Output levels fields, adjust the first value by clicking 0 and typing** 65, **or drag the black slider to the right until the first Output Level reads 65. Click OK to close the dialog box.**

   You remove some of the darker values from the clip by mapping the pixels to brighter values; you can see the clip overall is brighter. You don't adjust the light values; the default is 255.

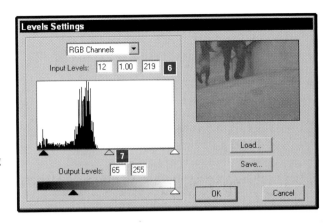

8. **Open the Tint effect controls. Click the Map Black to color swatch to open a Color Picker. Change the Map Black color to RGB=**202/5/0 **and click OK to close the Color Picker.**

   This is the red color used in the bar titles. Map Black to and Map White to specify to which colors dark and bright pixels are mapped or blended.

9. **Click the Map White to color swatch to open the Color Picker again. Choose RGB=**68/0/40 **and click OK to close the Color Picker.**

   This is a yellow from the lights in the street scene.

10. **Click the Amount to Tint, and type** 35.

    You want the black and white in the clip to blend with your chosen colors. The higher the tint amount, the brighter the color.

11. **Open the Luma Key effect. Set the Threshold to 75% and the Cutoff to 10%.**

    You can see some of the city traffic through the clip.

<NOTE>

You can see how different effects work on the same clip as you are setting values. Click the *f* to the left of the effect's name in the ECW to toggle the effect on and off.

12. **Save the project.**

    You adjusted the levels in the c_staircase.mov clip to increase the contrast by shifting the range of colors to brighter levels, tinted the clip using colors from other elements, and added transparency to blend the clip.

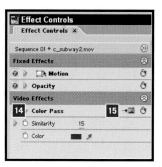

13. Select the `c_subway2.mov` in **Video 1** starting at **05:14.** Position the CTI within the clip, so you can see the effect as you are working.

14. In the **Effects** tab, choose **Video Effects→Image Control→Color Pass. Drag the effect to the ECW.**

15. In the **ECW,** click the **Setup** icon to open the **Color Pass Settings** dialog box.

    You can adjust settings on the ECW itself, but you can see the effects in the dialog box as you make adjustments.

Using the Levels Histogram

The Levels histogram in Premiere Pro is the same as that found in other Adobe products. You work with it for several clips, including the `c_staircase.mov` clip. Working with a histogram allows you to "see" the intensity of a clip's color. To adjust levels, you remap the Input Levels (those represented in the original image) and the Output Levels (those adjusted in the processed clip). You adjust the levels in the image to more evenly distribute the dark, medium, and bright values. The histogram represents brightness values ranging along the x-axis from dark (0) at the left to bright (255) at the right. The y-axis shows how how many pixels in the frame use a particular brightness value. The higher the spike, the more pixels in the image use a particular brightness value. The `c_staircase.mov` clip uses dark to medium brightness, with no lightness at all; that is why the clip appears quite dark overall.

As you move the sliders, you readjust the intensity of each pixel in the clip. Moving the black triangle right in the first Input Level field remaps the intensity of the darker pixels. All pixels that are darker than the new value you set are adjusted, or remapped, to lighter values. Dragging the white triangle left in the third Input Level field decreases the range of intensity to 219 from 255, which shifts or remaps some of the medium pixels into the lighter value range.

You decreased the pixel range used in the clip in the Input Levels histogram, shifting pixels to brighter values. You further adjust the contrast between brightness values using the Output Levels.

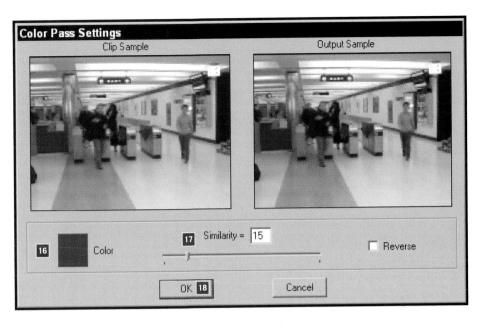

16. **Click the Color Swatch to open the Color Picker. Set the color to RGB=85/40/30 and click OK to close the Color Picker.**
The rust/brown color is chosen from the red turnstiles in the clip.

17. **Drag the Similarity slider right to 15, or type** 15 **in the field.**
The Output Sample image shows that most of the clip is grayscale except for the turnstiles, which are dark red.

18. **Click OK to close the dialog box.**

19. Save the project.
You adjusted one more clip. You replaced the color in the clip with shades of gray, except for a range of dark red colors.

Tutorial

» Focusing the Traffic Lights

You split the original traffic light clip into two clips when you edited it. In this tutorial, you apply the same effect to the two clips using different values controlled by keyframes. You apply the effects to the first clip and then copy them to the next. You work with a Radial blur, which blurs the edges of the clip to focus on the traffic lights. In the traffic light sequence, you also added frame hold copies of the clip before and after the pair of active clips to use for transitions. It isn't necessary to apply the effect to the first transition copy of the clip because the starting blur is quite small, but you need to add it to the final transition copy.

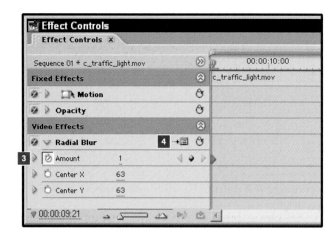

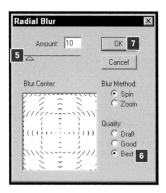

1. **On the Timeline, select the** c_traffic_light.mov **clip in Video 2 starting at 09:21. Move the CTI to the start of the clip at 09:21.**

   This is the first segment where the light changes from green to amber.

2. **In the Effects tab, choose Video Effects→Blur & Sharpen→Radial Blur. Drag the effect to the ECW.**

3. **In the ECW, click the spindown arrow to open the Radial Blur effect. Click Add Keyframe to add a keyframe to the clip's starting frame.**

   You can set the amount and center point for the blur.

4. **With the CTI at 09:21, click the Setup icon to open the Radial Blur dialog box.**

   You visually adjust the blur in the dialog box.

5. **Drag the value slider, or type** 10.

   The blur starts at a value of 10 percent.

6. **Click Best to increase the quality of the blur.**

   The higher the quality, the smoother the blur appears. You are using keyframes with this effect, so a high-quality blur also means that the changes in the blur amount are applied evenly over time.

7. **Click OK to close the Radial Blur dialog box.**

   The settings are applied to the keyframe.

8. **Move the CTI to the last frame of the clip at 10:17. Type** 15 **for the Amount value.**

   Another keyframe is added to the Timeline. The higher the number, the greater the blurring around the edges and the smaller the unblurred center of the image.

9. **Click the Radial Blur effect label to select it. Choose Edit→Copy, or use Ctrl+C, to copy the effect.**

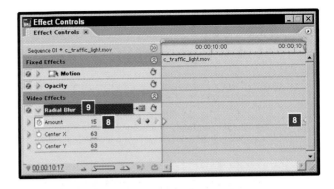

10. **On the Timeline, click the second part of the traffic light that shows the light changing from amber to red starting at 10:17. Choose Edit→Paste, or use Ctrl+V, to paste the effect.**

11. **Repeat Step 10 with the final copy of the clip starting at 11:07.**

    You applied the effect to two more copies of the clip.

12. **Select the** c_traffic_light.mov **clip starting at 10:17.**

    You modify the effect settings.

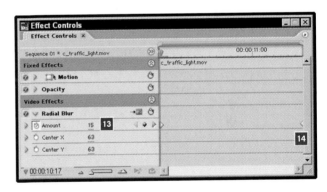

13. **In the ECW, select the first keyframe at 10:17. Increase the Amount from 10 to** 15.

    The clip's blur starts with the same amount of blurring with which the previous clip ended.

14. **Move the CTI to the final keyframe at the end of the clip at 11:07. Change the Amount to** 20 **to increase the blur over the duration of the clip.**

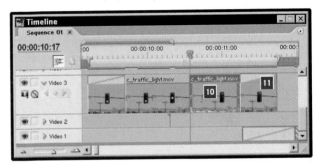

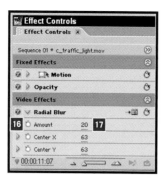

15. **On the Timeline, select the final copy of the c_traffic_light.mov clip starting at 11:07.**

16. **In the ECW, click the Amount Stopwatch icon to remove the keyframes. A notice asks if you want to delete them; click Yes.**

17. **Click the Amount, and type** 20.

    This copy of the clip is used for the transition and has a frame hold applied to the first frame. The only frame seen for the duration of the transition is the first frame, so it isn't necessary to use any keyframes.

18. **Preview the segment from 09:06 to 11:22.**

    Carefully watch how the blur is applied. The effect is smoothly applied from the beginning of the first copy to the end of the sequence.

19. **Save the project.**

    You worked with a simple keyframed effect in this tutorial. You added the same blur effect to three copies of the c_traffic_light.mov clip. When you edited the clips, you created two separate clips that together show the traffic lights changing from green to red, and then added copies of the clips before and after the original pair to use for transitions. Your effect settings were applied to make the set of clips appear unified.

Tutorial
» Adjusting the Drivethrough Traffic Clips

The city segment of the project contains a pair of drivethrough traffic clips. These clips are not of high quality. In this tutorial, you adjust their levels and then purposely decrease their clarity further by posterizing the images. The Posterize effect specifies the number of brightness levels in an image and maps the pixels to the closest level. Blocks of color in the image become more patchy the lower the value. A clip's Posterizing value range is from 2 to 32 levels. You change the opacity of the second clip to transition to the final sequence of the city segment of the project.

1. Select the `c_drive1.mov` clip in Video 1 starting at 11:08.

2. In the Effects tab, choose Video Effects→Adjust. Drag both the Posterize and Levels effects to the ECW.

3. Click the spindown arrow to open the Posterize effect. Click the Level value, and type 14.

4. Click the Setup icon to open the Levels Settings dialog box.
   You adjust the output levels only.

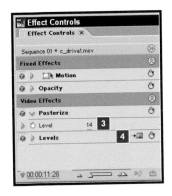

5. Drag the black Output slider right to 24. Click OK to close the dialog box.
   You increase the brightness of the clip.

6. Click the Posterize label, and Shift+click to select the Levels effect label. Choose Edit→Copy, or press Ctrl+C, to copy the effects.

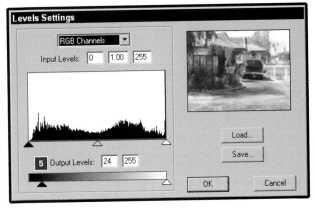

7. **Click the** c_drive2.mov **clip in Video 1 starting at 11:29; display the ECW. Choose Edit→Paste, or press Ctrl+V, to paste the effects.**

8. **Move the CTI to 12:14. Click the Opacity effect's Add Keyframe icon to add a keyframe at the CTI location.**
   The opacity is set at 100 percent by default.

9. **Move the CTI to 12:23. Click the Opacity value, and type** 50.
   Another keyframe is added to the end of the clip at a lower opacity.

10. **Preview the segment from 11:08 to 12:23.**
    The images in both clips are divided into blocks of color, giving them a bolder appearance. The second clip gradually darkens.

11. **Save the project.**
    You added effects to another pair of clips. The appearance of the drivethrough clips was altered using the Posterize effect. You also decreased the second clip's opacity. The second clip segues into the final sequence. You completed most of the effects for the city segment of the project. Other effects are added in the next sessions as you create and add nested sequences of animated bar graphics for impact.

Tutorial

» Ending the First Segment with Flair

Toward the end of the first segment of the movie, you see two traffic signs sweep across the screen as a man throws paper into the air. The starkness of the clip adds to the sense of frustration. In this tutorial, you add an effect to the two signs to add to the sense of motion. You next add noise to the man throwing paper to enhance the emotion conveyed by the clip—as if the poor man didn't already have enough problems! You also scale the ending titles to create a sense of motion.

1. Click the sign2.jpg clip on Video 2 starting at 13:07.
   You add the Wind effect to the clip.

2. **In the Effects tab, choose Video Effects→Stylize→Wind. Drag the effect to the ECW.**

3. **Click the Setup icon to open the Wind Settings dialog box.**
   You change the effect's direction.

<NOTE>
In the ECW, you can see that the Stopwatch icon isn't available for the effect. Wind is one of the effects that is absolute. That is, either the effect is applied or it isn't—it can't be changed over time, nor can you adjust its settings.

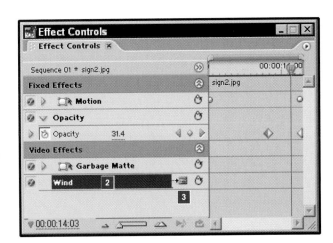

4. **Click From the left to change direction. Click OK to close the dialog box and apply the effect.**

5. **Click the Wind effect's title, and choose Edit→Copy or press Ctrl+C.**
   You copy the effect to use for the second sign.

6. **On the Timeline, click the sign1.jpg clip on Video 3 starting at 13:17 to select it. In the ECW, choose Edit→Paste, or press Ctrl+V, to paste the effect to the second sign.**

7. **Select the c_papers.mov clip in Video 1 starting at 12:23. Move the CTI to the starting frame of the clip at 12:23.**

8. **In the Effects tab, choose Video Effects→Stylize→Noise. Drag the effect to the ECW.**

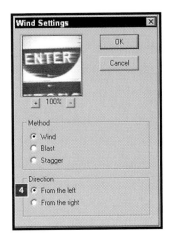

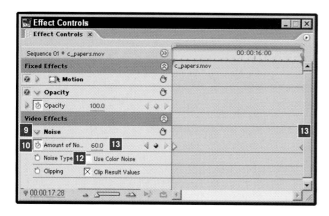

9. **Click the spindown arrow to display the Noise settings.**
   You add keyframes to control the amount of noise.

10. **Click the Stopwatch icon to activate the keyframes for the Amount of Noise value.**

11. **Type** 3 **for the Amount of Noise to start the effect with very little noise.**
   Noise randomly changes pixel values throughout the image, causing a speckled appearance.

12. **Deselect the Use Color Noise option.**
   Color noise adds a range of color to the image, distorting the central figure. Simple noise adds only black and white pixels.

13. **Move the CTI to the last frame of the clip at 17:28. Click the Amount of Noise value, and type** 60.
   Increasing to a higher level at the end of the clip gradually makes the image less distinct as the clip plays.

14. **On the Timeline, select the** you_forgot.prtl **title in Video 4 starting at 13:00.**
   You change the clip's scale over time.

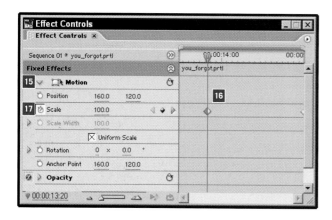

15. **In the ECW, click the Motion effects spindown arrow to display the values.**
   You adjust the scale.

16. **In the ECW, move the CTI to 13:20.**
   You start the scale change at the location where the clip's transition ends.

17. **Click the Scale Stopwatch icon to activate the keyframes.**
   Leave the default values for the first keyframe.

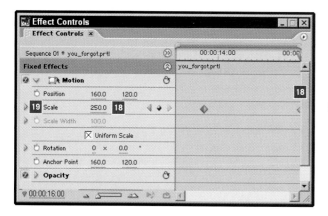

18. **Move the CTI to the final frame of the title clip at 16:00. Click the Scale value, and type** 250.
   You increase the title's size by 250 percent.

19. **Click the Scale value title. The keyframes turn blue. Choose Edit→Copy, or press Ctrl+C, to copy the keyframes.**

20. **On the Timeline, click the** didn't_you.prtl **title starting at 16:00 on Video 4.**
   You paste the keyframes to the second title.

21. **In the ECW, move the CTI to the start of the clip at 16:00.**
    Keyframes are pasted according to the CTI location; the first keyframe is placed at the CTI location.

22. **Click the Motion effects spindown arrow to display the values.**

23. **Click the Scale value's Stopwatch icon to activate the keyframes.**
    A keyframe is automatically added at the CTI location.

24. **Choose Edit→Paste, or press Ctrl+V, to paste the keyframes to the clip.**
    The two new keyframes use the scale values copied from the first clip.

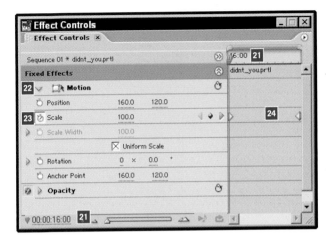

25. **Preview the segment from 13:07 to approximately 18:00.**
    The signs appear to move across the screen against the wind. The increase in noise added to the c_papers.mov adds an edgy look to the clip. As it plays, the image's pixels are progressively disrupted. Each title seems to gradually get larger on the screen as it plays.

26. **Save the project.**
    You added effects to a number of clips. You copied and p asted effects and fixed effects between clips. The sample clip session10A.wmv shows the city segment of the project from 00:00 to 18:15. Aside from nested sequences of bar titles and another nested image sequence that you create and add in the next two sessions, the city segment of the project is complete.

Tutorial
» Correcting and Modifying Color Using Effects

The city segment of the project uses a great deal of stark black, white, and red material. The beach segment, by contrast, uses lots of bright colors, including green and blue. The beach segment doesn't get off to a very bright start. In this tutorial, you work with the pale and faded-looking opening beach clip. You use Adjust and Image Control effects to correct the color of the clip. An additional effect named Color Corrector in the Image Control folder of the Video Effects combines the effects that you use along with many others. You work with the standard Effects workspace throughout; Premiere Pro also includes a Color Correction workspace. Read more about it in the *More Premiere Pro Features* Bonus Discussion on the CD.

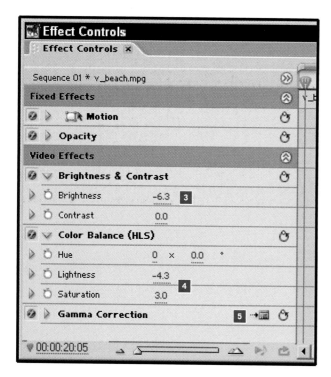

1. **Click the** v_beach.mpg **clip on Video 1 starting at 19:21.**
   You add several effects to the clip to correct the color.

2. **Drag these effects to the ECW from the Effects tab:**
   Adjust→Brightness & Contrast
   Image Control→Color Balance (HLS)
   Adjust→ Gamma Correction

3. **Click the spindown arrow to open the Brightness & Contrast effect. Click the Brightness value, and type** -6.3**.**
   The blue sky and water in the clip appear darker and richer.

4. **Click the spindown arrow to open the Color Balance (HLS) effect. Click the Lightness value, and type** -4.3**. Click the Saturation value, and type** 3**.**
   The HLS Color Balance effect modifies color based on the HLS (Hue/ Lightness/ Saturation) color model. Hue, which specifies the color scheme for the image, is unchanged. The clip is darkened slightly by decreasing the Lightness setting; the color is made more intense by increasing the Saturation setting.

< N O T E >
The Adjust effects folder also includes a Color Balance (RGB) effect. If you are more comfortable working with RGB color values than HLS values, you may prefer to use that effect.

5. **Click the Setup icon to open the Gamma Correction Settings dialog box.**
   You can use the Setup window to evaluate changes as you make adjustments.

6. Drag the slider to a Gamma value of 1.3.

The Gamma value of an image is the relative brightness of the midtones of an image and has no effect on either shadows or highlights. Increasing the Gamma value darkens the mid-gray levels (midtones), giving more fullness to the image.

7. Click OK to close the Gamma Corrections Settings dialog box.

8. Preview the clip from 19:21 to 26:21 in the Program view monitor.

The color is more rich and full with the settings that you applied.

9. Save the project.

You added three color correction effects to the same clip in this tutorial: adjusting the balance and contrast, correcting the color, and modifying the Gamma value to increase the brightness of the midtones. The original clip was very pale and indistinct; the corrected clip is a much more vibrant way to begin the beach segment.

Tutorial
» Brightening Palm Tree Backgrounds

A bit further down the Timeline, you added a track matte over the clip of the young lady running down the beach. The palm trees clip that displays behind the alpha channel of the letters needs some brightening. You adjust its colors using Brightness & Contrast, and then you apply the Tint effect. You use keyframes for the tint effect to gradually change the clip's color over time. When the effect is complete, you paste it to another palm tree background clip.

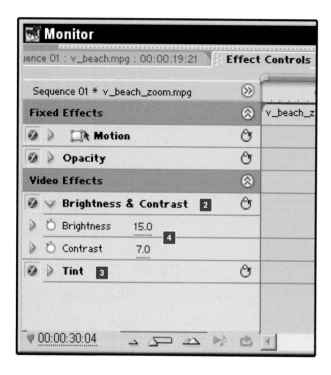

1. **Select the** v_beach_zoom.mpg **clip in Video 1 starting at 26:21. Move the CTI to the starting frame of the clip.**
   You brighten and tint the clip.

2. **In the Effects tab, choose Video Effects→Adjust→Brightness & Contrast. Drag the effect to the ECW.**

3. **Repeat Step 2 with the Tint effect from the Image Control folder.**
   You add two effects to the clip.

4. **Click the spindown arrow to open the Brightness & Contrast values. Click the Brightness value, and type** 15. **Click the Contrast value, and type** 7.
   The trees in the clip are much more distinct.

5. **Click the Brightness & Contrast effect's spindown arrow to close it.**
   Collapsing the effect makes it less distracting when working with another effect.

6. **Click the spindown arrow to open the Tint effect values.**
   Click the Stopwatch icons for all three Tint values.

7. **Click the Amount to Tint value, and type** 30.
   Leave the default colors for the Map Black to and Map White to values.

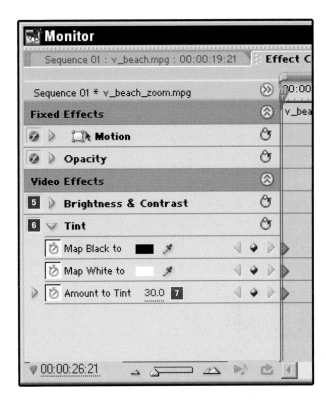

8. **Move the CTI to the last frame of the clip at 30:26.**
   You set new values and keyframes at the end of the clip.

9. **Click the Map Black to color swatch to open a Color Picker. Change the Map Black color to RGB=**60/140/30 **and click OK to close the Color Picker.**
   This is a medium green that blends with the black pixels in the clip.

10. **Click the Map White to color swatch to open the color picker again. Choose RGB=**70/130/200 **and click OK to close the Color Picker.**
    This is a clear blue color that blends with the white pixels in the clip.

11. **Click the Amount to Tint value, and type** 60.
    As the clip plays, the tint becomes more intense.

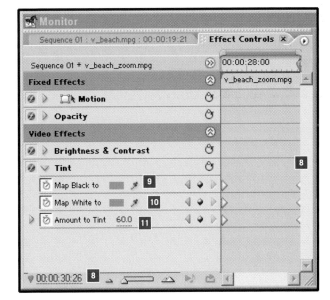

12. **Preview the clip from 26:21 to 30:26 in the Program view monitor.**
    The clip gradually changes in color and intensity.

13. **Click the Tint effect label in the ECW to select the effect. Choose Edit➙Copy, or press Ctrl+C, to copy the effect.**

14. **In the Timeline, click the** v_palms_rotate.mpg **clip on Video 1 starting at 39:06.**
    You add the Tint effect to the clip.

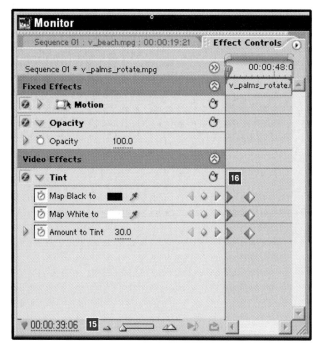

15. **In the ECW (or on the Timeline), click the current time indicator. Type** 3906 **to move the CTI to the starting frame of the clip.**

16. **Choose Edit➙Paste, or press Ctrl+V, to paste the effect to the clip.**
    The effect is added to the clip starting at the first frame of the clip. You see that the second keyframe for each value is not at the end frame in the clip because the v_palms_rotate.mpg clip is longer than the v_palms_zoom.mpg clip from which you copied the effect.

17. **In the ECW, drag each end keyframe from its pasted position to the end of the clip at 51:15.**

You reset the keyframe positions in accordance with the clip's duration.

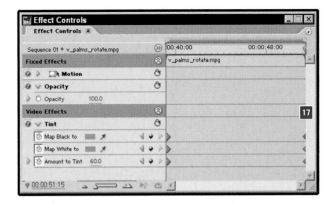

18. **Preview the Timeline segment from 39:06 to 51:15 in the Program view monitor.**

You see that the background palm trees gradually increase in color intensity as they rotate.

19. **Save the project.**

You applied two effects to two palm tree video clips, correcting brightness and contrast, and you added an interesting keyframed tint. Because the same effect is added to two background clips in various locations, it adds continuity to the project. Watch the preview clip, session10B.wmv, to see the Timeline segment from the start of the beach segment until the end of the v_palms_zoom.mpg clip.

Tutorial
» Combining Transparency Types

The final sequence with which you work in this session is the woman and the dog running down the beach. In this tutorial, you add transparency to the clip using the Luma Key effect. You are working with some complicated effects in this sequence. The clip of the woman and dog overlay one of the surfer clips. You want to see the surfer, but you also want to see the running figures clearly. You use both opacity and Luma keying to achieve some effective transparency.

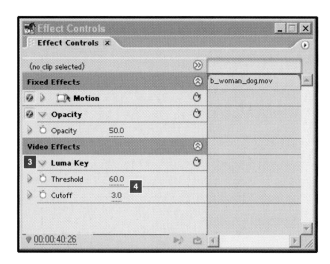

1. Select the b_woman_dog.mov clip in Video 3 starting at 37:27. You add an effect and transitions.

2. In the Effects tab, choose Video Effects→Keying→ Luma Key. Drag the effect to the ECW.

3. In the ECW, click the spindown arrow to open the Luma Key values.

4. Set the Threshold to 60 and the Cutoff to 3. Both the Threshold and Cutoff can be set in a range from 0 to 100 percent.
   A medium Threshold value creates some transparency in the clip, which is the desired effect. A low Cutoff value retains the visibility of the woman and dog in the clip.

< N O T E >
You set the clip's opacity to 50 percent in an earlier session. Adding luminance creates another type of transparency. In combination with the matte that you create later in the tutorial, you produce an interesting effect.

5. In the Effects tab, choose Video Transitions→Dissolve→Additive Dissolve. Drag the transition to the start of the b_woman_dog.mov clip at 37:27 on Video 3.
   The Additive Dissolve transition gradually displays the woman running down the beach, and the surfer is still clearly visible. The transition doesn't darken from the exiting clip or lighten from the entering clip.

6. Drag the sceneB.psd clip from Video 4 down to Video 3 to start after the b_woman_dog.mov clip at 40:26.
   You placed the clip in Video 4 when you added it to the project in a previous session. Now you move it into its final location following the b_woman_dog.mov clip.

7. Move the CTI to the end of the b_woman_dog.mov clip at 40:26. Repeat Step 5.
   Extend the transition to 30 frames (01:00), centered at the cut point. You add a dissolve from the woman running on the beach to the still image used with the picture in picture sequence.

8. **Preview the segment from approximately 37:00 to 41:15 in the Program view montior.**

You see the surfer gradually replaced by the woman and dog running, although neither clip gets as dark as with a cross dissolve.

9. **Save the project.**

You added some additional transparency to one clip and added transitions to both ends of the b_woman_dog.mov clip. In the next (and final) tutorial for this session, you add an underlying color layer for special effects.

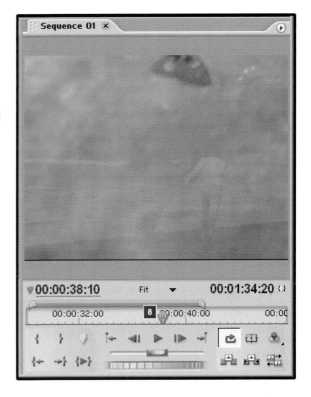

Tutorial

» Adding a Color Matte

This session's final tutorial ends the woman-and-dog-running-on-the-beach segment with a bang. You work with a color matte for more depth of color. A color matte is an object created internally in Premiere Pro—you cannot export it or save it as a separate file. You can create a solid color still image in an external program and import it to achieve the same outcome; using the Premiere Pro color matte is much simpler and quicker. You apply a Ramp effect to the matte, animate the effect, and then add some final transitions to finish the sequence. A Ramp effect uses a color ramp, or gradient, where colors blend from one to another across the screen.

1. **On the Project window, click New Item→Color Matte.**
   A Color Picker opens.

   < T I P >
   You can also select File→New→Color Matte.

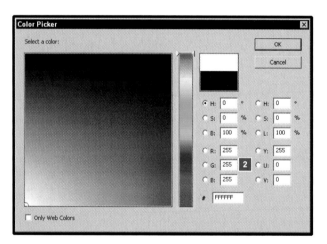

2. **In the Color Picker, type RGB=255/255/255 and click OK.**
   The Color Picker closes. The matte is white; the color for the matte isn't really important in this project because it is used with an effect and not blended with the effect.

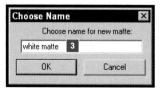

3. **In the Choose Name dialog box, type** white matte. **Click OK to close the dialog box**.
   The matte is added to the Project window. Store the matte in the titles bin.

4. **Move the CTI to 37:27.**

   You add the white matte at the same start location as the b_woman_dog.mov clip.

5. **Drag the white matte from the Project window to Video 2. Place the matte to start at 37:27. Drag the right margin to extend the clip to snap to the** v_resort.mpg **clip starting at 40:26 in the Timeline.**

   The final length of the white matte is 02:29, the same length as the b_woman_dog.mov clip in Video 3.

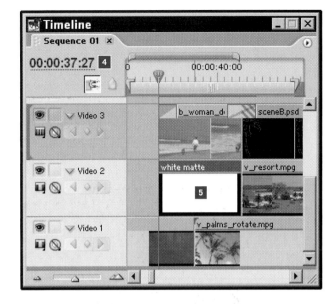

6. **In the ECW, click the spindown arrow to open the Opacity setting. Decrease the clip's opacity to 75%.**

7. **In the Effects tab, choose Video Effects→Render→Ramp. Drag the Ramp effect to the ECW.**

8. **Click the spindown arrow to display the Ramp effect's values.**

   You create a custom gradient. The default is a black to white gradient.

9. **Click the Ramp effect label in the ECW.**

   Positioning points display in the Program view monitor.

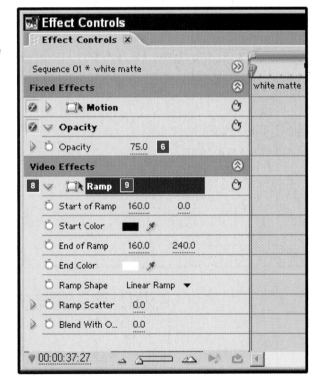

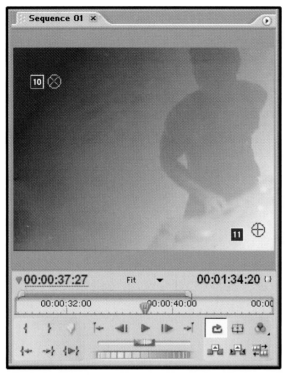

10. **Drag the upper positioning point left and downward until the Start of Ramp value is 50, 40.**

    You can also type the values into the ECW Start of Ramp fields.

11. **Repeat Step 10 with the lower positioning point. Drag it right and upward to an End of Ramp value of 300, 215.**

    The gradient is now angled from upper left to lower right.

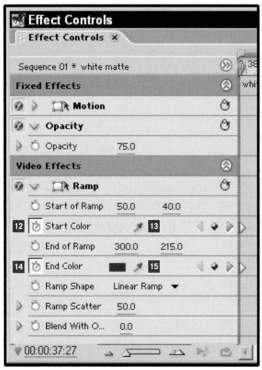

12. **Click the Stopwatch icon to activate the Start Color value keyframe.**

    You animate the start colors in the gradient.

13. **Click the color swatch to open the Color Picker. Type RGB=255/223/72.**

    The yellow is the same yellow used in the beach segment's main titles as the inner stroke on the text.

14. **Click the Stopwatch icon to activate the End Color value keyframe.**

    You animate the end color in the gradient.

15. **Click the color swatch to open the Color Picker. Type RGB=175/0/40.**

    The red color is the same red used in the main titles as the outer stroke on the text.

16. **Move the CTI to the last frame of the clip at 40:25. Repeat Steps 13 and 15, except reverse the colors.**

    Use the color that you set for the Start of Ramp color as the End of Ramp color, and vice versa.

17. **Click the Ramp Scatter value, and type 50.**

    The higher the Ramp Scatter value, the greater the number of random pixels blended, decreasing the appearance of distinct bands of color.

18. **In the Effects tab, choose Video Transitions→Dissolve→Additive Dissolve. Drag the transition to the start of the** white matte **clip at 37:27 on Video 2 in the Timeline.**

19. **In the Effects tab, choose Video Transitions→Dissolve→Cross Dissolve. Add the transition to the end of the** white matte **clip at 40:26 on Video 2, ending at the cut point.**

20. **Preview the segment from approximately 37:00 to 41:15 in the Program view monitor.**

    The colored background gradually changes from a yellow tint in the upper left to a red tint in the lower right of the screen over time. The luminance added to the b_woman_dog.mov clip adds interesting color tinting to the clip.

21. **Save the project.**

    You added a complex video effect to complete the first sports segment of the beach sequence and the segue into the scenery segment. The Ramp effect, one of the rendering effects, calculates color and generates an image—in this case, a yellow/red color gradient. The sequence with which you worked in the last two tutorials is shown in the session10C.wmv preview movie.

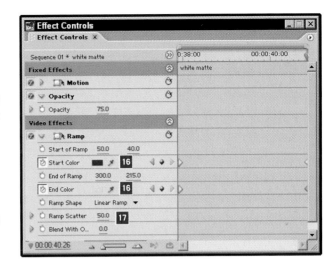

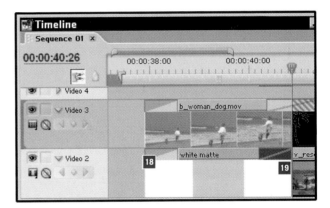

What Happened to the Solid White Matte?

The Ramp effect is a rendering filter (another name for an effect). This means that the original content of the clip remains as is and that changes are made to it based on the algorithms of the selected filter (in this case, creating a gradient). The gradient has its own values for color and distribution. In essence, it sits on top of the matte; for this reason, the underlying matte can be any color. The only time the matte color is important is if you use the Blending feature to blend the ramp and underlying matte colors.

» Session Review

In this session, you applied and configured a large number of effects such as those used to correct color or clarity problems in a clip. You worked with a number of effects that work with a clip's color in some way, such as the Color Pass effect, which makes a clip grayscale aside from a specified range of color. The opening image in the session shows a frame of one of the clips with which you worked in this session. I explained how to add a solid color matte to your project to serve as a background for a clip with luminance-based transparency. You learned how to modify the matte by adding a Ramp effect to it. The final image in this session shows the same frame at the end of the session's activities. What a difference!

In the Bonus Discussion called *The Finer Points of Premiere Pro Effects* found on the CD, you can find a top-level overview of the different categories of video effects. Taking the time to experiment with effects is very important. Certain effects are similar in their application and results, and others are wildly different—or just wild! Most clips can be modified in some way, such as with configurable parameters or custom colors. Other effects are absolute, in that they are applied or they are not applied.

Here are questions to help you review the information in this session. You'll find the answer to each question in the tutorial noted in parentheses.

1. What is shown on the histogram in the Levels effect? How do you use the information in the histogram to adjust the brightness of a clip? (See Tutorial: Adding Color Tint Effects.)

2. How do the selected Map Black to and Map White to colors relate to the clip's tint? (See Tutorial: Adding Color Tint Effects.)

3. Why is it important to adjust the quality of a blur when you use a large amount of blurring in a clip? (See Tutorial: Focusing the Traffic Lights.)

4. Can you add keyframes to an effect that has a frame hold applied to the In Point? Why or why not? (See Tutorial: Focusing the Traffic Lights.)

5. How does the Posterize effect apply color to a clip? (See Tutorial: Adjusting the Drivethrough Traffic Clips.)

6. How is an absolute effect different from other effects? (See Tutorial: Ending the First Segment with Flair.)

7. How do you correct the color of a clip? What kinds of effects are used for correction? (See Tutorial: Correcting and Modifying Color Using Effects.)

8. How does gamma correction work? What does it do to the colors in a clip? (See Tutorial: Correcting and Modifying Color Using Effects.)

9. How do keyframed tints affect a clip's coloring over time? (See Tutorial: Brightening Palm Tree Backgrounds.)

10. Can you combine different types of transparency in the same clip? (See Tutorial: Combining Transparency Types.)

11. What is a color matte? Where is it used? (See Tutorial: Adding a Color Matte.)

12. Why would you increase the Ramp effect's Scatter value? (See Tutorial: Adding a Color Matte.)

» Other Projects

Experiment with different Ramp effect colors and settings. Can you see how changing the coordinates alters the direction?

Use a clip that requires lots of correction. Experiment with the correction-type effects (such as those in the Adjust and Image Control folders) to see how they work. Try them in combination. Adjust their order in the Effect Controls panel list. Is there a difference in the appearance of the clip based on the effects' order? Try working with the Color Correction workspace and some of the waveform/vectorscope options. Refer to the Discussion: Color Correction Workspace in the *More Premiere Pro Features* Bonus Discussion on the CD.

More Video Effects

Tutorial: **Enhancing a Text Title**

Tutorial: **Finishing the Palm Tree Track Matte Overlay**

Tutorial: **Transitioning Clips Using Fixed Effects**

Tutorial: **Improving Color in Two Clips**

Tutorial: **Cropping the Content of Clips**

Tutorial: **Using Effects to Create Themes in the Movie**

Tutorial: **Adding a New Sequence to the Project**

Tutorial: **Creating Sequences for Animating Bar Titles**

Session Introduction

I hope you have watched the segments of your movie numerous times. You should; you have done lots of work. In this session, you work with more effects as you continue to make your way through the project. In this session, you look at the Color Corrector effect, which is an enormous effect used to overhaul a clip. Refer to the More Premiere Pro Features Bonus Discussion called *Color Correction Workspace* on the CD for more information on how to view color as you work with it. You also work with a series of effects on some of the sports clips to add some punch to the production.

After you reach the end of the project, you start preparing the last two items for your movie. You are going to create an image sequence for the city segment of the project using garbage mattes. You also make sequences of the animated bars for the opening section of the project. Rather than adding any clips to the Timeline, you build additional sequences. In the next session, you add multiple copies of the sequences to your main project's Timeline, creating some complex animation effects.

This session includes two preview files. The first preview, `session11A.wmv`, includes most of the beach segment of the project from the `life2.prtl` location at 27:15 to the end of the movie. The second preview file, `session11B.wmv`, shows you the contents of the three additional sequences that you add to the project.

TOOLS YOU'LL USE
Bevel Edges effect, Brightness & Contrast effect, Checker Wipe transition, Color Corrector effect, Color Offset effect, Crop effect, CTI, Drop Shadow effect, ECW, Effects tab, Fast Blur effect, Frame Hold command, Garbage Matte effect, In point and Out point, Levels effect, Motion effects, New Sequence command, Opacity effect, Opacity keyframe graph, Pen tool, Poster marker, Sharpen effect, Timeline

MATERIALS NEEDED
Session 10 project file that you created, or the `session10.ppj` file from the CD-ROM; `session11A.wmv` and `session11B.wmv` preview files

TIME REQUIRED
90 minutes

Tutorial
» Enhancing a Text Title

At the end of the preceding session, you had made your way from the start of the project to approximately the middle of the beach segment adding effects and adjusting clips. You corrected a number of clips, added a variety of effects, and completed some complex sequences, including one using a Ramp effect and color matte. In this tutorial, you back up slightly and add some effects to the red Life title and two more copies of the clip to the project.

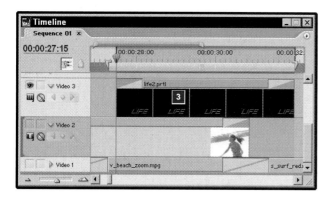

1. **Open Premiere Pro. When the Welcome window opens, choose** `session10.prproj`.
   The Welcome window closes, and the project is loaded into the program.

<NOTE>

If you didn't do the tutorials in Session 10, copy the `session10.prproj` file from the CD to your hard drive. In the Welcome window, choose Open Project. Browse to the location where you stored the copied project file, and select Open. Then resave the project in Premiere Pro as `session11.prproj` (or use another filenaming convention).

2. **Choose File➔Save As, and resave the project file as** session11.prproj.
   The name of the new project version displays at the top of the program window.

3. **In the Timeline, select the** `life2.prtl` **title on Video 3 starting at 27:15. Move the CTI to the start frame of the clip.**
   You add a keyframed effect.

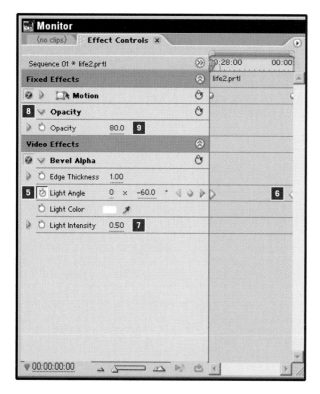

4. **In the Effects tab, choose Video Effects➔Perspective➔Bevel Edges. Drag the effect to the** `life2.prtl` **ECW.**
   You use many of the default settings.

5. **Open the Bevel Edges effect, and click the Light Angle value Stopwatch icon. Leave the starting Light Angle value at 0 revolutions, -60 degrees.**

6. **Move the CTI to the final frame of the clip at 32:00. Set the Light Angle value at 2 revolutions, 0 degrees.**
   The light rotates around the text twice as the text moves across the screen.

7. **Click the Light Intensity value, and type .5.**
   Don't keyframe the light intensity; you want to increase the contrast throughout.

8. **Click the spindown arrow to open the Opacity fixed effect.**
   You decrease the opacity of the entire clip.

9. **Click the 100.0 Opacity value, and type 80.**
   You decrease the clip's opacity. Don't use keyframes.

10. **Preview the segment from 27:15 to 32:00.**

You see the light rotate around the text as it moves across the screen.

11. **Save the project.**

You applied some subtle effects to a text title. Using the Bevel Edges effect, you added a light source to the text and rotated the light source over time causing a sense of motion as the clip moves across the screen.

Tutorial
» Finishing the Palm Tree Track Matte Overlay

In Session 9, you worked with a track matte to allow segments of one clip to display over another. You used a matte with a palm tree frame overlay. The overlay is pixelated. In this tutorial, you add a blur and a shadow to smooth the overlay and give it a professional finish.

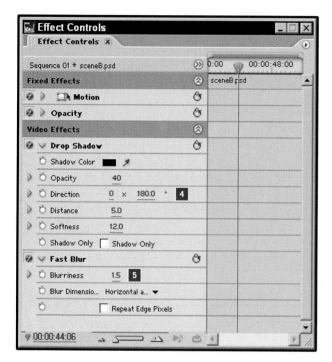

1. Select the sceneB.psd clip on Video 3 starting at 40:26. You add two effects to the clip.

2. In the Effects tab, choose Video Effects→Blur & Sharpen→Fast Blur. Drag the effect to the ECW.

<NOTE>

Blur effects produce blurring based on different mathematical processes. The Fast blur produces blurriness in a short distance. If you look closely at different types of blurs, you can see varying amounts of blurring depending on the distance from the object. A Fast Blur starts very close to the object, which is the desired effect.

3. In the Effects tab, choose Video Effects→Perspective→Drop Shadow. Drag the effect to the ECW.

4. In the ECW, click the spindown arrow to display the Drop Shadow values. Change these settings:
   Opacity = 40
   Direction = 0 (revolutions) x 180 (degrees)
   Distance = 5
   Softness = 12

5. In the ECW, click the spindown arrow to display the Fast Blur values. Set the blurriness to 1.5.

6. **Preview the Timeline segment from 40:26 to 51:15 in the Program monitor view.**

   You see that the edges of the palm tree matte overlay are much more attractive. The pixelated edges are smoothed, and the shadow adds some dimension to the image.

7. **Save the project.**

   You added two effects to the track matte overlay image to smooth its edges and give it some depth using a shadow. The Standard effects that you applied are rendered before the fixed effects are applied.

Rendering Order

Premiere Pro renders effects from the bottom up as they are listed in the ECW. Standard effects, those found in the Effects tab's folders, are rendered first. Opacity is rendered next, and the Motion effects last. You can change the order by using standard Video Effects rather than Fixed Effects. Instead of using the Motion fixed effects, choose Video Effects→Distort→Transform and add the effect to the ECW. Instead of using Opacity, choose Video Effects→Keying→Alpha Adjust.

Tutorial

» Transitioning Clips Using Fixed Effects

The second image matte sequence is now complete. Immediately following that sequence is a clip of a harbor and then the first of a series of sports clips. In this tutorial, you use fixed effects rather than a transition. When you are working with a pair of clips and using the start and end points of one clip as keyframe positions for the other clip, adjusting the CTI in the Timeline using the Page Up key or Page Down key is simpler. If you preview the Timeline segment from approximately 51:15 to 56:00, you hear the switch from the scenery to the sports scores. Adjust clips as you adjust effects to match the action more closely with the score for the movie.

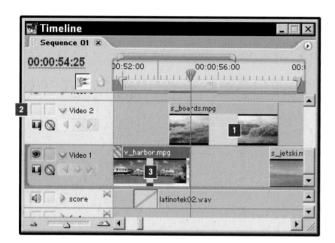

1. On the Timeline, drag the right margin of the s_boards.mpg clip in Video 2 right until the clip duration is 04:18. Drag the clip left along the Timeline to start at 53:28.

2. Toggle the visibility of Video 2 to off.
   You need to see the underlying clip to set its effects.

3. Click the v_harbor.mpg clip in Video 1 starting at 51:15. Drag the right margin of the clip to shorten it to 03:10, ending at 54:25.

4. In the ECW, click the spindown arrow to open the Motion effects.

5. Move the CTI to 53:10. Click the Stopwatch icon to activate keyframes for Position and Scale.

6. Move the CTI to the end of the v_harbor.mpg clip at 54:25. Click the Position values, and type 255 , -155. Click the Scale value, and type 400.

7. **On the Timeline, toggle Video 2 to on.**
   You work with the s_boards.mpg clip now that the harbor zoom is complete.

8. **Select the s_boards.mpg clip in Video 2 starting at 55:18.**

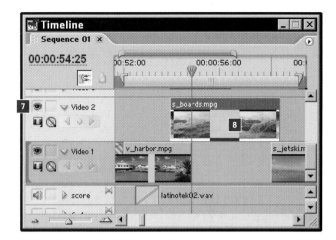

9. **In the ECW, click the spindown arrow to display the Opacity values.**
   The Stopwatch icon is automatically activated for Opacity.

10. **At the CTI position (which you set in Step 6), click Add Keyframe.**

11. **Add and adjust the Opacity keyframes. At the start of the clip, set Opacity to 10%; add a keyframe at 58:03 with 100% Opacity; add a final keyframe at 58:16 with 10% opacity.**
    You set the opacity to fade in and out corresponding with the clips on Video 1.

12. **Preview the sequence from 54:00 to 57:00, and save the project.**
    You see the harbor pass across the screen and then zoom into a segment of the water. The life.prtl title is visible in Video 3; it appears to start at the location into which you have zoomed. The surfer passing the screen gradually fades in as the music changes and replaces the harbor view, fading out to the jetski clip.

Tutorial
» Improving Color in Two Clips

Several of the sports clips use a special sequence of effects that you work with starting in the next tutorial. Two of the clips require some significant color correction first. In this tutorial, you use the Color Corrector effect for the sailing clip, which has a significant pink cast to it. You also adjust the windsurfer clip in this tutorial, using a combination of effects.

Click to open/close Keyframes display

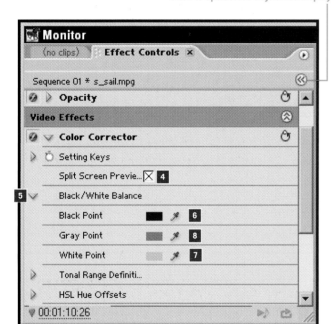

1. **Select the** `s_sail.mpg` **clip on Video 1 starting at 01:05:29.**

2. **Move the CTI to a frame that shows a medium shot of the sailboat. Choose a frame at approximately 01:08:00.**
   You want to see the people, the sailboat, and both the water and sky.

3. **In the Effects tab, choose Video Effects→Image Control→Color Corrector. Drag the effect to the ECW, and click the spindown arrow to open the list of settings.**
   The effect has many settings; as you work with the effect, toggle the spindown arrows to open and close different settings.

<NOTE>
You don't use any keyframes; click the Close Keyframes icon to collapse the keyframe area of the ECW.

4. **Click Split Screen Preview.**
   The view in the Program view monitor is split showing the original clip in the left side of the monitor and the corrected clip in the right side of the monitor.

5. **Click the Black/White Balance spindown arrow to display the three settings for Black, Gray, and White Point.**
   You set the Black Point and the White Point first and then the Gray Point.

6. **Click the Black Point eyedropper, and drag it over the image. Stop when the eyedropper is over a very dark section, like the underside of the boat.**
   The Black Point adjusts itself, and the image becomes lighter overall. The Black Point used in the sample is RGB=25/8/16, a very dark gray.

7. **Click the White Point eyedropper, and repeat Step 6. Drag the eyedropper over the bow of the boat or some of the brightest cloud areas.**
   The White Point adjusts itself, and the image brightens. The sample uses RGB=216/179/180, which is a pale pink.

8. **Repeat Step 6 one more time with the Gray Point. Move the eyedropper over the stripe along the side of the boat.**
   The sample uses RGB=123/104/107, which is a pinkish gray.

<NOTE>
You can also choose New Reference Monitor from the Monitor window menu to open the original clip in a new monitor. You can choose Gang to Reference Monitor to match the Reference window's timing to the Program view monitor. I prefer to use a split screen because additional monitors crowd the screen.

<NOTE>
You adjust the levels in the clip using the points. The Black Point is a sample of the darkest area of the image; the White Point is a sample of the lightest area of the image; the Gray Point is a medium value in the image. When you set the points, the range of darkness/lightness adjusts itself in the clip.

9. **Look at the split-screen view.**

   You can see that the uncorrected clip is very dark and the entire image, including the clouds, is quite pink. The color on the right side is clearer but still very dark.

10. **Move the CTI to approximately 01:09:22.**

    You want to see the colors of the sail in both sides of the split screen.

11. **Click the spindown arrow to open the HSL options.**

    You use the controls (either the HSL Hue Offsets or the HSL controls) to adjust the hue, saturation, and brightness of the clip.

12. **Adjust these settings in the HSL options:**
    Decrease Saturation to 90
    Increase Brightness to 2
    Increase Contrast to 5
    Increase Gamma to 1.4

    <**N O T E**>
    Brightness increases the brightness of the clip overall; gamma increases the brightness of the mid-range tones.

13. **Deselect the Split Screen Preview.**

    This returns you to the regular viewing mode.

14. **Preview the clip from 01:05:29 to 01:12:29.**

    The Program view monitor displays only the corrected clip. The colors are much clearer, but the figures are still blurry.

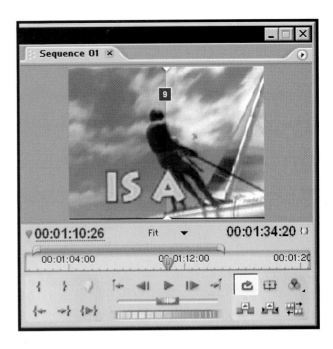

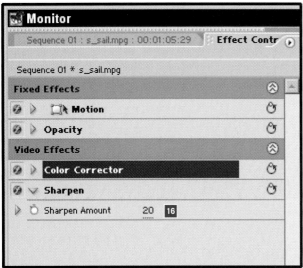

15. **In the Effects tab, choose Video Effects→Blur & Sharpen→Sharpen. Drag the effect to the ECW.**
    You sharpen the clip's content—that is, you increase the contrast between different color areas in the clip to offset some of the clip's blurriness.

16. **Click the Sharpen spindown arrow, and increase the Sharpen Amount to** 20.
    The contrast in the clip is increased to offset some of the blur.

17. **Preview the clip again in the Program view monitor**
    You see that the figures are more distinct in the clip.

18. **Save the project. You made multiple color adjustments for a clip in the beach segment of the project.**
    You used the Color Corrector effect to adjust several color characteristics and values. You also added a Sharpen effect to increase the clarity of the clip.

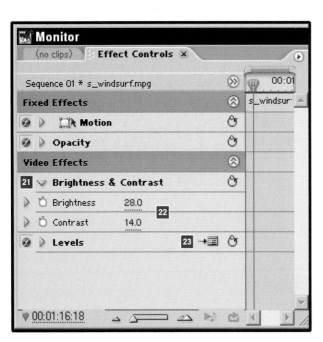

19. **In the Timeline, select the** s_windsurf.mpg **clip in Video 2 starting at 01:16:03.**
    You add two effects to the clip.

20. **In the Effects tab, choose Video Effects→Adjust. Select the Brightness & Contrast and Levels effects. Drag the effects to the ECW.**

21. **Click the spindown arrow to open the Brightness & Contrast effect.**

22. **Set the Brightness to** 28; **set the Contrast to** 14.
    The brightness and contrast of the clip are adjusted, making the images more distinct.

23. **Click the Setup icon to open the Levels Settings dialog box.**

24. **Set the Input Levels to** 17, 1.26, **and** 255.

    You can use the sliders under the histogram or type values into the fields above the histogram. The dialog box shows the histogram for a frame of the clip. The x-axis of the histogram shows brightness levels from darkest to brightest (values ranging from 0 to 255). The y-axis shows the number of pixels using each value. Dragging the black Input Level slider to the right increases shadow; dragging the white Input Level slider to the left increases highlights. The gray triangle controls midtones. In this case, you adjust only the shadow setting.

25. **Set the Output Levels to 30 and 255 by dragging the sliders or typing the values into the fields.**

    Moving the black triangle to the right decreases some of the dark values in the clip; moving the white triangle to the left removes some of the bright values from the clip. In this case, you adjust only the dark values.

26. **Click OK to close the dialog box.**

27. **Preview the clip in the Program view monitor.**

    You see that the clip is brighter and has less diffuse shadow than before adjusting the levels and brightness/contrast.

28. **Save the project.**

    You have added effects to one more clip. You made the clip brighter and clearer using the Levels and Brightness/Contrast effects. The windsurfer and the couple sailing are both clips of some length; correcting their appearance makes a more professional presentation.

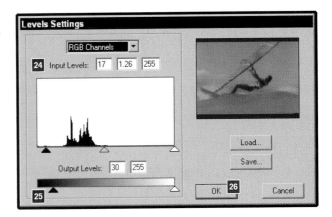

Reusing Settings

As you work with the effects, you may notice that some effects that include setup dialog boxes also include an option to Load or Save settings. For these effects, such as levels, you can set the effect for a clip in your project and then save the settings on your hard drive. This process is especially effective if you are working with several pieces of footage in different projects that were captured at the same time. Any settings that you require for one clip are generally required for another as well. Rather than writing the settings on a piece of paper (which you then lose!) or trying to guess what the settings were, you click the Load button and locate the saved file, and the settings are changed automatically.

Tutorial
» Cropping the Content of Clips

In this tutorial, you work with one of the Transform effects—the Crop effect. You use the effect on the two copies of the tropical drink clip and the final clip of palm trees at night at the end of the project. Trimming the clips centers the content better and also helps to decrease some of the visual shakiness caused by camera shake. You can experiment with an effect called SteadyMove to remove camera shake. Check out *Using the SteadyMove Effect to Decrease Camera Shake* in the Bonus Discussion called *The Finer Points of Premiere Pro's Effects* on the CD to learn how to install and use the effect.

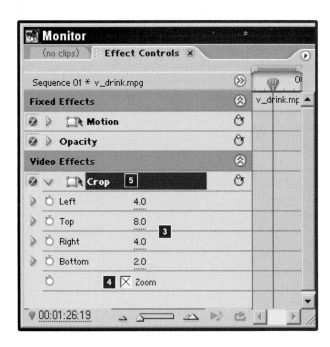

1. Select the first copy of the v_drink.mpg clip in Video 1 at 01:26:03.

2. In the Effects tab, choose Video Effects→Transform→Crop. Drag the effect to the ECW.

3. Click the spindown arrow to open the Crop effect settings. Type these values:
   Left = 4
   Top = 8
   Right = 4
   Bottom = 2
   You see the edges of the clip cropped.

4. Click Zoom.
   The clip resizes itself to fill the screen.

5. Click the effect's label, and choose Edit→Copy (or press Ctrl + C) to copy the effect.

6. In the Timeline, select the v_drink.mpg clip on Video 1 starting at 01:27:13. Choose Edit→Paste, or press Ctrl+V, to paste the effect.
   Leave the same settings because it is a copy of the clip used for transitioning.

7. Select the v_palms_night.mpg clip in Video 1 starting at 01:28:13, and repeat Step 6.

8. **Adjust the settings for the** v_palms_night.mpg **clip as follows:**
   Left = 15
   Top = 0
   Right = 15
   Bottom = 20

9. **Preview the Timeline segment from 01:26:03 to 01:30:28.**
   Both the tropical drink and palm tree clips are more evenly centered on the screen.

10. **Save the project.**
    You added the Crop effect to three clips. The two copies of the tropical drink clip were cropped, as was the final clip of palm trees at night. You have completed adjusting all the clips in the project, and have applied most of the effects to the current contents of the Timeline.

Tutorial
» Using Effects to Create Themes in the Movie

Your project contains several sequences, including a few that show people engaging in different sports. You have the score designed to use different music during the sports segments, and you also use different transitions. For the most part, the sports clips show the action and then end with splashing water. In this tutorial, you add effects to four clips to set off the groups of sports clips. You define a frame of each clip as a poster frame. You have worked with unnumbered markers, but poster frames are numbered 0. You also add second copies of the clips to the Timeline and apply frame holds. Finally, you add effects to the clip copies.

1. **In the Timeline, double-click the** s_surf_white.mpg **clip in Video 1 starting at 33:01 to open it in the Source view monitor.**

2. **Move the CTI to 04:11 in the Source view monitor. Right-click the monitor's Timeline, and choose Set Clip Marker→Other Numbered.** The Set Numbered Marker dialog box opens.

3. **Type O, and click OK to close the dialog box.** A marker numbered O is added to the clip. You use this location to identify the frame for the frame hold.

4. **In the Timeline, click the** s_surf_white.mpg **clip to select it. Choose Edit→Copy, or press Ctrl + C, to copy it.** You paste the clip at the CTI location.

<NOTE>
The marker O you added in Step 3 is shown on the s_surf_white.mpg clip on the Timeline.

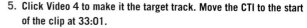

5. **Click Video 4 to make it the target track. Move the CTI to the start of the clip at 33:01.** You add the copy of the clip to the track.

6. **Choose Edit→Paste, or press Ctrl+V, to paste the copy to the designated space on Video 4.** The copy is pasted to Video 4 at the CTI location.

7. **Right-click the copy that you added in Step 6, and choose Frame Hold from the menu that appears.** The Frame Hold Options dialog box opens. You designate a holding frame for the clip.

8. **In the Frame Hold Options dialog box, click Hold On. Choose Marker O from the drop-down list, and click OK to close the dialog box.**

9. **On the Timeline, drag the In point for the clip to snap to the marker 0 location.**

   The clip plays only the designated frame; you want the copy to appear at the same time as the frame in the original.

10. **Drag the Out point for the clip left until the final length is 01:00.**

    In the next tutorial, you set the opacity to fade the clip out using some of the total length. The clip copies use different durations depending on other tracks' content.

11. **Repeat Steps 1 through 6 with the clips listed in Table 11-1. The table defines the clip, the marker location, and the track in which to place the copy of the clip.**

    For some clips, sufficient room exists for a copy of the clip in the track immediately above the orginal clip. In others, there isn't enough room. Place the copy on the designated track at the same start location as the original clip. For example, the `s_jetski.mpg` original clip starts at 01:01:20 in Video 1; place the copy in Video 2 starting at 01:01:20. When the In point is trimmed to the marker 0 location, the clip starts at 01:00:20. Trim the Out point of the clip so the final duration is 01:20.

12. **Repeat Steps 7 and 8 to apply a frame hold to each of the clip copies. Choose Hold On, and choose Marker 0 from the dropdown options.**

13. **In the Timeline, click the `s_surf_white.mpg` clip copy in Video 4 starting at 37:06.**

    You add an effect to the clip copy and modify its opacity.

14. **In the Effects tab, choose Video Effects→Image Control→Color Offset. Drag the effect to the ECW.**

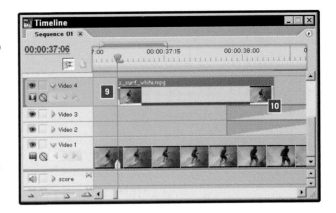

<TIP>

You can test the trimmed copies of the clips to see if you have placed them correctly. Advance the CTI one frame at a time in the area of the marker. You should not be able to tell whether you are seeing the original clip or the copy. If the copy is placed correctly, it seamlessly replaces the original in your Program view monitor.

Table 11-1: Duplicate Clips and Locations in the Timeline

Clip Name	Track	Start Time	Marker	Track for Copy	Paste Copy Starting At	Trim In Point to Start At	Trim Out Point to Final Duration
s_jetski.mpg	Video 1	01:01:20	03:03	Video 2	01:01:20	01:00:20	01:20
s_sail.mpg	Video 1	01:05:29	05:07	Video 2	01:05:29	01:10:12	02:00
s_windsurf.mpg	Video 2	01:16:03	03:07	Video 3	01:16:03	01:18:04	01:17*

* The `s_windsurf.mpg` clip doesn't need the Out point trimmed.

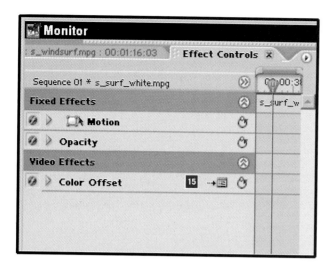

15. Click the Setup icon to open the Color Offset Settings dialog box.

16. In the Color Offset Settings dialog box, click Red and click Right.
The Red channel displaces to the right, showing the red layer in the clip's frame. The other channels automatically displace to the right as well.

17. Drag the Offset slider to a value of 4, or type 4 in the field. Click OK to close the dialog box.
You want the effect sufficiently visible. The Color Offset effect is used for creating a color ghosting effect, as you are using here, or for creating material used with 3-D glasses.

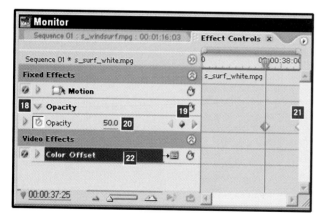

18. Click the spindown arrow to open the Opacity effect.
The Stopwatch icon is selected by default, with a default value of 100.

19. Move the CTI to 37:25. Click the Add Keyframe icon.
A keyframe displays on the ECW.

20. Click the Opacity value, and type 50 to decrease the clip's opacity.

21. Move the CTI to the final frame of the clip at 38:06. Add another keyframe. Set the Opacity of this keyframe to 10.

22. Click the Color Offset effect's label to select it. Choose Edit→Copy, or press Ctrl+C, to copy the effect.

23. Paste the effect to the clips listed in Table 11-2.
The set of four clip copies now contain the Color Offset effect.

24. Repeat Steps 18 through 21 with the clips and times listed in Table 11-2.
Use the same opacity settings as in Steps 18 through 21, and set the keyframes as listed in the table.

25. Preview the clip segments to test each effects clip.

You see the original clip's action, and then the action pauses and fractures into color at the marker frames; the action continues through the colored frame, and the effects clip fades out.

26. Save the project.

You completed some intricate edits and effects settings. You added copies of four sports clips to the Timeline, setting poster frames and trimming the clips according to the poster frame locations. You added a Color Offset effect to add a colored pause in the action, and you modified the opacity to see the underlying clip and faded out the effect.

27. Take a short break. You deserve it.

You have completed the work in the beach segment of the project. In the next tutorial, you start something completely different—you add more Timelines to the project.

Table 11-2: Keyframe Locations and Opacity Settings for Three Clips

Clip Name	Track	Start Time	Keyframe Location for 50% Opacity	Keyframe Location for 10% Opacity
s_jetski.mpg	Video 2	01:00:20	01:01:15	01:02:10
s_sail.mpg	Video 3	01:10:12	01:11:07	01:12:11
s_windsurf.mpg	Video 3	01:18:04	01:19:00	01:19:21

Tutorial
» Adding a New Sequence to the Project

In this tutorial, you work with four copies of the same still image. You use the sequence in the final session to finish off the city segment of the project. Working with a Garbage Matte Key effect, you create the appearance of a clockwise cycling image as the cropped segments of the image appear and disappear. The Garbage Matte Key effect, also used in Session 4, is used to crop out portions of a clip. You create a new sequence, which is displayed in the Timeline tabbed with the original sequence. For more information on creating and using nested sequences, read *Nesting Sequences in Your Project* in the More Premiere Pro Features Bonus Discussion on the CD.

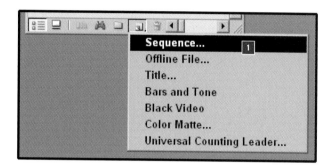

1. **In the Project window, click the New Item icon and choose Sequence.**
   The New Sequence dialog box opens.

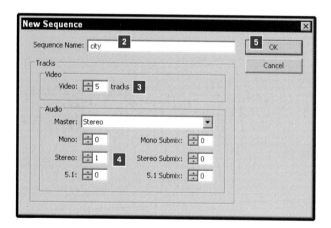

2. **Click the Sequence Name field, and type** city.

3. **Click the Video tracks field, and type** 5.
   You use four tracks to assemble the image and one to hold the matte.

4. **Click the Audio Stereo track, and type** 1.
   Although you don't use audio, the default requires at least one audio track.

5. **Click OK to close the dialog box.**
   The new sequence opens in the Timeline and is listed in the Project window.

6. In the Project window, select the `city1.jpg` clip in the stills bin and drag it to Video 4 in the new city sequence starting at 00:00. Drag the Out point for the clip to 10 frames, ending at 00:10.

7. In the Project window, select the `white_matte` matte file in the titles bin. Drag the clip to Video 5 of the new sequence, placing it at 00:00. Drag the Out point left to 01:00.

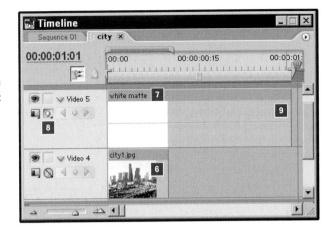

<NOTE>

You need guidelines for arranging the garbage mattes; you use the white matte that you created in an earlier session and then apply and freeze a transition. The borders of the transition are used to organize your garbage matte segments. Perhaps using transitions as guidelines is not as the program designers intended, but it works very well.

8. In Video 5, click the Show Keyframes icon and select Show Opacity Keyframes by clicking its icon.
   You see the gold opacity graph line display across the clip.

9. Click the Pen tool on the toolbar, and drag the Opacity graph line for the white matte clip down to approximately 50 percent.
   You want the clip to be semitransparent so you can see the underlying clips as you apply the garbage mattes.

10. Click the Select tool on the Toolbar to deselect the Pen tool.

11. Click the Show Keyframes icon on Video 5, and select Hide Keyframes by clicking its icon.

12. In the Effects tab, choose Video Transitions→Wipe→Checker Wipe and drag the transition to the white matte in Video 5. Drag its right margin to extend the full length of the clip.

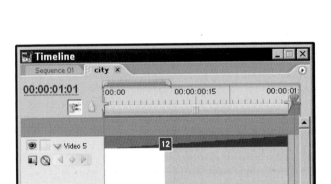

13. In the ECW, modify the transition's settings. Click Custom to open the Checker Wipe settings dialog box. Type 2 for the Horizontal and Vertical slices, and click OK to close the dialog box.

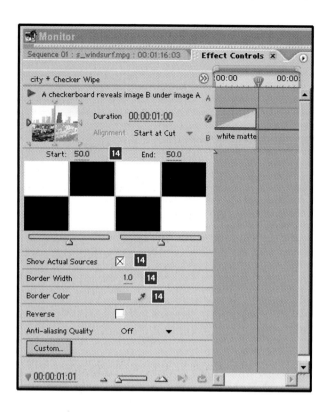

14. In the ECW, modify the transition's settings:
    Set the Start and End values to 50 to freeze the transition.
    Set the Border width to 1 to show the edges of the slices.
    Click Show Actual Sources to see the city image in the top pre-
    view area.
    Click the Border Color Color Swatch, and choose a bright color to
    frame the edges.

<NOTE>
The sample uses RGB=89/237/26 for the bright color framing
the edges.

15. In the Timeline, select the city1.jpg clip.

16. In the Effects tab, choose Video Effects→Keying→Garbage Matte
    and drag the effect to the ECW.

17. Click the spindown arrow to display the Garbage Matte settings.
    Click the Garbage Matte title to display the handles on the
    Program view monitor.
    You resize the matte to the upper-left segment of the window.

18. The top-left location remains stationary. Drag the other handles:
    Move the top-right handle to 160, 0; move the bottom-right handle
    to 160, 120; and move the bottom-left handle to 0, 120.

19. Open the Opacity fixed effect. Set keyframes at 00:00 and 00:10
    with an opacity of 10%. Set keyframes at 00:02 and 00:08 with
    an opacity of 100%.

20. In the Timeline, copy the `city1.jpg` clip in Video 4 starting at 00:00. Paste copies into Video 1 starting at 00:06, Video 2 starting at 00:04, and Video 3 starting at 00:02.

21. In Video 1's copy, revise the Garbage Matte effect's settings: Move the top-left handle to 0, 120; the top-right handle to 160, 120; and the bottom-right handle to 160, 240.
The bottom-left handle doesn't change.

22. In Video 2's copy, move the top-left handle to 160, 120; the top-right handle to 320, 120; and the bottom-left handle to 160, 240.
The bottom-right handle doesn't change.

23. In Video 3's copy, move the top-left handle to 160, 0; the bottom-right handle to 320, 120; and the bottom-left handle to 160, 120.
The top-right handle doesn't move.

24. **Delete the white matte that you added.**
You used it for placement only.

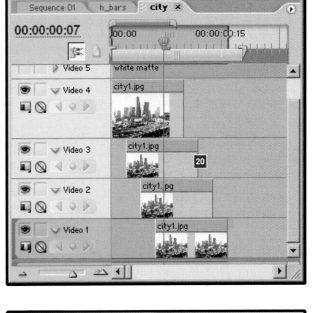

25. **Preview the Timeline in the Program view monitor.**
You see that the clips fade in and out in a clockwise direction as the sequence plays.

26. **Save the project.**
You added another sequence to the project. You created a cyclical animation using copies of the same image and the Garbage Matte Key effect. You used a transition in an unusual way to serve as guidelines for setting the garbage matte dimensions.

Tutorial

» Creating Sequences for Animating Bar Titles

In this tutorial, you add two more sequences to your project. One is for a group of animated horizontal bar titles; the other is for a group of animated vertical bar titles. In the next session, you add several copies of the sequences to the original sequence and apply some effects, change durations, and so on. Using just two additional sequences can create a very sophisticated and complex animation, as you will see.

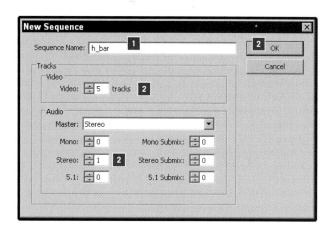

1. **In the Project window, click the New Item icon and choose Sequence. In the New Sequence dialog box, type** h_bars **to name the sequence.**

2. **Click the Video field, and type** 5**; click the Stereo field, and type** 1. **Click OK to close the dialog box.**
   You want five video tracks, and you must have one audio track by default.

3. **In the Timeline, click the tab for the city sequence to make it active and then click x on the tab to close it. Repeat these actions to close Sequence 01.**
   You are finished working with these sequences for now.

4. **Click the h_bar sequence to make it the active sequence.**

5. **Drag a copy of the** h_bar.prt1 **title clip from the titles bin in the Project window to Video 1 at 00:00.**
   Leave the clip selected and the CTI at 00:00.

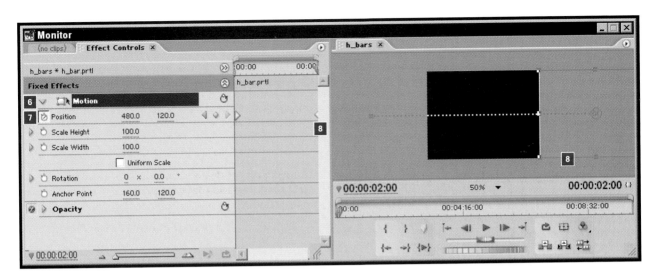

6. **In the ECW, click the spindown arrow to open the Motion settings.**

7. **Click the Position Stopwatch icon to add a Position keyframe at 00:00. Set the position values to** -160, 120.
   The start of the bar is to the left of the screen.

8. **Move the CTI to the end of the clip at 02:00. Set the position values to** 480, 120.
   The bar passes to the right of the screen, as you can see in the Project view monitor with the Motion title selected to highlight the placement handles.

9. **Copy the** h_bar.prtl **on Video 1. Paste copies to Video 2 through Video 5.**
   You adjust their horizontal locations and then make more copies.

10. **In the Timeline, select the** h_bar.prtl **clip on Video 2.**
    You change the bar's y-coordinate position.

11. **In the ECW, change the position at the 00:00 keyframe to** -160, 20 **and the position of the 02:00 keyframe to** 480, 20.
    The animation uses the same x-coordinates; the changes move the path of the bar vertically on the screen.

12. **Repeat Step 11 with the** h_bar.prtl **clips on Video 3, Video 4, and Video 5 with these coordinates:**
    On Video 3, set the y-coordinate to 90 **for both keyframes.**
    On Video 4, set the y-coordinate to 180 **for both keyframes.**
    On Video 5, set the y-coordinate to 220 **for both keyframes.**
    Leave the x-coordinates as they are.

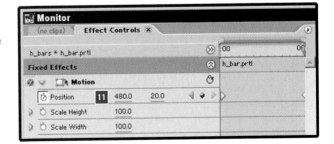

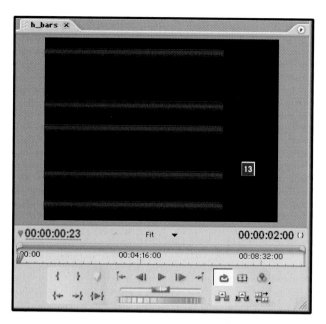

13. **Preview the Timeline from 00:00 to 02:00.**

    You see the set of five lines moving equally from left to right across the screen, distributed vertically.

14. **Copy the clip in each track, and paste two additional copies of each on the Timeline. You have a total of 15 copies of the clip.**

    Stagger the spacing between the clips and the clips' durations. The precise location and duration of each copy isn't critical; the more important factor is to stagger the sequence and duration along the Timeline. The locations used in the sample are shown on the figure.

    <NOTE>

    Experiment with changing the In and Out points on the Timeline and modifying the clip's duration. In the Timeline, when you reset the In or Out points, the animation appears to start and stop at the new In and Out point locations; when you adjust the duration, the entire animation speeds up. Use either or a combination of both methods to stagger the clips.

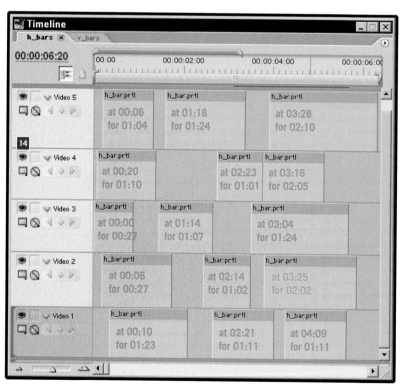

15. In the Project window, click the **New Item** icon and choose **Sequence**. In the New Sequence dialog box, type v_bars to name the sequence.

16. Click the **Video** field, and type 3; click the **Stereo** field, and type 1. **Click OK to close the dialog box.**
    You use fewer tracks for the vertical bar sequence than the horizontal bar sequence.

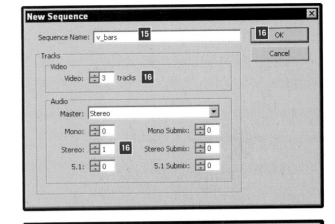

17. Drag the v_bars.prtl clip from the titles bin in the Project window to Video 1 in the new **v_bars** sequence.

18. In the ECW, click the spindown arrow to open the Motion settings.

19. Click the **Position Stopwatch** icon to add a Position keyframe at **00:00.** Set the position values to 160, 120.
    The start of the bar is to the left of the screen.

20. **Move the CTI to the end of the clip at 02:00. Set the position values to** 480, 120.
    The animation shows the vertical bar moving across the screen from left to right, as you can see in the Project view monitor with the Motion title selected to highlight the placement handles.

21. **Copy the** v_bar.prtl **clip in Video 1. Paste two more copies of the** v_bar.prtl **clip on to Video 1.**

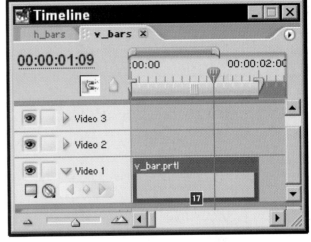

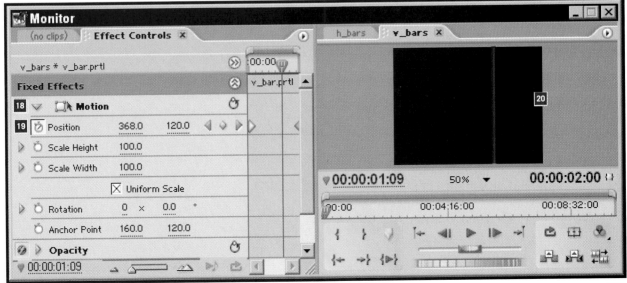

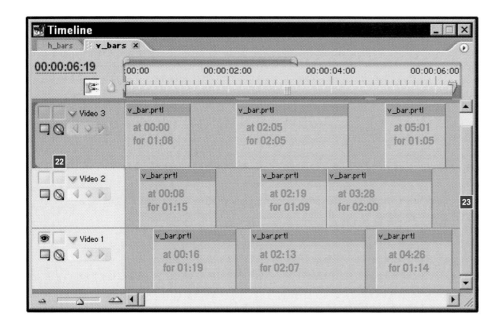

22. **Paste three copies of the** v_bar.prtl **clip to each of Video 2 and Video 3.**

    You have a total of nine copies of the v_bar.prtl clip in the sequence.

23. **Stagger the spacing between the clips and the clips' durations. The precise location and duration of each copy isn't critical.**

    As with the horizontal bar clips, the locations used in the sample are shown on the figure.

24. **Preview the sequence in the Program view monitor.**

    You see the staggered clips moving across the screen from left to right.

25. **Save the project.**

    You added two sequences and animated numerous copies of the title clips.

» Session Review

This session covered some sophisticated clip manipulation. First, you worked with a variety of effects to enhance, correct, and adjust several of your project's clips. You worked with the Color Corrector and other color correction effects to improve the quality of your clips' appearance. You worked with the Color Offset effect to create an unusual effect for several of the sports clips. The first image in this session shows a frame of the jetski clip. The final image in this session shows the same frame, but this time with the second copy of the clip and the Color Offset applied. The effect enhances the sense of motion in an artistic way. You created three additional sequences for your project. You created one sequence using four copies of the same clip, using a garbage matte to create a cycling image. You used a transition as a frame for organizing your matte. You created sequences using both the bar title clips and animated groups of the titles.

As a review of the information in this session, answer the following questions. The answer to each question is in the tutorial noted in parentheses.

1. What effect does keyframing the angle of a light have in an effect such as the Bevel Edges effect? (See Tutorial: Enhancing a Text Title.)

2. How are blur effects different? What does a fast blur refer to? (See Tutorial: Finishing the Palm Tree Track Matte Overlay.)

3. How are effects rendered, or applied, to the frames of your project? (See Tutorial: Finishing the Palm Tree Track Matte Overlay.)

4. Is the Opacity keyframing activated by default? Are other effects, either fixed or standard? (See Tutorial: Finishing the Palm Tree Track Matte Overlay.)

5. Why should you use the Split Screen setting when working with the Color Corrector effect? (See Tutorial: Improving Color in Two Clips.)

6. Why do you sample the image for Black, White, and Gray Points? (See Tutorial: Improving Color in Two Clips.)

7. What is the difference between brightness and gamma? (See Tutorial: Improving Color in Two Clips.)

8. What Input Level slider corresponds with the white triangle in the Levels effects settings dialog box? (See Tutorial: Improving Color in Two Clips.)

9. What effect does selecting the Zoom setting have on a cropped clip? (See Tutorial: Cropping the Content of Clips.)

10. What is a poster frame? How do you define it? (See Tutorial: Using Effects to Create Themes in the Movie.)

11. What is the Color Offset effect used for? (See Tutorial: Using Effects to Create Themes in the Movie.)

12. How can you use a transition as a way to add guidelines for performing other functions in your project? (See Tutorial: Adding a New Sequence to the Project.)

13. Which position coordinate controls the vertical orientation of a clip? (See Tutorial: Creating Sequences for Animating Bar Titles.)

14. How are clips affected visually by setting the In and Out points on the Timeline compared to resetting the duration in the Clip Speed/Duration dialog box? (See Tutorial: Creating Sequences for Animating Bar Titles.)

» Other Projects

Create an alternate way to cycle the clips in the city sequence. Experiment with "unusual" ways to use transitions as you did in the tutorial creating the cycled clips. You can use vertical blinds, for example, for a very different layout.

Experiment with the color correction and image adjustment effects. Correct other clips in your project.

Part VIII

Final Edits
and Exporting

Session 12 **Nesting Sequences and Exporting Your Movie** p 336

Nesting Sequences and Exporting Your Movie

Tutorial: **Nesting Video Sequences in the City Segment**

Tutorial: **Exporting Single Frames from the Project**

Tutorial: **Making a Final Splash**

Tutorial: **Reviewing Your Project**

Tutorial: **Exporting a Movie Segment**

Tutorial: **Sharing Your Movie!**

Tutorial: **Cleaning and Archiving Your Project**

Discussion: **Exporting and Archiving Checklist**

Session Introduction

Your project is nearly complete. At the end of the preceding session, you created several new sequences in the project. In the first tutorials in this session, you add copies of the sequences to the project for some final visual interest in the city segment of the project. Then you check through the project and add a sequence in the beach segment of the project for a final splash.

In this session, you also prepare the project for export and for storage. A checklist is included at the end of the session for you to refer to when you prepare this and future projects. Project cleanup includes several tasks. You remove extra files and remove preview files. The point of cleanup is to minimize storage requirements.

You can export a project from Premiere Pro in many formats. In this session, you export segments of the project in different ways. Using the standard Export Settings, you export six single frames to compose a final sequence. Each frame is exported individually and saved as a bitmap. You export the city segment of the project using the standard Windows AVI file format. You use the Adobe Media Encoder to create a movie using a format native to Windows Media Player. This session has two sample movies: session12.avi, a sample of the completed city segment of the project, and life is a beach.wmv, a Windows Media Player movie of the entire project.

In More Information on Exporting from Premiere Pro, one of the Bonus Discussions on the CD, you will find three discussions about different types of exporting. One discussion provides more information on the basic export process, the second is about the Adobe Media Encoder, and the third is a discussion on how to export to DVD.

TOOLS YOU'LL USE
Adobe Media Encoder, Brightness & Contrast effect, Crop effect, Delete Render Files command, ECW, ECW effect toggle, Export Movie command, Export Movie Settings, New Sequence command, Screen Key effect, Sharpen effect, Timeline, Tint effect, Transcode settings, Unlink Audio and Video command, Windows Explorer, Work Area bar

MATERIALS NEEDED
Session 11 project file that you created, or the session11.prproj file; life is a beach.wmv, session12.avi, girl.bmp, jetski.bmp, surf1.bmp, surf2.bmp, surf3.bmp, woman_dog.bmp

TIME REQUIRED
90 minutes

Tutorial

» Nesting Video Sequences in the City Segment

In the preceding session, you created three new sequences. The first was the city sequence. In this tutorial, you add two copies of that sequence to the main sequence of the project, Sequence 01. Adding sequences into other sequences is called nesting. You treat a sequence like any other type of footage. That is, you can change its duration and speed, add effects, use Fixed Effects, and so on. Be careful when nesting sequences: A sequence includes both audio and video components by default; you use only video components of new sequences in your project. For more information on working with, creating, and using nested sequences, read *Nesting Sequences in Your Project* in the More Premiere Pro Features Bonus Discussion on the CD.

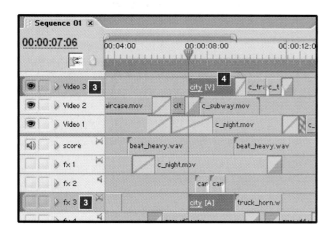

<NOTE>
When the sequence is added to the Timeline, you see that the titles of both the video and audio components are underlined because the two segments are linked, and their format (V) or (A) is shown to the right of the sequence name.

1. **Open Premiere Pro. When the Welcome window opens, choose** `session11.prproj`.
   The Welcome window closes, and the project is loaded into the program.

<NOTE>
If you didn't do the tutorials in Session 11, copy the `session11.prproj` file from the CD to your hard drive. In the Welcome window, choose Open Project. Browse to the location where you stored the copied project file, and select Open. Then resave the project in Premiere Pro as `session12.prproj` (or use another filenaming convention).

2. **Choose File→Save As, and resave the project file as** session12.prproj.
   The name of the new project version displays at the top of the program window.

3. **In the Sequence 01 Timeline (your main project sequence), click the header areas of Video 3 and fx 3 as the target tracks for inserting the new sequence.**
   The targeted track headers are dark gray. Targeting the track prevents adding content to another track accidentally and overlaying existing material.

4. **Select the city sequence in the Project window. Drag it to Video 3 starting at 07:06.**
   The sequence clips are colored gray on the Timeline. You use the sequence to add interest and improve the segue into the picture-in-picture traffic light clips.

5. **Right-click the city sequence, and click Unlink Audio and Video on the menu.**
   The two components are separated.

6. **Select the audio component in fx 3, and delete it.**
   You had to add an audio track when creating the sequence, but you don't use any audio in the sequence.

7. **Drag the right margin of the city sequence clip left to move its Out point. Shorten the sequence to 16 frames.**
When you add the sequence to the Timeline, it uses the program preference of 2 seconds.

8. **Copy the city sequence clip. Click the blank space on the Video 3 track next to the copied clip, and paste a copy of the sequence.**

9. **Move both copies of the clip right on the Timeline.**
The first copy starts at 08:04, and the second ends at 09:06 when the traffic light transition clip begins.

10. **In the Project window, select the h_bars sequence. Drag it to the Sequence 01 Timeline to the gray area below the time ruler.**
A new track is added for the video named Video 10. In addition, a new audio track, Audio 6, is also added.

11. **Right-click the h_bars sequence, and click Unlink Audio and Video on the menu. Delete the audio component in Audio 6.**

12. **In the Project window, select the v_bars sequence and drag it to the Sequence 01 Timeline to the gray area below the time ruler to add one more track.**
The clip is added to Video 11; the v_bars sequence's audio is added to Audio 6.

13. **Right-click the v_bars sequence, and click Unlink Audio and Video on the menu. Delete the v_bars sequence's audio on Audio 6.**

14. **Right-click the h_bars sequence on Video 10 to open the shortcut menu. Choose Speed/Duration to open the Clip Speed/Duration dialog box.**

15. **In the Clip Speed/Duration dialog box, click the Speed field and type 40. Click OK to close the dialog box.**
The clip's duration extends to 15:20.

16. **Repeat Steps 14 and 15 using the v_bars sequence in Video 11. Set the speed to 50%.**
The duration extends to 12:20.

17. **Move v_bars on Video 11 right to start at 01:17.**

18. **Click the h_bars sequence to select it. In the Effects tab, choose Video Effects→Keying→Screen Key. Drag the effect to the ECW.**

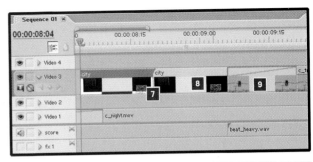

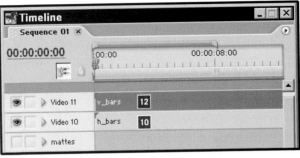

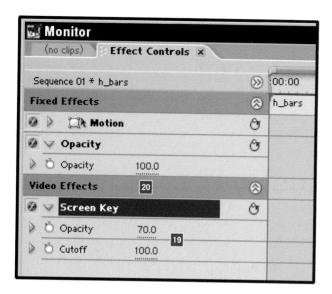

19. Click the spindown arrow to open the Screen Key effect's settings. Click Opacity, and type 70; leave the Cutoff at its default value of 100.

20. Click the Screen Key effect label, and copy the effect.

21. Click the v_bars sequence on Video 11 to select it. Choose Edit→Paste to paste the effect.

22. Preview the city segment of the movie in the Program view monitor. You see the sequences of stripes moving across the screen coordinating the picture-in-picture areas and adding to the overall effect.

23. Save the project. You added the three sequences that you created in the preceding session to the project. Experiment with the sequences. Add more video tracks and use multiple copies of the sequences. Adjust durations for additional effect. Speaking of effects, try some other effects with the sequences as well.

Tutorial
» Exporting Single Frames from the Project

Now that you have added the sequences to the city segment of the movie, it looks quite active. In this tutorial, you learn your first way to export content from Premiere Pro—a single frame. The clips that you create in this tutorial are assembled in a short sequence in the next tutorial to give the beach segment of the project some final punch. In order to activate the Export commands, the Timeline window must be the active window. The set of six images created in this tutorial is on the CD in the frames folder.

1. **Choose Edit→Preferences→Still Images. In the Preferences dialog box, click the Default Duration set at 60 frames and type** 4. You are working with several very short stills; changing the default makes it quicker to work with the set of clips rather than changing durations later.

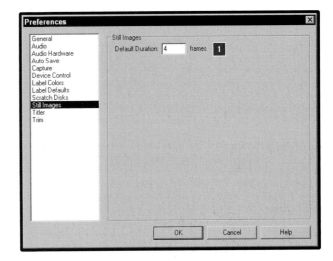

2. **On the Timeline, move the CTI to 30:22 and press * (asterisk) to add an unnumbered marker.**
The marker identifies the location where the first sequence ends.

3. **Move the CTI to 53:12, and press * (asterisk) again to mark the start of the second location to place the sequence.**

4. **Move the CTI to 32:02.**
You export the frame of the s_surf_red.mpg clip at 32:02.

5. Choose File→Export→Frame to open the Export Frame dialog box, and click New Folder. Name the folder frames.

You store the set of six frames in this folder; each frame is added to the Project window as you export it.

The Export settings are listed in the Summary area.

6. Double-click the new folder to open it. Name the exported frame surf1. **Click Save to save the frame.**

<NOTE>

Scroll down the Summary at the bottom of the Export Frame dialog box to see the export settings for the frame. You use the default frame export options, which include the file format (you export as a bitmap), frame size, compressor, and so on.

7. **Move the CTI to 36:23. Choose File→Export→Frame to open the folder that you created in Step 5. Save the frame as** surf2.
The frame is exported and added to the Project window.

<NOTE>

You don't have to add the file format extension; it is added automatically when the frame is saved.

8. **Move the CTI to 40:05. Toggle the visibility of Video 1 and Video 2 to off. Click the** b_woman_dog.mov **clip on Video 3 starting at 37:27.**

   You export a frame of the woman and dog running on the beach, and you don't want any background image or effects.

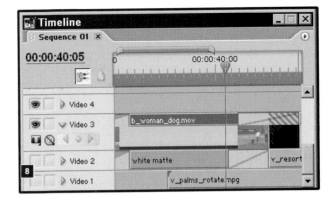

9. **In the ECW, click the** *f* **to the left of Luma Key to toggle the effect to off. Click the 50% Opacity value, and type** 100.

   You remove the effects temporarily.

10. **Choose File→Export→Frame to open the frames folder that you created earlier. Name the frame** woman_dog, **and save it in the frames folder.**

    The still image is added to the Project window.

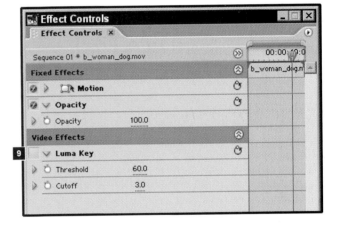

11. **In the ECW, toggle the Luma Key effect to on. Click the 100% Opacity value, and type** 50.

    You restore the effects to the clip.

12. **On the Timeline, toggle Video 1 and Video 2 to on.**

    You exported the frame and now return the Timeline to its original configuration.

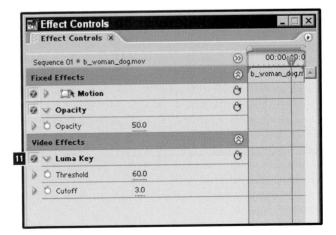

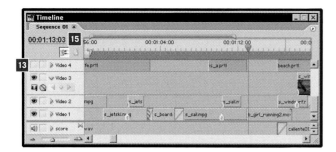

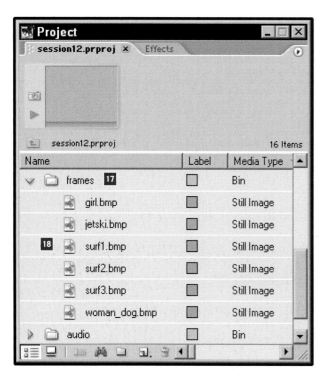

13. **Move the CTI to 01:00:17. Toggle Video 4 to off. Choose File→ Export→Frame to open the frames folder. Name the clip** jetski **and save it in the frames folder. Toggle Video 4 to on again.**
The clip is added to the project.

14. **Move the CTI to 01:03:16. Choose File→Export→Frame to open the frames folder that you created earlier. Name the clip** surf3 **and save it in the frames folder.**
The still image is added to the project.

15. **Move the CTI to 01:13:03. Choose File→Export→Frame to open the** frames **folder. Name the clip** girl **and save it in the frames folder.**
The still image is added to the project.

16. **Toggle Video 4 to on.**
You completed the frame exports.

17. **On the Project window, click New Bin. Name the bin** frames.

18. **Drag the set of six exported still images to the new bin.**

19. **Save the project.**
You exported six frames from the project to use for a final sequence. You used the default export settings, which include adding the exported product back into the open Project window. You created a new bin in the project to hold the new clips.

Which Settings Are Used for Exporting?

You can export material from your project for use on other devices and in other programs in many, many ways. You work with exported frames in this tutorial; Premiere Pro processes the frames using the original Project Settings that you established when you started the project and then adjusts them depending on what you choose in the Export Settings dialog box. In this tutorial, you used the defaults, so you made no changes to the Export Settings. In this session, you export your movie in both standard export formats (as frames and an AVI movie) and Windows Media format.

For DVD recordings, you start with the options selected in your original project settings, and then the project is processed using the settings in the Export to DVD dialog box. Web media and MPEG formats start with the settings in the Project Settings, and then the project is processed using settings from the Adobe Media Encoder dialog box. For other types of output, such as recording to tape, you use the Project Settings only. For more information on exporting, see the More Information on Exporting from Premiere Pro Bonus Discussion on the CD.

Tutorial
» Making a Final Splash

The beach segment features a very definite sound change when the score changes from the beach to sports music. The options for adding something visually exciting are almost endless. Whatever you decide to use should correspond and coordinate both with the existing material and the music. In this tutorial, you create one final sequence. Although you could use copies of the original clips and apply frame holds, you exported a set of clips from the original Timeline in the preceding tutorial. You use the set of new clips for the final sequence.

1. **In the Project window, choose the New Item icon and click Sequence on the menu to open the New Sequence dialog box. Use these settings:**
   Name the new sequence beach**, type** 1 **in the Video tracks field, and type** 1 **in the Audio tracks field. Click OK to close the dialog box.**
   The sequence is added to the project and opened in the Timeline.

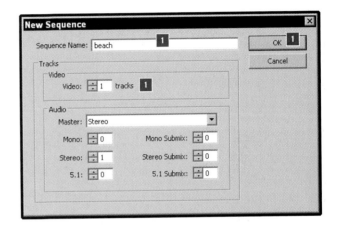

2. **In the beach sequence, add the new clips to Video 1 in this order:**
   jetski.bmp
   surf1.bmp
   girl.bmp
   surf2.bmp
   woman_dog.bmp
   surf3.bmp

3. Click `jetski.bmp` starting at 00:00 to select it. In the ECW, add these effects from the Video Effects folder in the Effects tab (in this order):

Blur & Sharpen→Sharpen
Adjust→Brightness & Contrast
Image Control→Tint
Transform→Crop

4. Adjust the settings for each clip as listed in Table 12-1.

All six clips use the same four effects. In all cases, click the Zoom setting in the Crop effect to resize the image. All Tint values are shown as RGB values.

Table 12-1: Video Effects Settings for the Beach Sequence Clips

Effect	Value	jetski.bmp	surf1.bmp	girl.bmp	surf2.bmp	woman_dog.bmp	surf3.bmp
Sharpen	Amount	10	30	30	15	60	50
Brightness & Contrast	Brightness	25	40	30	65	20	30
	Contrast	45	45	60	60	60	50
Tint	Map Black to	128/62/169	199/38/57	199/102/22	42/42/71	255/255/255	20/115/20
	Map White to	222/47/255	154/182/173	241/229/63	37/55/219	224/96/36	116/201/115
	Amount to Tint	50	65	50	45	50	60
Crop	Left	11	0	24	17	24	6
	Top	20	7	15	9	20	15
	Right	5	19	1	17	13	15
	Bottom	7	0	2	26	16	6

5. **Preview the sequence in the Program view monitor.**
   You see a rapid change from one high-contrast and highly colored image to the next. The set of clips is 00:24 in length.

6. **In Sequence 01, click Video 4 and fx 3 to target the tracks.**
   You add the first copy of the beach sequence to the targeted tracks.

7. **Drag the beach sequence from the Project window to Video 4 starting at 29:28 and ending at the unnumbered marker at 30:22.**
   The audio and video segments of the sequence are added to the Timeline.

8. **Right-click the beach sequence, and choose Unlink Audio and Video. Click the audio track in fx 3 starting at 29:28, and press Delete.**
   The video segment of the sequence remains.

9. **Preview the sequence in the Program view monitor from 29:28 to 30:22.**
   You see that the new sequence hides the title in Video 3.

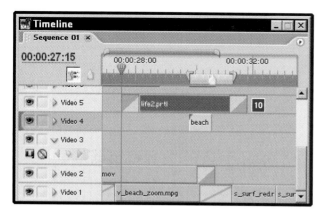

10. **Drag** life2.prt1 **from Video 3 starting at 27:15 to Video 5 starting at 27:15.**

    You superimpose the title on top of the beach sequence. Now the title plays on top of the beach sequence. If you want, you can move both the beach sequence and life2.prt1 clips down one track to fill the gap in Video 3. It depends on your sense of neatness!

11. **Copy the sequence in Video 4.**

    You paste a second copy of the sequence at the second unnumbered marker; use the unlinked copy on the Timeline.

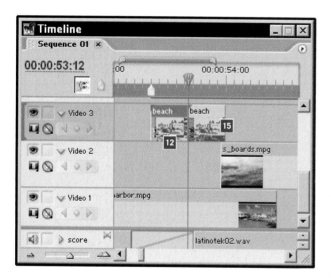

12. **Move the CTI to the unnumbered marker at 52:24. Paste the copy of the sequence on Video 3 starting at 52:24.**

13. **Right-click the beach sequence starting at 52:24, and choose Speed/Duration from the menu.**

    The Clip Speed/Duration dialog box opens.

14. **In the Clip Speed/Duration dialog box, decrease the duration to 00:18.**

    The clip shortens on the Timeline.

15. **Copy the shortened beach sequence ending at 53:12. Paste a copy next to the first one, starting at 53:12 and ending at 54:00.**

16. **Preview the segment in the Program view monitor from approximately 50:00 to 55:00.**

    You see the sequence's images flash, and the sequence plays twice as the music changes from the beach theme to the sports theme.

17. **Save the project.**

    You added the final sequence to your project. You adjusted and modified the sequence of stills to add a final graphical flash to the project.

Tutorial

» Reviewing Your Project

Before you export a finished movie, go through the project slowly and carefully. Look for inconsistencies, adjust settings if necessary, and nudge clips as necessary. In this tutorial, you move through your project one last time. No hard and fast rule exists for how to do a final project check, but this is one way.

1. **Display all the tracks in your project.**
   You need to see the entire Timeline to evaluate its contents.

2. **Check the coordination of the audio and video tracks.**
   Check that the audio and video portions of clips start at the same location on the Timeline. The project includes one instance of an out-of-sync clip. You will recall that the sound of the street was shifted to start before the video starts at the beginning of the project.

3. **Check all audio clips containing effects.**
   Test and adjust effect sequences as necessary. For clips with both track and clip effects, make sure that the overall outcome is correct.

4. **Check the audio transitions.**
   Check that crossfades are present between audio clips where they should be and that their lengths coordinate with the clips.

5. **Open the video tracks.**
   Click the arrows to the left of the track names to expand the tracks.

6. **Check all clips containing video effects.**
   All clips with applied effects have a colored stripe below the clip's name on the Timeline. Test and adjust effects as necessary. Check the clips with multiple effects. Effects effects render in the order listed in the ECW; make sure you are satisfied with the application sequence. For example, a clip with both a shadow and a blur effect looks different depending on the order of the effects in the ECW listing.

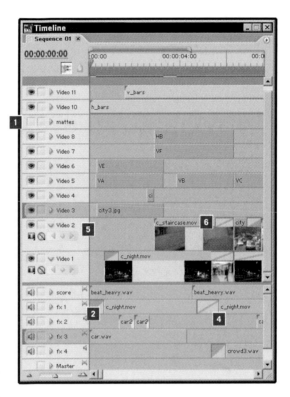

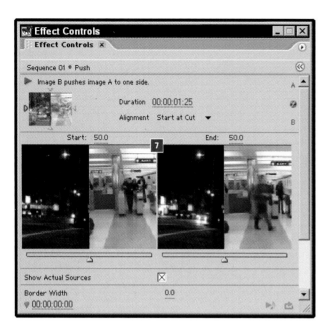

7. **Check the transitions for length and settings.**
Open the ECW for each transition and check the settings, in particular the start/end points. If you have previewed any transition in the Transition Settings dialog box, check that you returned the slider to the correct start/end points. The exceptions are the frozen transitions.

8. **Preview any segments of the project that you changed in the Program view monitor.**
Check the movie one last time.

9. **Save the project.**
You reviewed the content of the project, opening and displaying tracks looking for inconsistencies that could create errors when you export the project.

View the Final Sequences

You can see a copy of the finished project's Timelines on the CD. The file, timelines.pdf, is in the samples folder. It includes the Sequence 01 Timeline, as well as the additional sequences that you created in the last sessions. You cannot export the content from Premiere Pro as you see in the file; it was composited from a number of screenshots.

Tutorial

» Exporting a Movie Segment

In the first session, you chose project settings that you have used throughout the project. In this tutorial, you learn how to format your movie for export using a basic Microsoft AVI format. You export the movie after modifying some of the original project settings. In this tutorial, you modify the settings for using the movie in a smaller, compressed version. Due to the size of the finished file, the tutorial and the sample file describe how to export the city segment only—that is, the first 18:15 of the movie. Although AVI files are large in size, they are quickly processed and good for testing output. If you choose to open the movie in your project when it is rendered, you can easily view it.

1. **On the Sequence 01 Timeline, drag and resize the Work Area bar to include the segment from 00:00 to 18:15.**
   You export only the city segment of the movie using the Work Area as a defined segment for export.

2. **Choose File→Export→Movie to open the Export Movie dialog box.**

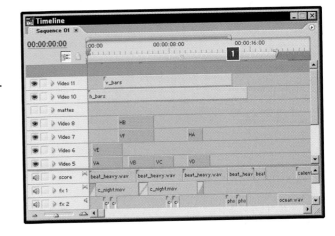

3. **The file is named** session12.avi **by default. Name your movie** city.avi. **Click Settings to open the Export Movie Settings dialog box.**
   The dialog box is composed of four panels.

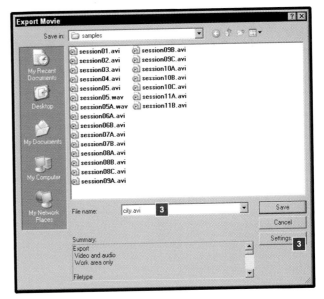

4. **The General panel is displayed. Choose these settings (or leave the defaults):**
   File Type: Microsoft AVI (default)
   Range: Work Area Bar
   Export Video, Export Audio, Add to Project When Finished (default)

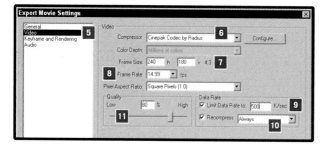

5. **Click the Video listing at the left of the Export Movie Settings dialog box.**
   The Video options display in the dialog box.

6. **Select Cinepak Codec by Radius from the Compressor drop-down menu.**
   A codec compresses the video data for saving, and then decompresses it for playback. The Cinepak codec offers good general compression.

< T I P >

Click Configure to display the settings if the codec you choose is configurable; the option is grayed out for nonconfigurable codecs. The Cinepak codec, for example, allows you to choose from either color or black and white output.

7. **Set the Frame Size to** 240 **pixels horizontally (h) and** 180 **pixels vertically (v) in the Export Movie Settings window.**
   The frame size is adequate for clear viewing and saves file space by being smaller than the default frame size. As you change the values, you see the ratio next to the v value change as well. You maintain the project's 4:3 aspect ratio.

8. **Choose 14.99 from the Frame Rate drop-down menu.**
   The 14.99 frame rate is precisely half the original project rate, which contributes to speedier processing.

9. **Click the check box to the left of the Limit Data Rate option, and type** 500 **in the Limit Data Rate to field.**
   Playback may be smoother if you limit how much data is processed at one time.

10. **Select Recompress, and choose Always from the drop-down menu.**
    Each frame of the project is compressed when it is exported.

11. **Drag the Quality slider left to 80%.**
    The exported movie is at high quality, which is adequate.

Tradeoffs

The Microsoft AVI movie that you produce in this tutorial is small in dimension but over 6MB in file size. You must always weigh file size against image quality, sound quality, and smooth motion. File size increases with a larger frame size. If you use a low data rate, the output is pixelated. If you use a codec for the audio or a high interleave setting, you may have a smaller file size but poor sound quality. For example, the project settings that you use may result in some audio pops due to the interleave and low sample rate; the video may stutter or skip frames. Experiment with different settings using a few seconds of the movie. In the next tutorial, you prepare another copy of the movie, this one using a WMV (Windows Media Video) format that is smaller in size, but it allows for a larger frame size and higher frame rate for more clarity.

12. **Click Keyframe and Rendering to display Keyframe and Rendering settings.**

13. **Select Optimize Stills.**
Optimizing stills saves processing time. Rather than rendering a still image once for each frame for the length of time it appears, the image is rendered only once.

14. **Click Add Keyframes at Edits.**
Rendering keyframes refers to producing output. The codec you chose for the export allows for setting keyframes, which is an efficient way to process information. Rather than processing all the information in all the frames, each edit is rendered, and then only changes between keyframes are processed.

15. **Click Audio to display the Audio options.**

16. **Choose the Microsoft ADPCM from the Compressor drop-down menu.**
You can use several different audio codecs; they compress and decompress the audio information just as the video codecs do.

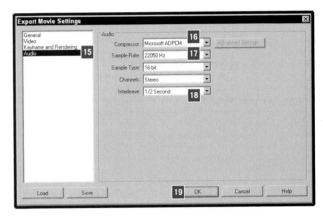

17. **Choose 22050 Hz from the Rate drop-down menu.**
The project settings used a 44100 Hz rate, which works well for screen playback, but it isn't necessary for Web playback. The higher rate adds to file size. Your project uses 16-bit Stereo format, so you don't have to change the settings.

18. **Set the Interleave rate to** 1/2 Second.
The interleave rate specifies how often audio information is inserted into the video frames in the exported movie. For every one-half second of video playback, one-half second of audio is loaded into RAM and plays.

19. **Click OK to close the Export Movie Settings dialog box and return to the Export Movie dialog box.**

20. **Click Save on the Export Movie dialog box.**
A Rendering dialog box displays.

21. **Click the Spindown arrow to view the details of the render.**
The render time depends on the speed of your processor, memory available, and the impact of any other programs that you may have running. Click Cancel if you want to stop the process.

22. **Preview the finished movie, which is added to the Project window.**
You chose Export Settings and produced a small movie using the default AVI export format. For information on exporting to other standard formats, see *Other Export Formats* in the More Information on Exporting from Premiere Pro Bonus Discussion on the CD.

Tutorial
» Sharing Your Movie!

In the preceding tutorial, you exported a segment of the movie using the basic Export Settings, which are based on the Project Settings that you chose when you first started the project. Premiere Pro contains the Adobe Media Encoder, which is a separate exporting engine. The Adobe Media Encoder has an astoundingly large range of options that you can use for exporting in MPEG, QuickTime, RealMedia, and Windows Media formats. In this tutorial, you export your entire project in a format for playback on the Windows Media Player. The format chosen is designed for Windows Media Player 9. If you have Version 8, choose the preset listed in the tutorial; upgrade to a new version if you are using Version 7 or older.

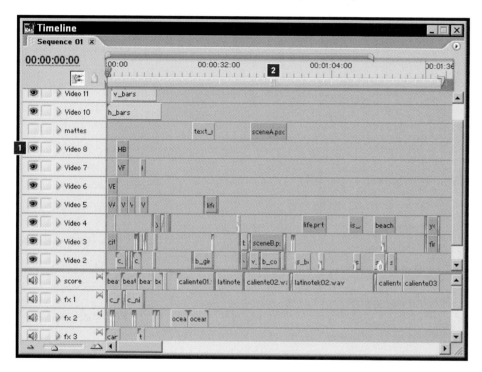

1. **Make sure that all the tracks that you want included in the movie are toggled on.**

   The video tracks should display the eye icon, and the audio tracks the speaker icon. Remember that the mattes track is turned off in order to work correctly.

2. **Double-click the beige Work Area bar to extend it the length of the project.**

   The export is based on the defined work area.

3. **Choose File→Export→Adobe Media Encoder.**

   The Transcode Settings dialog box opens.

Exporting Your Movie to Other Programs

You may want to use your movie in other programs such as Adobe After Effects, Adobe Acrobat, or Macromedia Flash. Plan for use in other programs before you export. If the receiving project is intended for cross-platform use, use codecs and formats such as QuickTime. If your movie needs transparency for use in another program, maintain alpha channel transparency on export. If you have the hard drive space, export your Premiere movie without any compression. This preserves the best picture quality. In addition to using your finished movie as part of an After Effects project, you can export an entire Premiere project for use in After Effects.

Settings for the chosen preset are listed here.

The audience corresponding to the selected preset is listed here.

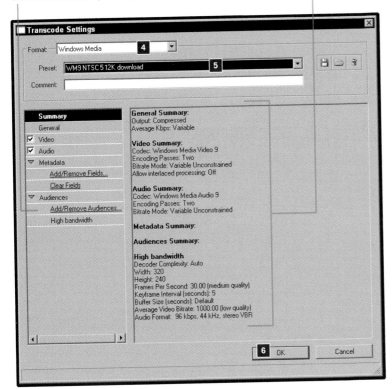

4. Click the Format drop-down menu, and choose Windows Media.
The Preset options change to the Windows Media presets.

<NOTE>
You can also choose different MPEG1 and MPEG2 formats, QuickTime, and RealMedia. If you choose QuickTime, you must have QuickTime 6.0 components installed in your system.

5. Click the Preset drop-down menu, and choose WM9 NTSC 512K download.
This format is a cable modem or broadband-level output. It uses NTSC format because you chose NTSC-format options when the project was started. If you used a PAL preset when you created the project, you have PAL-format options. The same applies if you use a DV (digital video) preset.

<NOTE>
If you don't have Windows Media Player 9 installed, choose a Windows Media Player 8 preset or upgrade to version 9.

<NOTE>
The basic settings for the preset are constant in the Windows Media format. The option chosen in the tutorial is compressed and uses a variable bit rate. It uses the Windows Media Video 9 and the Windows Media Audio 9 codecs. The movie output uses your project's size, 320 x 240 pixels, a frame rate of 30 fps, and keyframes every 5 seconds.

6. Click OK to close the Transcode Settings and open the Save File dialog box.

7. **Browse to the location where you want to store the finished movie. In the File Name field, type** Life is a Beach**. Choose Work Area from the Export Range drop-down menu.**
   The only Save As type available is based on your Transcode Settings options—in this case, Windows Media.

<TIP>

If you click Settings, you reopen the Transcode Settings dialog box.

8. **Click Save to close the dialog box and start the rendering process.**
   The Rendering dialog box displays.

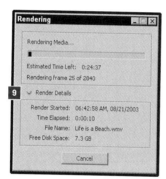

9. **Click the spindown arrow to display information about the rendering process.**
   Click Cancel if you need to stop the rendering process.

10. **Take the dog for a walk.**
    The Render process can be quite lengthy (up to an hour or more) depending on your computer's capacity, other programs running, the settings chosen, and the length and complexity of the movie. The WMV format uses two encoding passes for each of the video and audio components. That is, the entire movie is rendered twice, and then the information combined.

11. **On the desktop, choose Start→Programs→Windows Media Player.**
    Now that the movie is rendered, you can view the movie in the external player.

<NOTE>

You can also import the movie into Premiere Pro for playback. It won't automatically be added to the project as with the AVI or frames that you exported earlier in the session by leaving the default to place a copy into the open project.

12. **Choose File→Open. Browse to the location where you stored the movie. Select it, and open it in the Windows Media Player.**

13. **Click Play to play the movie.**

Send copies to friends and family! You created a Windows Media version of the movie using the Adobe Media Encoder. For information on exporting the movie directly to DVD, see *Exporting to DVD* in the More Information on Exporting from Premiere Pro Bonus Discussion on the CD.

Customizing Settings

In the Transcode Settings dialog box, you can choose from a vast array of options. You can also define custom settings for Metadata and the Audience. Metadata is information about the project that is stored in its file as XML data. Click the Metadata spindown arrow to display options, and click Add/Remove Fields to open the dialog box shown here. You can select from the range of options or add a new field. Click New Field to open a small dialog box for identifying the type of data and a description. In this case, the metadata is named "project name" and the description is "Life is a Beach" as shown in the dialog box. Click OK to close the dialog box. If you make changes to the metadata, you are instructed to name the preset before you can process the file.

The general audience is displayed based on the settings chosen. In the project, you use the Broadband or cable modem settings for that audience. Click Audience in the Summary list to open a dialog box listing the options shown here. If you choose another audience, you must again name the preset before processing.

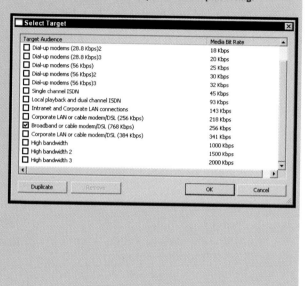

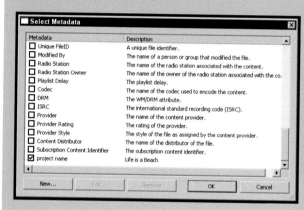

Tutorial

» Cleaning and Archiving Your Project

In this tutorial, you clean up the project and prepare it for archiving by deleting files created as you developed your project. Each time you create a new project file, as with the series of sessions in this book, a new auto-save, preview, and CFA (Conformed Audio) folder is created. Each project file auto-saves up to five copies, depending on the preference setting; each project file creates its own preview folder, and each project file creates its own CFA folder, as each audio file used in the project file is reprocessed. The conformed audio for session 12, for example, is over 50MB in size. If you are storing your project at completion, delete the files to save hard drive space. The folders removed from my hard drive, for example, were .97GB in size, which is lots of hard drive space devoted to unnecessary storage.

1. **Right-click the time ruler on the Timeline, and choose Clear Timeline Marker→All Markers.**
   All markers on the Timeline are removed, including In and Out point markers and both unnumbered and numbered markers.

2. **Choose Sequence→Delete Render Files.**
   A confirmation dialog box opens. The confirmation dialog box explains that preview files are rendered files saved on disk and that deleting the files means you will have to render them again.

3. **Read the confirmation dialog box. Click OK.**
   The dialog box closes, and the files are removed from your hard drive.

<NOTE>
Don't delete the rendered files unless your movie is complete to your satisfaction. Otherwise, if you make changes and then have to export the file again, the project must be rendered again, which may take a lot of time.

4. **Expand the Project window. Open each folder. Scroll right to display the Video Usage column.**
   As you scroll down the list, you see that all files are used except the city.avi movie that you created earlier in the session. The additional sequences that you created were added to Sequence 01 and defined as video clips.

5. **Repeat Step 4 for the Audio files, using the Audio Usage column.**
   If you have a number of clips to delete, click the Video Usage or Audio Usage column heading to sort the contents of the project based on the number of times the clip is used in the project. Select the clips that aren't used, and press Delete to remove them from the project.

6. **Click the city.avi clip in the Project window, and click Delete to remove it.**

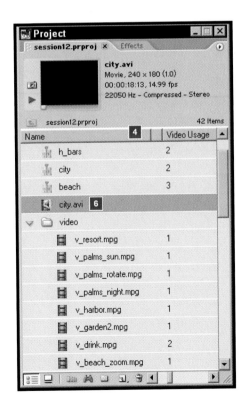

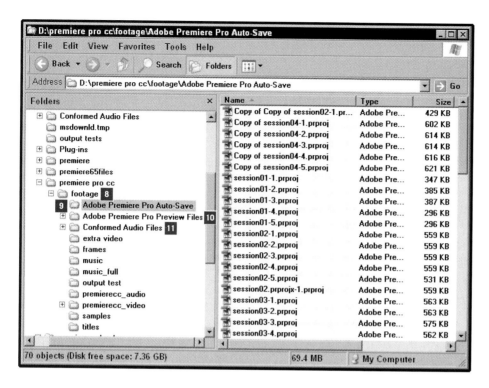

7. **Save the project, and close Premiere Pro.**
You cleaned the final project file.

8. **On the desktop, right-click Start and choose Explore.**
Windows Explorer opens. Browse to the location where you stored your project files.

9. **Click Adobe Premiere Pro Auto-Save to display the files for each session.**
Select the group of files and delete them.

10. **Click Adobe Premiere Pro Preview Files to display folders for each session. Select the group of files, and delete them.**
The number of files varies with the number of previews that you made.

11. **Click Conformed Audio Files (a folder is added for each project file) to display the folders for each session. Select the group of files, and delete them.**
The Conformed Audio Files are stored on your hard drive. Each time you make a new project file, each audio file is processed and information stored in this folder. Once you have finished working with a project file, you no longer need its conformed audio files.

Discussion
Exporting and Archiving Checklist

At the start of this session, I suggested that you use a checklist to prepare your project for export and archiving. You have followed that checklist as you worked through this session. Table 12-2 lists the items to check before you finish your project.

Table 12-2: Exporting and Archiving Checklist

Be sure to ...	Because ...
Turn on tracks	Only visible tracks are exported.
Take one last, slow look	You may see inconsistencies when you view the entire project in total that you didn't notice when working on different segments.
Delete markers	Markers aren't required for a completed project.
Define output requirements	Defining the criteria for exporting makes the most efficient and effective file depending on the type of output.
Export and test	Testing the output settings and adjusting and rebuilding until you are pleased with the results is your safest bet.
Remove extra files	You want to save storage space.
Delete previews	Previews aren't required, and they take lots of room to store.
Delete auto-save files	You have final copies of each session's project, and you don't need copies.
Delete conformed audio folder	Audio is reconformed when a project is reopened, so it isn't necessary to save the stored copies.

» Session Review

This session brings your first adventure in video-making to a close. I am sure it has been a worthwhile and interesting experience for you; my hope is that I have been able to share some of my enthusiasm for the art and science involved.

In this session, you learned a method for making a final review of the project before exporting. Why review before export? As you learned when you finished defining the export settings and clicked that Save button, producing the finished movie can take a significant amount of time depending on the rendering circumstances. Waiting for a movie to render and then finding an error when you run the movie isn't a pleasant experience, especially when you are working to meet a deadline.

In this session, you learned how to nest sequences within one another. The image at the start of this session shows the city segment of the project before adding the nested sequences. You saw how much time can be saved constructing a sequence and then reusing it within another sequence as you would any other type of clip. The effects that you created with the bar title animations, like those shown in the final image in this session, would be very time consuming if you had to build them manually. You also learned to export single frames for a new sequence, and then you nested the sequence to finish the beach segment.

You made two movies in this final session. Along with the excitement of producing a finished product, you learned how to prepare the project for archiving.

Here are questions to help you review the information in this session. You'll find the answer to each question in the tutorial noted in parentheses.

1. Is a sequence created as a movie clip? How does it appear when added to another sequence? (See Tutorial: Nesting Video Sequences in the City Segment.)

2. Can you define the tracks to which a clip is added? How? Can you define both audio and video? (See Tutorial: Nesting Video Sequences in the City Segment.)

3. When is it a good idea to change the project preferences for still image length? (See Tutorial: Exporting Single Frames from the Project.)

4. When you resize a clip using the Crop effect, how can you expand the remaining clip to fill the screen? (See Tutorial: Making a Final Splash.)

5. In what order do effects render in a clip? (See Tutorial: Reviewing Your Project.)

6. Why do you use a codec when exporting a movie? (See Tutorial: Exporting a Movie Segment.)

7. What does it mean to optimize a still? (See Tutorial: Exporting a Movie Segment.)

8. How are the Transcode Settings defined? How do the settings that you can choose relate to the project settings that you used when the project was created? (See Tutorial: Sharing Your Movie!)

9. Can you change the individual settings in the Transcode Settings dialog box? (See Tutorial: Sharing Your Movie!)

10. If you delete render files, can they be restored? (See Tutorial: Cleaning and Archiving Your Project.)

11. Why will some sequence files display Video Usage while others don't? (See Tutorial: Cleaning and Archiving Your Project.)

» Other Projects

Before you started the sessions, you created an animated logo. Revisit that project. Make changes and modifications based on your newly acquired skills. Customize the logo, and attach it to your book project for a complete presentation.

View and review the project carefully. Where can you change the clip's arrangements? What other effects can you use to enhance the project? Please experiment with more effects. The effects used were chosen partially for what they could demonstrate as well as how they impact the project within the time limits allotted for each session.

Part IX
Bonus Material:
CD-ROM Only

Bonus Session 1 **Creating Project Titles and Graphics**   see CD-ROM

Bonus Discussion 1 **More Premiere Pro Features**   see CD-ROM

Bonus Discussion 2 **More Information on Exporting from Premiere Pro**
see CD-ROM

Bonus Discussion 3 **The Finer Points of Premiere Pro Effects**
see CD-ROM

Appendix A

What's on the CD-ROM?

This appendix provides you with information on the contents of the CD-ROM that accompanies this book. For the latest and greatest information, please refer to the ReadMe file located at the root of the CD-ROM. Here is what you find:

» System Requirements

» Using the CD-ROM with Windows XP

» What's on the CD-ROM

» Troubleshooting

System Requirements

Make sure that your computer meets the minimum system requirements listed in this section. If your computer doesn't match up to these requirements, you may have a problem using the contents of the CD-ROM.

For Windows XP

» Intel® Pentium® III 800MHz processor (Pentium 4 3.06GHz recommended)

» Microsoft® Windows® XP Professional or Home Edition with Service Pack 1

» 256MB of RAM installed (1GB or more recommended)

» 800MB of available hard-disk space for installation

» CD-ROM drive

» Compatible DVD recorder (DVD-R/RW+R/RW) required for Export to DVD

» 1,024x768 32-bit color video display adapter (1,280x1,024 or dual monitors recommended)

» For DV: OHCI-compatible IEEE 1394 interface and dedicated large-capacity 7200RPM UDMA 66 IDE or SCSI hard disk or disk array

» For third-party capture cards: Adobe® Premiere® Pro certified capture card

» Optional: ASIO audio hardware device; surround speaker system for 5.1 audio playback

Using the CD-ROM

To install the items from the CD-ROM to your hard drive, follow these steps:

1. Insert the CD-ROM into the CD-ROM drive.

2. The interface launches. If you have autorun disabled, click Start→Run. In the dialog box that appears, type D:\setup.exe. Replace *D* with the proper letter if the CD-ROM drive uses a different letter. (If you don't know the letter, see how the CD-ROM drive is listed under My Computer.) Click OK. A license agreement appears.

3. Read through the license agreement, and then click the Accept button if you want to use the CD-ROM. (After you click Accept, the License Agreement window never bothers you again.) The CD-ROM interface Welcome screen appears.

4. The interface coordinates installing the programs and running the demos. The interface basically enables you to click a button or two to make things happen.

5. Click anywhere on the Welcome screen to enter the interface. This next screen lists categories for the software on the CD-ROM.

6. For more information about a program, click the program's name. Be sure to read the information that appears. Sometimes a program has its own system requirements or requires you to do a few tricks on your computer before you can install or run the program. This screen tells you what you may need to do.

7. If you don't want to install the program, click the Back button to return to the previous screen. You can always return to the previous screen by clicking the Back button. Using this feature, you can browse the different categories and products, and then decide what you want to install.

8. To install a program, click the appropriate Install button. The CD-ROM interface drops to the background while the CD-ROM installs the program you chose.

9. To install other items, repeat Step 8 for each program.

10. When you finish installing programs, click the Quit button to close the interface. You can eject the CD-ROM now. Carefully place it back in the plastic jacket of the book for safekeeping.

<NOTE>

Use the interface to install the project files on your hard drive rather than installing them directly from the CD-ROM. Do not work on the project using the files directly from the CD-ROM. Premiere Pro doesn't store content in project files, but uses links to file locations. Unless you copy the session project files and the footage files to your hard drive, each time you start working on your project, you have to use the book's CD-ROM. You save your project files locally as well. I suggest that you instruct Windows to display the filename extensions of the copied tutorial files, if it isn't already set up to show them, so that you can see the file formats (e.g., .ppj, .mpg, and .mov, and so on). Find your Folder Options dialog box in the Appearance and Themes Control Panel. Click the View tab. Click Hide File Extensions for Known File Types to deselect it.

Each session has its own project file. When you first open a project file, Premiere Pro may ask you for file locations. This is so Premiere Pro can establish links to the files it needs. If you work on a single session more than once, you won't have to identify file locations.

What's on the CD-ROM

The following sections provide a summary of the software and other materials you find on the CD-ROM.

Author-created materials

All author-created material from the book, including project files, source material, and samples, are on the CD-ROM in the folder named Footage. This folder contains numerous files and subfolders.

Files within the main footage folder include:

» `session01.prproj` through `session12.prproj`. These are the 12 Premiere Pro project files created for each session.

» confidence builder—This folder contains five files; the sound, image, title and project file required to complete the introductory tutorials as well as a movie of the completed logo.

» extra music—This folder contains the two pieces of source music used to create the clips you use in this project. It also contains one additional piece of music in its entirety supplied by Studio Cutz music library.

» frames—This folder contains six exported frame image files used as a separate sequence in the final session of your project.

» music—This folder contains five music clips used for the beach segment of the project.

» premierecc_audio—This folder contains eight sound effects files used in the project.

» premierecc_video—This folder contains 36 files used in your project. The folder includes movie and video clips as well as several still images.

» samples—This folder contains different types of files used as samples to show you different aspects of the project as you are working through the sessions. All sessions have at least one sample file; some have as many as three sample files. The folder also includes a PDF file showing the finished Timeline for the project.

» titles—This folder contains fourteen files used as titles or masks in your project. One of the Photoshop files is used for extra work in the bonus discussion on the CD.

Bonus Material

There is a Bonus Material folder on the CD. It contains four bonus documents with additional information about the project and about working with Premiere Pro. The four files are:

» Bonus Session 1, Creating Project Titles and Graphics

» Bonus Discussion 1, More Premiere Pro Features

» Bonus Discussion 2, More Information on Exporting from Premiere Pro

» Bonus Discussion 3, The Finer Points of Premiere Pro's Effects

Applications

The following applications are on the CD-ROM.

Studio Cutz Music Library demo from Mediatone Music, Inc.

Listen to the wide range of music available from Studio Cutz to use in your projects. Music is available in a number of formats, and you can choose from individual selections for immediate download or order CD compilations. The music used in the book's project is from Studio Cutz. For more information, visit their site at www.studiocutz.com.

Adobe Reader 6.0 from Adobe Systems, Inc.

Freeware version—For Windows. This is the reader required to view PDF files. For more information, check out www.adobe.com/products/acrobat/readermain.html.

Adobe Audition from Adobe Systems, Inc.

Tryout version—Adobe Audition is part of the Adobe Video Collection. Audition is an audio editing program that allows you to record, mix, edit, and apply effects to audio files.

Boris FX and Boris CONTINUUM from Boris FX

Demo—Fully functional but does not render. For Windows XP. Boris FX is a plug-in that offers hundreds of customizable effects, lighting and particle filters, and keying and color control. Boris CONTINUUM is another plug-in used to integrate particle effects such as snow, clouds, and fire into your video; it also includes a range of filters such as Burnt Film and Cartooner. Find out more about these and other Boris products at www.borisfx.com.

SpiceMASTER 2.0 from Pixelan Software

Demo—For Windows. SpiceMaster is a plug-in that customizes, controls, and manages a wide range of transitions called spice effects. It can also animate/flow Premiere video filters. Find out more information on SpiceMASTER and Spices in general at www.pixelan.com.

Troubleshooting

If you have difficulty installing or using anything on the companion CD-ROM, try the following solutions:

» **Turn off any antivirus software that you may have running.** Installers sometimes mimic virus activity and can make your computer incorrectly believe that it is being infected by a virus. (Be sure to turn the antivirus software back on later.)

» **Close all running programs.** The more programs you're running, the less memory is available to other programs. Installers also typically update files and programs; if you keep other programs running, the installation may not work properly.

» **Reference the ReadMe:** Please refer to the ReadMe file located at the root of the CD-ROM for the latest product information at the time of publication.

If you still have trouble with the CD-ROM, please call the Wiley Publishing Customer Care phone number: (800)762-2974. Outside the United States, call 1(317)572-3994. You can also contact Wiley Publishing Customer Service by e-mail at techsupdum@wiley.com. Wiley Publishing will provide technical support only for installation and other general quality control items; for technical support on the applications themselves, consult the program vendor or author.

Index

»A«

Add Tracks dialog box, 139

Additive Dissolve transition
    introduction, 124
    transparency and, 298–299

Adjust effect, color and, 292–293

Adobe Acrobat, exporting movies for use in, 354

Adobe After Effects
    motion graphics, 26
    color channels and, 197
    exporting movies for use in, 354

Adobe Audition, 184

Adobe Encore, 29

Adobe Media Encoder, 354–358

Adobe Title Designer
    custom text, 230–233
    fills, 231–232
    fonts, 226
    frames, 233
    Properties drop-down list, 226
    Show Safe Titles, 232
    styles, 227
    templates, 244–245
    window, opening, 224

aliases, clips, 267

alpha channel, matte keys, 253, 255

animation
    bar titles, sequences for, 328–332
    clips, tutorial, 14–16
    graphics, tutorial, 17–19
    rotation value, 238
    titles, Fixed effects and, 236–240, 241–243
    titles, layers, 256–259

archiving, 359–361

audio
    adding trimmed clips to Timeline, 145–148
    bit depth, 143
    clip loops, 153
    Constant Power transition, 157

audio *(continued)*

Cutoff setting, 178

editing clip groups, 152–156

editing clips, 149–150

effects in tracks, Audio Mixer and, 176–179

fades, 160

file preparation, 141–142

format, 143

ignoring, 64

loudness versus volume, 151

Master audio track, 144

organization, 138–140

processing sequence, 175

reasons to use, 136–137

review process and, 349

sample rate, 143

signal adjustments, 151

Submix, 144

surround sound, 144

transitions, 157–160

transitions, reviewing and, 349

trimming clips, 141–142

waveforms, 149

Audio Mixer window

audio effects in tracks, 176–179

Automation modes, 172

clips, panning, 180–183

editing and, 165

editing music clips, 187–190

introduction, 135

Lowpass effect, 178

music clips, 184–186

Mute icon, 167

playing multiple tracks, 167

resizing, 166

Solo icon, 167

track volume adjustments, 166–168

volume, 191–192

VU meters, 167

audio options, General settings, 44

Audio Transitions folder, 158

Automate to Sequence dialog box, 63

Automation modes, Audio Mixer window, 172

»B«

background

brightening, 294–297

frame from Video, Title Designer, 230

templates, Title Designer, 244–245

balance, panning and, 182

bar titles, animated, sequences for, 328–332

Bevel Edges effect, 308–309

bit depth (audio), 144

Black Point eyedropper tool, 314

blank spaces, duration, 89

Blue Screen Key effect, 218

brightness

background, 294–297

Posterize effect and, 287–288

Brightness & Contrast effect

background and, 294–297

brightness value, 292

Browse For Folder dialog box, 39

»C«

Capture options, General settings, 44

CD-ROM, material on, 5

center point, transitions, 122

CFA (Conformed Audio) folder, 359

checklists

archiving and, 361

exporting and, 361

cleaning up project, 359–360

Clip Gain dialog box, 151

Clip Speed/Duration dialog box, 52

clips

adding to Timeline, 11–13, 260–261

adjustments, 96–97

aliases, 267

animating, tutorial, 14–16

audio, adding trimmed to Timeline, 145–148

audio, editing, 149–150

audio, editing groups, 152–156

audio, loops, 153

audio, trimming, 141–142

color, improvements, 314–317

content cropping, 318–319

cut point, transitions and, 114

duration, setting in Project window, 52–23

editing, 91–92

editing, groups, 76–80

editing, multiple windows and, 98–100

editing, opening, 70–71

editing in Source View monitor, 68–69

extract edits, 92

graphic title bar clip placement, 269

groups, adding to Timeline, 62–64

layering, 197

length, adjusting in Project window, 65–67

lift edits, 92

margins, viewing, 209

matte keys, applying multiple, 262–265

modifying, 89–90

moving, recording keyframe values, 256

music, adding, 184–186

opacity, 202–206

opening, 70–71

ordering, 64

organization, 123–125

organization, Project Window Name column, 54

Out points, adding, 99

overlays, 64

panning, 180–183

In points, adding, 99

Project window and, 49–51

ripple edits, 91

scale, 207–210

segments, editing, 104–106

segments, extracting in Program View monitor, 101–103

sizing, Fixed effects and, 198–201

slip edits, 91

speed reversal, previewing results, 72–75

stacking order, 202–206

superimposition, 197

transferring to Timeline, 54–57

transitions, fixed effects and, 312–313

transitions, multiple clips and, 116–118

unlinking, 89–90

volume fading over multiple, 171–175

codecs

custom color palettes, 45

editing mode and, 44

video rendering and, 44

color

Adjust effect, 292–293

Black Point eyedropper tool, 314

color keying effects, 218

correcting with effects, 292–293

depth, setting, 45

HSL options, 315

Image Control effect, 292–293

improvements, 314–317

intensity, Levels histogram and, 282

Keying effects and, 197

modifying with effects, 292–293

palettes, custom, 45

Posterize effect and, 287–288

Ramp effect, 300–303

RGB, 197

Tint effects, 280–283

White Point eyedropper tool, 314

Color Balance effect, 292

Color Corrector effect

color improvements and, 314–317

introduction, 307

color mattes, 300–303

Color Offset Settings dialog box, 322

Color Pass Settings dialog box, 282

Confidence Builder, logo introduction, 7

Conformed Audio Files, 143

Constant Power transition, 157

correcting color, effects and, 292–293

Crop effect, 318–319

cropping clip content, 318–319

Cross-Dissolve transitions

title sequences and, 246–247

Video Transitions folder, 113

crossfades, 160

CTI (Current Time Indicator)

clip starts, 54

Constant Power transition, 157

Iris Round transition, 128–130

keyframes and, 240

rolling edits and, 93–95

Source view monitor, 69

transition preview and, 122

Work Area bar and, 153

cut point, transitions snapping to, 114

Cutoff setting, 178

##

decibels (dB), 168

default sequences, General settings, 46

depth of color, 45

dialog boxes

Add Tracks, 139

Automate to Sequence, 63

Browse For Folder, 39

Clip Gain, 151

Clip Speed/Duration, 52

Color Offset Settings, 322

Color Pass Settings, 282

Frame Hold Options, 126

Gamma Correction Settings, 292–293

Import, 47

Levels Settings, 287

New Sequence, 324–325

Radial Blur, 284

Rename Clip, 267

Setup, 280

Show/Hide Tracks, 171

Wind Settings, 289

Zoom Trails Settings, 271

directional transitions, 117

**Display Format option, General
   Settings, 43**

dissolves, applying, 123–125

duration of clips

blank spaces, 89

extract edits and, 92

frames, 67

lift edits and, 92

rolling edits and, 91

setting, Project window, 52–23

DV editing, codecs, 44

»E«

ECW (Effect Controls window)

keyframe volume, 191–192

keyframes, title animation and,
   236–240

layout, 112

Timeline, keyframes, 169

Timeline coordination, 206

zooming and, 102

editing

clips, groups, 76–80

clips, opening from Timeline, 70–71

clips, Source View monitor, 68–69

extract edits, 92

Insert edits, 64

lift edits, 92

mode, codecs and, 44

Overlay edits, 64

RAM and, 46

ripple edits, 91

rolling edits, 91

slide edits, 92

slip edits, 91

Source view monitor and, 106

split edits, 138

Editing workspace, 95

effects

Adjust, 292–293

Bevel Edges, 308–309

Blue Screen Key, 218

Color Balance, 292

color correction and, 292–293

Color Corrector, 307, 314–317

color modification and, 292–293

copying, 284–286

Crop, 318–319

Fast Blur, 310–311

fixed, transitioning clips and, 312–313

Garbage Matte, 213–217, 324–327

Green Screen Key, 218

HLS Color Balance, 292

Image Control, 292–293

introduction, 197

Lowpass, 178

Luma Key, 211–212

Motion effects, 237–240

Noise, 290–291

Non-Red Screen Key, 218

Posterize, 287–288

Ramp, 300–303

review process and, 349

Screen Key, 211–212

settings, reusing, 317

Setup icon, 280

SteadyMove, 318–319

theme creation and, 320–323

Tint, 279

Wind, 289–290

Effects tab, enabling, 112

Effects workspace, adding titles to Timeline, 228–229

exporting

Adobe Media Encoder and, 354–358

checklist, 361

frames, single, 341–344

movie segments, 351–353

projects, Export Settings, 337

settings for, 344

extract edit, 92, 101–103

»F«

fades

audio, 160

volume, multiple clips, 171–175

Fast Blur effect, 310–311

Fields option, General Settings, 43

files

audio, preparation, 141–142

movie, 48

naming, 48

storage, 46

tutorial, working with, 33–34

video, 48

fills, Adobe Title Designer, 231

Fixed effects

animating titles and, 236–240, 241–243

categories, 197

clip resizing, 198–201

motion effects, 197

Opacity, 202–206

transitioning clips and, 312–313

folders, Video Transitions, 113

fonts, Adobe Title Designer, 226

Frame Hold Options dialog box, 126

Frame Size option, General Settings, 43

frames

Adobe Title Designer, safe areas, 233

content location, defining, 201

dropping, 40

duration, 67

exporting single from project, 341–344

graphics, split screens and, 266–270

Non Drop-Frame Timecode option, 40

poster, 320–321

size, 43

video, freezing, 126–127

freezing, video frames, 126–127

frozen transitions, 117

»G«

Gain values, audio clips, 151

Gamma Correction Settings dialog box, 292–293

Garbage Matte Key effect, 213–217, 324–327

garbage mattes, sequence creation and, 307

General settings

audio options, 44

Capture options, 44

default sequences, 46

video options, 43–44

video rendering, 44–45

graphics

animation, tutorial, 17–19

frames, split screens and, 266–270

horizontal clips, keyframes, 270

split screens, 251

title clip placement, 269

vertical clips, keyframes, 270

Green Screen Key effect, 218

groups

audio clips, editing in Timeline, 152–156

clips, adding to Timeline, 62–64

clips, editing, 76–80

»H«

handles, transition handles, 120

histograms

Levels histogram, 282

x-axis, 281

y-axis, 281

HLS Color Balance effect, 292

horizontal graphic clips, keyframes, 270

»I«

icons, sizes, 63

ignoring audio, 64

Image Control effect, color and, 292–293

Image Matte, 251

images, titles, 244–245

Import dialog box, 47

importing, footage for projects, 47–48

In point
  adding, 99
  clips in Timeline, 96–97
  viewing transitions and, 117

Insert edits, 64

Iris Round transition, 128–130

Iris Square transition
  adding, 121–122
  multiple, 128–130

»J«

J-cut edit, 138

»K«

keyframes
  Adobe Title Designer, 238
  CTI location and, 240
  interpolation, 170

opacity graph line, 205

position, start/end points and, 312

Timeline, 169

values, recording while moving clips, 256

volume, ECW, 191–192

keying, luminance and, 197

Keying effects, color and, 197

»L«

layers
  animated titles, 256–259
  clips, 197
  importing layered images, 224
  superimposition, 197

layout of book, 2–5

L-cut edit, 138

length, clips, adjusting in Project window, 65–67

Levels histogram, color intensity, 282

Levels Settings dialog box, 287

lift edit, 92

logo, Confidence Builder and, 7

loops
  audio clips, 153
  Timeline, 117

loudness versus volume, 151

Lowpass effect, 178

Luma Key effect
  Threshold value, 212
  Tint effect and, 281
  tinting, 279
  transparencies, combining, 298–299
  transparency and, 211–212

luminance
  Tint effect and, 280–283
  transparency and, 197, 211–212

»M«

Macromedia Flash, 354

margins, clips, 209

markers, unnumbered
  adding to timeline, 65–66
  adding to source clip, 76–77

Master audio track, 144

matte keys
  alpha channel, 253
  applying to multiple clips, 262–265
  color mattes, 300–303
  Image mattes, 255
  Track mattes, 255
  transparency and, 251
  Tree Track Matte, 310–311

Microsoft AVI movies, 351–353

Monitor window, 71

mono sound versus stereo, 144

Motion effects, 237–240

movie files, 48

movies

exporting segments, 351–353

tutorial, 20–21

music clips

adding, 184–186

synchronization, 345–348

Mute icon, Audio Mixer window, 167

»N«

naming

files, 48

workspaces, 95

sequences, 324

tracks, 140

nesting, sequences, 338–340

new features, 27–29

New Project window, 38

New Sequence dialog box, 324–325

Noise effect, 290–291

Non Drop-Frame Timecode option, 40

Non-Red Screen Key effect, 218

numbered markers, themes and, 320

»O«

opacity

clips, 202–206

graph line, adding keyframes, 205

Show Opacity keyframes setting, 217

value, 202

Opacity setting, values, 202

ordering

clips, 64

rendering order, 311

organization

audio, Timeline and, 138–140

clips, 123–125

Out point

adding, 99

clips in Timeline, 96–97

viewing transitions and, 117

Overlay edits, 64

»PQ«

panning

balancing and, 182

clips, Audio Mixer and, 180–183

picture-in-picture effect, 262–265

pixels, distribution in a histogram, 282

pixels, frame size, 43

pixels aspect ratio, general settings, 43

Play In to Out button (Timeline), 118

Posterize effect, 287–288

positioning handle, 102

previews

clip speed reversal, 72–75

files, 307

Project window, 51

transitions, 118

Program View monitor

content played, 73

extracting clip segments, 101–103

monitor window menu, 314

overview, 71

view zoom level setting, 201

viewing Garbage Matte effect handles, 214–215

viewing Motion Fixed Effects handles, 204

viewing transitions, 118

Project window

clip duration, setting, 52–23

clip length, adjusting, 65–67

clip organization, 49–51

Name column, clip organization, 54

previewing in, 51

reorganizing, 64

resizing, 47

projects

archiving, 359–360

cleanup, 359–360

content organization, 64

development, 31–32

exporting, 337

files, naming, 48

footage, importing, 47–48

General settings, 42–44

overview, 31–34

reviewing, 349–350

starting, tools needed, 37

starting, tutorial, 8–10, 38–41

Properties drop-down list, Adobe Title Designer, 226

Push transition, applying, 116

push transitions, 119–120

»R«

Radial blur, 284–286

Radial Blur dialog box, 284

RAM (Random Access Memory), editing and, 46

Ramp effect, 300–303

Razor tool, 90

reasons to use book, 2

Rename Clip dialog box, 267

rendering
codecs, 44
definition, 153
order, 311

Reveal in Project command, 73

reviewing projects, 349–350

RGB color, 197

Ripple Delete command, 71, 80
edit process, 91

ripple edits, 91

Ripple Trim tool, 130

rolling edits
description, 91
Timeline, 93–95

»S«

safe areas, General Settings, 44

sample rate settings (audio), 143

scale
adjusting, 207–210
General Settings, 44
titles, 237

Screen Key effect, 211–212

screen location, defining, 201

scrolling, Timeline window, 56

segments of clips
editing, 104–106
extracting, Program View monitor and, 101–103
loops, 117

sequences
adding, 324–327
animating bar titles, 328–332
music synchronization, 345–348
nesting, 338–340

settings
exporting and, 344
reusing, 317

Setup dialog boxes, 280

Setup icon, effects, 280

Show Head and Tail menu option, 101

Show/Hide Effects and Sends (Audio Mixer window), 166–167

Show/Hide Tracks dialog box, 171

Show Opacity keyframes setting, 217

Show Safe Titles (Adobe Title Designer), 232

size, frames, 43

slide edit, 92

Slide folder, Video Transitions folder, 116

slip edit, 91

Solo icon, Audio Mixer window, 167

sound. *See* audio

Source view monitor
audio and, 135
clip editing, 68–69
clip margins, 209
CTI, 69
editing tips, 106

speed of clips
adjusting in Timeline, 96–97
reversing and previewing, 72–75

split edits, 138

split screens
graphic frames, adding, 266–270
graphic titles, 251

stacking order, clips, 202–206

starting project, tools needed, 37

static titles, creating, 224–227

SteadyMove effect, 318–319

stereo versus mono sound, 144

strokes, Adobe Title Design, 232

Studio Cutz Music Library, music clips and, 184

styles, Adobe Title Designer, 227

Submix audio, 144

superimposition, 197

surround sound, 144

system requirements, 29

»T«

Take Audio Video command, 78

templates, Adobe Title Designer, 244–245

text, crawling, 252, 254

text in titles
Bevel Edges effect, 308–309
customization, 230–233
enhancement, 308–309

themes, effects and, 320–323

Threshold value, Luma Key effect and, 212

timebase
notation, 41
Video for Windows and, 42

timecode, Non Drop-Frame Timecode option, 40

Timeline
audio clips, editing groups, 152–156
audio clips, editing in, 149–150
audio clips, organization, 138–140
audio clips, trimmed, 145–148

clip editing, opening from Timeline, 70–71

clips, adding (tutorial), 11–13

clips, adding groups to Timeline, 62–64

clips, adding to Timeline, 260–261

clips, adjustments to, 96–97

clips, copying, 145

clips, opening from Timeline, 70–71

clips, pasting, 145

clips, transferring to Timeline, 54–57

Collapse/Expand arrow, 87

drag and drop, 145

ECW coordination, 206

keyframes, 169

layout configuration, 86–88

loops, 117

rolling edits, 93–95

scrolling, 56

Show Head and Tail menu option, 101

titles, adding, 228–229

tracks, 54

tracks, additional, 76–80

tracks, locking, 87

tracks, visibility, 86

unnumbered markers, 65–66

Work Area bar, 54

zooming, 101

Tint effect
adding, 280–283
introduction, 279

Title Designer window
static titles and, 224–227
text customization, 230–233

titles
adding messages, 234–235
adding to Timeline, 228–229
animated, layering, 256–259
animation, Fixed effects and, 236–240, 241–243
bar titles, animating, 328–332
Bevel Edges effect, 308–309
graphic, resize handles, 245
static, 224–227
templates and, 244–245
text customization, 230–233
text enhancement, 308–309
title sequences, 246–247
Track Mattes, 252–255

Track Mattes
introduction, 251
title Track Mattes, 252–255
visibility and, 252

tracks
audio effects, Audio Mixer and, 176–179
locking, 87
pan/balance, 181
volume, Audio Mixer and, 166–168

transitions
Additive Dissolve, 124, 298–299
audio, reviewing and, 349
center point, 122
complex, 271–273
Constant Power, 157
Cross Dissolves, title sequences and, 246–247

transitions (continued)

directional, 117

fixed effects and, 312–313

frozen, 117

handles, 120

inserting, 112–115

introduction, 111

Iris Round, 128–130

Iris Square, 121–122

Iris Square, multiple, 128–130

locating, 115

multiple clips and, 116–118

previewing, 118

Push, 116

push transitions, 119–120

snapping to cut point, 114

sound, 157–160

viewing, In point/Out point and, 117

Zoom Trails, 271

transparency

Additive Dissolve transition and, 298–299

Luma Key effect and, 211–212

matte keys, 251

Screen Key effect and, 211–212

tinting and, 280–283

types, combining, 298–299

Trim view, 102

trimming audio clips, 141–142, 145–148

Type tool, Adobe Title Designer, 225

»U«

Unlink Audio and Video command, 78

effect on clip titles, 89

»V«

vertical graphic clips, keyframes, 270

Video Duration, viewing, 66

video files, 48

video folder, contents, 48

Video for Windows

codecs, 44

timebase and, 42

video frames

freezing, 126–127

review process and, 349

Video In point, viewing, 66

video options, General Settings

Display Format, 43

Fields, 43

Frame size, 43

Pixel Aspect Ratio, 43

safe areas, 44

scaling, 44

Video Out point

resetting, 66

viewing, 66

Video rendering, General settings, 44–45

Video Transitions folder

Cross-Dissolve transition, 113

Slide folder, 116

volume

Audio Mixer and, 191–192

fading, multiple clips, 171–175

versus loudness, 151

tracks, Audio Mixer and, 166–168

VU meters, Audio Mixer window, 167

»W«

waveforms, audio editing and, 149

Welcome window, 38

White Point eyedropper tool, 314

Wind effect, 289–290

windows

Adobe Title Designer, 224–227

clip editing using multiple, 98–100

Monitor window, 71

New Project, 38

resizing, 47

Welcome, 38

Work Area bar, exporting and, 54, 352

setting, 155

workspaces

creating/saving, 95

named, 95

»X«

x-axis, histogram, 281

x-axis, location, 201

»Y«

y-axis, histogram, 281

y-axis, location, 201

»Z«

Zoom Trails Settings dialog box, 271

Zoom Trails transition, 271

zooming

    Effect Controls window, 102

    Timeline, 101

About Seybold Seminars and Publications

Seybold Seminars and Publications is your complete guide to the publishing industry. For more than 30 years it has been the most trusted source for technology events, news, and insider intelligence.

SEYBOLD
CONSULTING PUBLICATIONS℠

SEYBOLD
SEMINARS

SEYBOLD
CONSULTING PUBLICATIONS℠

PUBLICATIONS

Today, Seybold Publications and Consulting continues to guide publishing professionals around the world in their purchasing decisions and business strategies through newsletters, online resources, consulting, and custom corporate services.

○ ***The Seybold Report: Analyzing Publishing Technologies***
The Seybold Report analyzes the cross-media tools, technologies, and trends shaping professional publishing today. Each in-depth newsletter delves into the topics changing the marketplace. *The Seybold Report* covers critical analyses of the business issues and market conditions that determine the success of new products, technologies, and companies. Read about the latest developments in mission-critical topic areas, including content and asset management, color management and proofing, industry standards, and cross-media workflows. A subscription to *The Seybold Report* (24 issues per year) includes our weekly email news service, *The Bulletin,* and full access to the seyboldreports.com archives.

○ ***The Bulletin: Seybold News & Views on Electronic Publishing***
The Bulletin: Seybold News & Views on Electronic Publishing is Seybold Publications' weekly email news service covering all aspects of electronic publishing. Every week *The Bulletin* brings you all the important news in a concise, easy-to-read format.

For more information on **NEWSLETTER SUBSCRIPTIONS,**
please visit **seyboldreports.com**.

CUSTOM SERVICES

In addition to newsletters and online information resources, Seybold Publications and Consulting offers a variety of custom corporate services designed to meet your organization's specific needs.

○ **Strategic Technology Advisory Research Service (STARS)**
The STARS program includes a group license to *The Seybold Report* and *The Bulletin*, phone access to our analysts, access to online archives at seyboldreports.com, an on-site visit by one of our analysts, and much more.

○ **Personalized Seminars**
Our team of skilled consultants and subject experts work with you to create a custom presentation that gets your employees up to speed on topics spanning the full spectrum of prepress and publishing technologies covered in our publications. Full-day and half-day seminars are available.

○ **Site Licenses**
Our electronic licensing program keeps everyone in your organization, sales force, or marketing department up to date at a fraction of the cost of buying individual subscriptions. One hard copy of *The Seybold Report* is included with each electronic license.

For more information on **CUSTOM CORPORATE SERVICES,** please visit **seyboldreports.com**.

SEYBOLD
SEMINARS

EVENTS

Seybold Seminars facilitates exchange and discussion within the high-tech publishing community several times a year. A hard-hitting lineup of conferences, an opportunity to meet leading media technology vendors, and special events bring innovators and leaders together to share ideas and experiences.

Conferences

Our diverse educational programs are designed to tackle the full range of the latest developments in publishing technology. Topics include:

- Print publishing
- Web publishing
- Design
- Creative tools and standards
- Best practices
- Multimedia
- Content management
- Technology standards
- Security
- Digital rights management

In addition to the conferences, you'll have the opportunity to meet representatives from companies that bring you the newest products and technologies in the publishing marketplace. Test tools, evaluate products, and take free classes from the experts.

For more information on **SEYBOLD SEMINARS EVENTS,**
please visit **seyboldseminars.com.**

Wiley Publishing, Inc.
End-User License Agreement

READ THIS. You should carefully read these terms and conditions before opening the software packet(s) included with this book "Book". This is a license agreement "Agreement" between you and Wiley Publishing, Inc. "WPI". By opening the accompanying software packet(s), you acknowledge that you have read and accept the following terms and conditions. If you do not agree and do not want to be bound by such terms and conditions, promptly return the Book and the unopened software packet(s) to the place you obtained them for a full refund.

1. **License Grant.** WPI grants to you (either an individual or entity) a nonexclusive license to use one copy of the enclosed software program(s) (collectively, the "Software," solely for your own personal or business purposes on a single computer (whether a standard computer or a workstation component of a multi-user network). The Software is in use on a computer when it is loaded into temporary memory (RAM) or installed into permanent memory (hard disk, CD-ROM, or other storage device). WPI reserves all rights not expressly granted herein.

2. **Ownership.** WPI is the owner of all right, title, and interest, including copyright, in and to the compilation of the Software recorded on the disk(s) or CD-ROM "Software Media". Copyright to the individual programs recorded on the Software Media is owned by the author or other authorized copyright owner of each program. Ownership of the Software and all proprietary rights relating thereto remain with WPI and its licensers.

3. **Restrictions On Use and Transfer.**

   (a) You may only (i) make one copy of the Software for backup or archival purposes, or (ii) transfer the Software to a single hard disk, provided that you keep the original for backup or archival purposes. You may not (i) rent or lease the Software, (ii) copy or reproduce the Software through a LAN or other network system or through any computer subscriber system or bulletin-board system, or (iii) modify, adapt, or create derivative works based on the Software.

   (b) You may not reverse engineer, decompile, or disassemble the Software. You may transfer the Software and user documentation on a permanent basis, provided that the transferee agrees to accept the terms and conditions of this Agreement and you retain no copies. If the Software is an update or has been updated, any transfer must include the most recent update and all prior versions.

4. **Restrictions on Use of Individual Programs.** You must follow the individual requirements and restrictions detailed for each individual program in the About the CD-ROM appendix of this Book. These limitations are also contained in the individual license agreements recorded on the Software Media. These limitations may include a requirement that after using the program for a specified period of time, the user must pay a registration fee or discontinue use. By opening the Software packet(s), you will be agreeing to abide by the licenses and restrictions for these individual programs that are detailed in the About the CD-ROM appendix and on the Software Media. None of the material on this Software Media or listed in this Book may ever be redistributed, in original or modified form, for commercial purposes.

5. **Limited Warranty.**

   (a) WPI warrants that the Software and Software Media are free from defects in materials and workmanship under normal use for a period of sixty (60) days from the date of purchase of this Book. If WPI receives notification within the warranty period of defects in materials or workmanship, WPI will replace the defective Software Media.

   (b) WPI AND THE AUTHOR(S) OF THE BOOK DISCLAIM ALL OTHER WARRANTIES, EXPRESS OR IMPLIED, INCLUDING WITHOUT LIMITATION IMPLIED WARRANTIES OF MERCHANTABILITY AND FITNESS FOR A PARTICULAR PURPOSE, WITH RESPECT TO THE SOFTWARE, THE PROGRAMS, THE SOURCE CODE CONTAINED THEREIN, AND/OR THE TECHNIQUES DESCRIBED IN THIS BOOK. WPI DOES NOT WARRANT THAT THE FUNCTIONS CONTAINED IN THE SOFTWARE WILL MEET YOUR REQUIREMENTS OR THAT THE OPERATION OF THE SOFTWARE WILL BE ERROR FREE.

   (c) This limited warranty gives you specific legal rights, and you may have other rights that vary from jurisdiction to jurisdiction.

6. Remedies.

(a) WPI's entire liability and your exclusive remedy for defects in materials and workmanship shall be limited to replacement of the Software Media, which may be returned to WPI with a copy of your receipt at the following address: Software Media Fulfillment Department, Attn.: *Adobe Premiere Pro Complete Course*, Wiley Publishing, Inc., 10475 Crosspoint Blvd., Indianapolis, IN 46256, or call 1-800-762-2974. Please allow four to six weeks for delivery. This Limited Warranty is void if failure of the Software Media has resulted from accident, abuse, or misapplication. Any replacement Software Media will be warranted for the remainder of the original warranty period or thirty (30) days, whichever is longer.

(b) In no event shall WPI or the author be liable for any damages whatsoever (including without limitation damages for loss of business profits, business interruption, loss of business information, or any other pecuniary loss) arising from the use of or inability to use the Book or the Software, even if WPI has been advised of the possibility of such damages.

(c) Because some jurisdictions do not allow the exclusion or limitation of liability for consequential or incidental damages, the above limitation or exclusion may not apply to you.

7. U.S. Government Restricted Rights.
Use, duplication, or disclosure of the Software for or on behalf of the United States of America, its agencies and/or instrumentalities "U.S. Government" is subject to restrictions as stated in paragraph (c)(1)(ii) of the Rights in Technical Data and Computer Software clause of DFARS 252.227-7013, or subparagraphs (c) (1) and (2) of the Commercial Computer Software - Restricted Rights clause at FAR 52.227-19, and in similar clauses in the NASA FAR supplement, as applicable.

8. General.
This Agreement constitutes the entire understanding of the parties and revokes and supersedes all prior agreements, oral or written, between them and may not be modified or amended except in a writing signed by both parties hereto that specifically refers to this Agreement. This Agreement shall take precedence over any other documents that may be in conflict herewith. If any one or more provisions contained in this Agreement are held by any court or tribunal to be invalid, illegal, or otherwise unenforceable, each and every other provision shall remain in full force and effect.

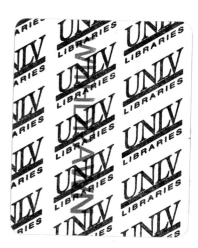